D1253866

DARWIN AMONG THE POETS

DARWIN
AMONG THE POETS

By LIONEL STEVENSON

New York

RUSSELL & RUSSELL

1963

FOREWORD

THE following study was originally submitted to the graduate division of the University of California in partial fulfilment of the requirements for the degree of Doctor of Philosophy. It has since been extensively revised. I am happy to acknowledge my deep indebtedness to Professor Garnet G. Sedgewick, of the University of British Columbia, in whose classes the principal ideas herein embodied were first suggested to me, and to Professor Benjamin H. Lehman, of the University of California, for his generous advice and encouragement throughout the writing of the book.

My thanks are also due to the following firms for permission to quote from copyright works which they publish: Doubleday, Doran and Company for selections from *Rudyard Kipling's Verse*; Henry Holt and Company for selections from *Collected Poems of Walter de la Mare*; The Macmillan Company for selections from *Poetical Works of Matthew Arnold*, *Complete Poetical Works of Robert Browning*, *Collected Poems of Thomas Hardy*, *The Dynasts*, *The Early Life of Thomas Hardy*, by Florence Emily Hardy, *Poems of John Masefield*, and *Works of Alfred, Lord Tennyson*; The Oxford University Press for selections from *Poetical Works of Robert Bridges*; Charles Scribner's

Sons for selections from *Poetical Works of George Meredith* and *Letters of George Meredith;* and Frederick A. Stokes Company for selections from Volume I of *Collected Poems of Alfred Noyes;* also to Sir William Watson personally for similar courtesies.

CONTENTS

vii

Chapter I

POETRY IN RELATION TO THE
EVOLUTIONARY THEORY

IN ITS simplest terms, the grievance of the New Humanists against modern literature is that it has surrendered itself root and branch, in methods and in philosophic outlook alike, to the habits of scientific research. The Humanists regard this as an intolerable affliction, and hope to apply a remedy. But no one seems to have realized that for a full diagnosis the first step ought to be an investigation of how the condition originated. The irruption of science is probably the most interesting phenomenon in nineteenth-century literature; and indeed that is only one chapter of the change which was then affecting every province of human thought, and of which the reverberations still surround us. As an area that can be conveniently isolated for analysis, none could be better than English poetry, for in it all the present shades and species of opinion, ranging from fundamentalism through humanism and other compromise theories to radical iconoclasm, were displayed. One is amazed to discover how many of to-day's new creeds and revised philosophies of life were first proposed by Victorian poets.

Mr. H. G. Wells, for instance, professes to present in *The World of William Clissold* the independent cogitations on the problem of existence of an intelligent Englishman in the year 1926. "He is," the novelist says, "a specimen of modern liberalism." The story aims to give "the full effect of contemporary life in which living ideas and movements play a dominant part." Yet Clissold's essential ideas turn out to be identical with those advanced two generations earlier, and advanced particularly in poetry. Seeking a working philosophy of life consistent with current science, and explicitly proclaiming his independence of precedent, Clissold reproduces the main tenets of the leading literary idols of Victorianism. The commentary on the modern mind is more subtle, perhaps, than Mr. Wells realized.

Clissold, although a scientist and a rationalist, cannot ignore the intuitive flashes which give him a "sense of externality" from "the common-sense world" and make him doubt whether it be "ultimately true"; he admits the "insufficiency" of the human brain and the possibility of powers beyond our comprehension; and he seeks to formulate a creed harmonizing these intuitions with the scientific outlook. He perceives that the orthodox religions have lost their authority and that belief must be based on the evolutionary view of the world and human life. But he gives no indication of knowing that these conclusions were reached by Alfred Tennyson the better part of a century ago.

Furthermore, the suggestions and hesitations of Clissold can all be paralleled specifically in the work of Tennyson and his contemporaries. His introduction of the scientific viewpoint—"I doubt if man had quite the same sense of abbreviation before this measuring by astronomical distances and geological ages began"—is to be found identically in the Epilogue to *The Charge of the Heavy Brigade*. He stresses the universality of change as the essential fact of existence, and Tennyson did likewise throughout his career; the motto of Wells's novel, the πavτa ρει of Heraclitus, was the theme of a poem in Tennyson's earliest volume (1830), which developed precisely Wells's statement, "In truth there is no underlying permanent stratum to the changes of our world; it all changes, root as well as flower." And Wells goes on to paraphrase the hundred and twenty-third section of *In Memoriam* thus:

> I can discover in all my world nothing enduring, neither in the hills, nor in the sea, nor in laws and customs, nor in the nature of man, nothing steadfast except for this—a certain growth of science, a certain increase of understanding, a certain accumulation of power.

"Is there a plot to the show?" Clissold demands; "is it a drama moving through a vast complexity to a definite end, or at any rate moving in a definite direction?" His answer to the question includes elements from the creeds of Tennyson, Meredith, Hardy, and Browning. His kinship with Meredith is particularly close in his concept of "a collective human person"; like that poet, he discards belief in personal immortality, and substitutes a "Racial Man to which all our individual lives consciously or unconsciously are contributory and subordinate," so that "I am not merely myself but a participator in a Being that has been born but need not die." And there is a reminiscence of the more hopeful moments of Thomas Hardy when he says, "We are all presented as contributory units to a Titanic being which becomes conscious and takes hold of this planet." Like Meredith, too, he deduces an ethical code; there could scarcely be a better summary of Meredith's teaching of the individual's responsibility than this:

Let us gather knowledge and power, let us communicate and learn to co-operate, let us lay hands on life and fate. Let us at any rate make the attempt. . . . . Since we are obliged willy-nilly to participate in the increase and application of knowledge to human ends, we may as well give our lives cheerfully and take a conscious share in the process. We shall be happier to extend our motives and desires beyond the tragic uncertainties of the purely egotistic life. We shall be broadened and steadied by that participation, we shall be released from the worst intensities of personal desire and passion and from the bitter fear and still bitterer realization of futility that haunt self-centred minds.

One reverts to Tennyson in reading that "progressive life" is the story of the universe:

There have been secular massacres of animal and vegetable life, in comparatively brief geological phases thousands of species and genera have been swept away, but . . . . the geological record, the archives of life's adventures, does certainly seem to so amateurish a reader as I a straightforward story of expansion and progress—and particularly of expanding intelligence. Mind grows—and grows at an ever-increasing pace.

And he shares Tennyson's sanguine hopes for the future glories of human achievement.

Finally, and most surprisingly of all, it is the mystical optimism of Browning that appears in Clissold's summary of his faith:

> There is no enduring pain, there is no eternal tragedy. Toil passes like the straining of a rootlet or the opening of a bud. Supreme above wars and disasters, surpassing and at last redeeming all the present torments of man, is the growth of a being of thought. . . . . It is because our light is growing that we at last apprehend the shadows. To realize the unacceptable evil in a thing is to begin its cure. Great as are the evils that we can see in life, the power of the will in us grows greater.

This is the doctrine of encouragement inseparable from imperfection, which was Browning's constant evangel.

These and other amazing parallels of thought show that a common basis of outlook and purpose existed between Mr. Wells and the Victorian poets, and that a common element united the poets themselves sufficiently to permit of them all being echoed by a single successor. In Darwin's hypothesis of evolution the essentials of modern science were epitomized and their radical implications most fully displayed. This theory was the most potent foe to the older creeds and their literal interpretation of the Bible; it entailed a complete revaluation of all mental equipment and an utterly changed perspective in man's view of the universe. The Victorian poets, whose "high seriousness" was particularly concerned with the didactic and elevating mission of their art, were prompt in proffering suggestions calculated to reconcile the new principle with some sort of spiritual system, and their efforts pervade all their work to such an extent that the gulf separating their poetic outlook from that of all antecedent poets is probably the most abrupt in the whole record of human thought. Mr. Wells's sole innovation is the applying of the same purpose to fiction. But the fact that neither William Clissold nor the critics of the book remarked upon the absence of novelty in the views propounded—whether or not Mr. Wells was cognizant of it—suggests that the antecedent utterances are unduly neglected.

THE MATING OF POETRY AND SCIENCE

Certain critics have, from time to time, asserted that the modern scientific point of view is fatally antagonistic to poetic inspiration and that the era of science is bound to witness the extinction of poetry. The more general belief, however, and that which now seems to be generally accepted, is expressed in Walter de la Mare's sonnet *The Happy Encounter:*

I saw sweet Poetry turn troubled eyes
  On shaggy Science nosing in the grass,
   For by that way poor Poetry must pass
On her long pilgrimage to Paradise.
He snuffled, grunted, squealed; perplexed by flies,
  Parched, weatherworn, and near of sight, alas,
   From peering close where very little was
In dens secluded from the open skies.

But Poetry in bravery went down,
  And called his name, soft, clear, and fearlessly;

Stooped low, and stroked his muzzle overgrown;
  Refreshed his drought with dew; wiped pure and free
  His eyes: and lo! laughed loud for joy to see
In those gray deeps the azure of her own.

Such a view is not merely theoretical; for nearly a century now the manifold development of scientific theory has been paralleled by constant discussions and interpretations of its pronouncements on the part of the poets.

To be sure, poetry cannot simply phrase scientific formulas in metrical lines; the material must be subjected to the processes of emotion and imagination, so that when the original austere ideas of science emerge in poetry they are fantastically masked and robed. A very brief scrutiny, however, reveals the ascetic beneath the mummer's garb.

Wordsworth wrote prophetically in the Preface to *Lyrical Ballads* (1802):

If the labours of the Men of Science should ever create any material revolution, direct or indirect, in our condition, and the impressions which we habitually receive, the Poet will sleep then no more than at present; he will be ready to follow the steps of the Man of Science, not only in those general indirect effects, but he will be at his side, carrying sensation into the midst of the objects of science itself. The remotest discoveries of the Chemist, the Botanist, or the Mineralogist, will be as proper objects of the Poet's art as any upon which it can be employed, if the time should ever come when these things shall be familiar to us, and the relations under which they are contemplated by the followers of these respective sciences shall be manifestly and palpably material to us as enjoying and suffering beings. If the time should ever come when what is now called science, thus familiarized to men, should be ready to put on, as it were, a form of flesh and blood, the Poet will lend his divine spirit to aid the transfiguration and will welcome the Being thus produced, as a dear and genuine inmate of the household of man.

Even within Wordsworth's lifetime his prediction attained a measure of fulfilment, and nine years after his death a book was published in which "the remotest discoveries of the chemist, the botanist, and the mineralogist" were synthesized in a theory of existence gravely affecting the material of poetry. The Victorian poets were not necessarily possessed of accurate information on all the individual discoveries of science, but in common with the general public they received an adequate conception of the theories advanced by the scientists in attempted explanation of the nature and source of life. Although the whole century was characterized by this broadening of the interest in science, the year 1859 marks the crucial event: *The Origin of Species* summed up the previous researches in various branches of science, and in its turn became the progenitor of many new branches. The thesis of the book impressed itself upon the public mind with sudden violence, and the resulting deductions had far-reaching effects in almost every department of intellectual activity. In this disturbance poetry was not immune from contagion.

Never before had any scientific theory penetrated deeply enough into the general imagination or aroused strong enough emotional reactions to storm poetry's ivory tower. Writing at the beginning of the nineteenth century, Wordsworth was justified in assuming that poetry and science had little in common. Of all attempts to embody a scientific view of the universe in metrical form, probably the *De Rerum Natura* of Lucretius alone could have won the title of genuine poetry from many critics. During the eighteenth century, in spite of the widespread interest in science among cultivated men, even the essentially cerebral poetry of that age balked at the topic. The chief poets, such as Butler, Prior, and Pope, found in the new science material only for satire and burlesque; and, on the other hand, the register of versified scientific treatises, from *The Ecstasy* of John Hughes, through *The Spleen* and *The Art of Preserving Health*, to Erasmus Darwin's *Botanic Garden*, is not exhilarating. In reaction against such ponderous expositions, the romantic poets discarded scientific discussion along with other Augustan traits, as hopelessly antagonistic to imagination.

Nevertheless, a few decades later the debating of scientific discoveries, and the philosophic interpretation of them, like a barbarian invader rudely banished the noncombatant exquisites—beauty and love—from their placid monopoly. The reason for this revulsion was precisely what Wordsworth had indicated: science had become familiarized, and had produced a "material revolution in the impressions which we habitually receive" by proffering a new explanation of the universe and man's place in it. For many centuries science had been permitted only a harmless toying with phenomena, because, in explaining man's place in the universe, poetry—the lofty poetry of the Hebrew Scriptures—admitted no rival. The scientific cosmogony of Lucretius was contemned, not as inexact science, but as pagan materialism; and the imaginative cosmogony of the Book of Genesis reigned unchallenged as a literal record of the creative process. So long as man was held to have been shaped in the image of God, to rule over the whole natural order which had been expressly arranged to serve him, poets accepted the orthodox belief without question. The greatest reflective poem of the Christian tradition, *Paradise Lost*, in undertaking to justify the ways of God to man, employed the Genesis legend as expanded during centuries by accretions of dogma and fantasy.

To this orthodoxy the early stages of modern science were not seriously destructive. The most important discovery, the Copernican system, tended to make the universe more anthropocentric than ever, by revealing the vastitude of the scene created for man's benefit. In *Paradise Lost* can be seen the transitional stage between the old Ptolemaic astronomy and the new Copernican, with some confusion, it is true, but with no perception that the orthodox idea of creation might be imperiled. In the eighteenth century, the concept of astronomical space enabled such devout poets as Young and Akenside to describe the firmament as "the garden of the Deity," giving new cause for adoration of the Creator. Even Wordsworth, despite his instinctive sense of communion with external nature, treated natural phenomena as a mere background for human thoughts and emotions, assuming an essential difference to exist between mankind and all other phenomena. The outlook is not a matter of orthodoxy, but of knowledge; it was shared by the atheistic Shelley, simply because no other probability entered his head.

The primary postulate, as stated in the *Ode on Intimations of Immortality*, was that man is a sojourner upon earth who never quite forgets his celestial source or feels at home in his incarnation. Nature is no more than a nurse or foster-mother who provides for him materially. Such a view is as consistent with the Genesis story as Milton's was. Until the beginning of the nineteenth century the poets took for granted the validity of the conventional dualism which distinguished man from external nature by a definite separate creation. As the final masterpiece of God, the human race was necessarily ideally perfect for its function of controlling the lower orders.

And yet, the poets must have been, for a long time, subconsciously aware of the impending change of theory. None of Milton's successors, in their references to the creation, gave such free range to the poetic faculty of concrete visualization as he had done in *Paradise Lost*, Book vii:

> The earth obeyed, and straight
> Opening her fertile womb teemed at a birth
> Innumerous living creatures, perfect forms
> Limbed and full grown: out of the ground uprose

As from his lair the wild beast where he wonns . . . .
The grassy clods now calved, now half appeared
The tawny lion, pawing to get free
His hinder parts, then springs as broke from bonds,
And rampant shakes his brinded mane; the ounce,
The libbard, and the tiger, as the mole
Rising, the crumbled earth above them threw
In hillocks; the swift stag from under ground
Bore up his branching head. . . . .

Dryden, for example, in *The Hind and the Panther*, in discussing the same event, passed over it in cautious figurative terms and focused his attention on the problems involved. He clearly indicated his perception of the "struggle for survival" (so momentous to the evolutionists), although denying that it extended to the human species; and he faced the difficulty of reconciling man's present shortcomings with his original creation as a perfect being:

Beasts are the subjects of tyrannic sway
Where still the stronger on the weaker prey.
Man only of a softer mould is made,
Not for his fellows' ruin, but their aid.
Created kind, beneficent and free,
The noble image of the Deity.
One portion of informing fire was given
The brutes, the inferior family of heaven:
The smith divine, as with a careless beat,
Struck out the mute creation at a heat:
But when arrived at last to human race,
The Godhead took a deep considering space:
And, to distinguish man from all the rest,
Unlocked the sacred treasures of his breast . . . .
And like his mind his outward form appeared
When issuing naked to the wondering herd
He charmed their eyes, and for they loved they feared.

Not armed with horns of arbitrary might,
Or claws to seize their furry spoils in fight . . . .
Thus kneaded up with milk, the new made man
His kingdom o'er his kindred world began:
Till knowledge misapplied, misunderstood,
And pride of empire soured his balmy blood.

On passing over a century, one finds in Coleridge an indication of how far the process of modification had advanced. Just as Milton, without knowing it, had mingled the old Ptolemaic system with the Copernican which was superseding it, so Coleridge, without knowing it, mingled the old scriptural idea of man as an originally perfect image of God with the new scientific idea of man as an animal endowed with reason by the struggle for survival. In *Religious Musings* Coleridge at one moment declares that Christ "uncharmed the drowsed soul" of the skeptic "till of its nobler nature it 'gan feel dim recollections," and goes on to indicate, just as Dryden did, man's decline from primitive altruism:

In the primeval age a dateless while
The vacant shepherd wandered with his flock,
Pitching his tent where'er the green grass waved.
But soon Imagination conjured up
An host of new desires: with busy aim,
Each for himself, Earth's eager children toiled.

Yet in the very next breath Coleridge says that these new ambitions were the direct cause of progress:

Wide-wasting ills! yet each the immediate source
Of mightier good. Their keen necessities
To ceaseless action goading human thought
Have made Earth's reasoning animal her Lord.

Apparently oblivious to the inconsistency of regarding man as a reasoning animal propelled by economic
necessity and simultaneously as having been originally endowed by heaven with a "nobler nature,"
Coleridge held to the static axioms of man's place in
the world. If both Wordsworth, with his intuitive
sense of identity with nature, and Coleridge, with his
insatiable appetite for metaphysical theories, were
unaware of any challenge to the orthodox dualism,
we may assume that the materialistic ideas of scientific research had made no impression on the poetic
mind.

To all this established certainty the evolutionary
theory was immediately destructive. Even before
Darwin had written his second epochal book, *The
Descent of Man*, applying specifically to the human
race his principles of selection and development, the
iconoclastic implications of his theory were widely
recognized. If all the varied forms of life could be
traced back to some rudimentary prototype, the
biblical account of a special creation was obviously
contradicted. Above all, if man had been produced
by the same forces as the other species, he was reduced to essential similarity with the animal kingdom; and in this case, how could he claim to possess
an immortal soul? His so-called "spiritual qualities"
might be nothing more than physiological processes.
Indeed, since the concept of a creative God was replaced by that of certain natural laws acting mechanically, there seemed to be no place for any spir-

itual element in the universe. Thus, suddenly deprived of the accustomed confidence in religious explanations of the meaning of life, many people became depressed and passive, or frankly materialistic.

Such opinions were particularly obnoxious to the poets. They felt themselves to be in a very special sense the apostles of the spiritual view of life. Materialism and poetry seemed to be antithetical. Nevertheless, they were not so constituted that they could withdraw from the painful controversies into an ideal world of imagination. The whole romantic generation had been supremely interested in ideas: Wordsworth and Coleridge, Byron and Shelley, were intensely concerned, in their various ways, with the place of man in the cosmos. To Byron and Shelley the social problem was paramount; but Wordsworth and Coleridge were especially devoted to man's connection with nature, and announced the discussion of it to be an essential theme of poetry. Coleridge declared: "Believe me, you must master the essence, the *natura naturans*, which presupposes a bond between nature in the higher sense and the soul of man." Wordsworth said in the Preface already quoted: "Poetry is the breath and finer spirit of all knowledge; it is the impassioned expression which is in the countenance of all science." To these assertions made by the poets themselves, the other formulators of critical theory added their support. Hazlitt describes the poet: "He sees things in their eternal beauty, for he sees them as they are; he feels them in their universal interest, for he feels them as they affect the first principles of his and our common nature." Carlyle uttered similar opinions in discussing the poet as *Vates*. Clearly a single principle underlies these critical dicta, namely, that the function of poetry is primarily interpretation: poetry reveals to man his own relationship with external phenomena.

The romantic critics having thus prepared the way, poetry during the Victorian period was permitted to concern itself extensively with the speculations of science. Tennyson and Browning, for example, were fully conscious of a mission to fulfil. They felt an intellectual pleasure in the discoveries of science, and they shared the general sense of encouragement arising from the material advance entailed. But they also considered that the purely materialistic view must be discredited. Accordingly, they set about explaining the theories of science in terms of mysticism; to them the evolutionary theory seemed to deal only with processes and not with first-causes, and so they found that there was still ample room for a spiritual principle in the universe. It was merely necessary to reclassify the attributes of this spiritual entity in conformity with scientific hypotheses. The problem was of such immediate interest to all thinking men that it was accepted without cavil as suitable material for poetry; and the poets were so deeply moved by the seriousness of the situation that they treated it with the intensity of emotion necessary for poetic effectiveness.

As early as 1847 the question of the scientific influence upon poetry was sufficiently prominent to evoke from Leigh Hunt a significant comment:

> It is, in fact, remarkable, that the growth of science and the reappearance of a more poetical kind of poetry have accompanied one another. . . . . We reason to a certain point, and are content with the discoveries of second causes. We reason farther, and find ourselves in the same airy depths as of old. The imagination recognizes its ancient field. Soul, and not body, is her pursuit; the first cause, not the second; the whole effect, not a part of it; the will, the invention, the marvel itself. As long as this lies hidden, she still fancies what agents for it she pleases.

A more concise summary of the aim of the Victorian poets would be hard to find: they were fancying an agent for the process of evolution, and their whole outlook on the universe was affected by the effort.

FORERUNNERS OF DARWIN

When the idea of evolution became an exciting topic in the nineteenth century and forced itself upon the attention of the poets, their knowledge of it was not restricted to the hypothesis of Charles Darwin. *The Origin of Species* does not derive its importance from being an entirely new and unprecedented idea: in various forms the concept of evolution had appeared recurrently in philosophy from the early Greek period onward. On the one hand, scientists had approached it in the course of their experiments and classifications; on the other hand, philosophers had conceived something resembling it as a metaphysical principle, apart from physical processes. But Darwin was the first to see the immense importance of the idea, and to formulate it by means of laborious and extensive demonstrations. He perceived the common principle underlying the separate theories of development which scientists had already advanced in astronomy and geology. And he made the concept a vital concern to the general public: as touched unconsciously or suggested tentatively by previous thinkers, it had not revealed its significance, but in the hands of Darwin it became a dynamic and positive thing which could not be ignored.

The poets, being well-informed people, were acquainted with many of the earlier suggestions of evolution, and reverted to them with fresh interest in the effort to estimate Darwin's hypothesis. Not only were many echoes of the earlier theories incorporated into the poetic commentary, but in the case of both Tennyson and Browning the poets had actually forestalled Darwin in recognizing the importance of the idea for themselves.

The philosophers of Greece and Rome, speculating before the ascendancy of the Mosaic records had precluded investigation of first-causes, came close to the evolutionary idea. The earliest important figures were Heraclitus, who saw the universal law as movement—the perpetual transposition of everything into new shapes—and Empedocles, who held that the four elements are formed into phenomena by the combining force, or love, and the separating force, or hate. Although believing in abiogenesis—spontaneous generation—he described a gradual and painful progression by which vegetable life was succeeded by animal life after many trials and abortions. All the forms occurred by the chance combination of elements, and the monstrous forms gradually became extinct, giving way to those which happened to be adapted efficiently. Thus he shadowed forth the idea of natural selection.

Modern scientists find the best anticipation of Darwinism in Aristotle's *Physics* and *Natural History of Animals*, with his concept of a single chain of development from the polyps to man, and his idea of the "perfecting principle" in nature. Working from his experiments, he constructed an evolutionary theory upon the Socratic and Platonic doctrines, explaining that nature proceeds constantly from the most imperfect to the most perfect, just as the soul advances toward fuller knowledge of transcendent reality. Aristotle held that the process was directed by Intelligent Design, all the imperfections of nature being due to the resistance of matter against the form which sought embodiment. The significance of Aristotle's point of view is that many of the nineteenth-century thinkers followed the same course in turning to Platonic idealism as a spiritual counterpart of physical evolution.

The later classical philosophers, however, reverted to the theory of Empedocles. Through Epicurus the ideas of atomic mechanism and spontaneous generation came to the Roman poet Lucretius, who is particularly important because the literary excellence of his poem *De Rerum Natura* made his theories extremely familiar to succeeding generations. In some respects he seems very close to present-day science, particularly in the concept of all matter being formed from atoms of the same nature—the diverse substances resulting from different arrangements and motions of the atoms; but elsewhere he is definitely contrary to the Darwinian theory, explicitly describing in Book v the separate origin of all species: earth produced "all kinds of herbage, next gave birth to the races of mortal creatures springing up many in number in many ways after divers fashions. For no living creature can have dropped from heaven, nor can those belonging to the land have come out of the salt pools." The least plausible passage of all is that describing the spontaneous generation of human beings from the earth, by a process reminiscent of the modern euphemism about "finding babies among the cabbages."

When Christianity prevailed, the whole mechanistic theory of Epicurus and Lucretius was supplanted. In its Aristotelian form, however, the evolutionary concept survived for some time among certain Fathers of the Church, notably Augustine, who gave a naturalistic interpretation of the Mosaic record. His suggestion, which has been phrased as "potential rather than special creation," was that in the original creation the earth was given merely seminal power, whence natural phenomena developed as the tree from the seed. But these ideas vanished as the scholastic devotion to Aristotle weakened, and we may consider this as the point where the evolution theory of the ancients was defunct and the precursors of the modern theory incipient.

In seeking early traces of the theory one must, of course, beware of *post facto* judgment. An evolutionary significance can be read into many ideas where it was probably accidental, as when Gauguin thought he recognized it in the mythology of the Tahitian natives. One need not linger, therefore, over such isolated trifles as Sir Walter Raleigh's passing comment on the variability of species: such details, no matter how specific, are less important than apparently less relevant ideas which eventually had a more direct bearing on the concept. So the starting-point of modern evolution may be sought in the starting-point of nearly all modern science—the alchemists. However much the savants of today may ridicule those strange speculations, they were the direct precursors of the inductive method and all that it produced. Moreover, they form the link with the ancient theories, for they join hands with the Arabic scientists, who derived directly from Aristotle. Avicenna in the tenth century discussed fossils and geological changes; Avempace said that between men, animals, plants, and minerals there existed strong relations binding them into a single united whole, and that through various grades of development the human soul rises from the level of the instincts which it shares with animals to the "acquired intellect." These ideas reappear in the weird mingling of chemistry and occultism which constituted alchemy.

Both the scientific and the mystical elements of alchemy have a bearing on the later vicissitudes of the evolutionary idea. Since the basic assumption of alchemy was the transmutability of metals, the idea of the four elements, variously combined to constitute all matter, was axiomatic. Again, the homunculus experiments, seeking the artificial propagation of life, dealt with the transmutation idea, this time on the plane of living beings instead of metals. Thus the essential distinctions of species were disregarded in favor of a belief in transformation and development. But the alchemists did not restrict their theories to physical phenomena; they were also mystics, explaining their physical theories by a form of pantheism. They believed in a life-force or vital principle permeating all nature, manifesting itself in a graduated scale of being. Through this force God sustains the universe. Thus divested of its absurd jargon and superstitions, the basic creed is quite in accord with various modern metaphysical doctrines.

Although the Renaissance brought a more materialistic type of science, the esoteric beliefs of Raimon Lull and Paracelsus and the other alchemists were inherited by such avid knowledge-seekers as Giordano Bruno. Later the mystical side of their speculations was expanded by visionaries like Boehme—who formulated his revelations in the jargon of the alchemists—and Swedenborg—who had anticipated many modern scientific discoveries, such as the nebular hypothesis, before he developed his mystical religion. These men were essentially pantheists, proclaiming the progressive character of manifestation, with the quality of divine love as the self-subsisting life of the universe.

It is not to be inferred that these metaphysical systems contributed directly to the scientific concept of evolution; but in the nineteenth century, when Darwinism was supreme and a readjustment of spiritual principles was urgent, men saw a new significance in the mystics; and the poets, being men of wide reading, were particularly acquainted with them. Swedenborg, for instance, exerted a strong influence on Coleridge, Carlyle, Emerson, the Brownings, and others. To the alchemists and mystics, then, more than to any other single source, may be attributed the pantheistic and transcendental concepts which were advanced as consistent with the evolutionary idea.

A few of the more intellectual of the poets may have been aware of the German philosophers, Leibnitz, Kant, and Herder, who inclined to doctrines of continuous development from lower to higher types by natural—possibly mechanical—processes. But the abstruse phraseology and inflexibly abstract methods would be anything but stimulating to the poetic mind, and I doubt very much whether Tennyson or Browning or their contemporaries derived any imaginative value from "perfectability of the monads" or "mechanical causation" even if they had heard of them. Infinitely more effective were certain other movements in eighteenth-century thought, mainly emanating from France, not explicitly evolutionary in themselves, but bringing the mind of the ordinary thinking man to a point from which the step to perception of evolution was easy. On the one hand Voltaire, potent assailant of orthodox religion, set philosophic speculation free from the dominance of ecclesiastical dogma; on the other, Rousseau proclaimed the gospel of progress, exhorting mankind toward a golden age. Their doctrines, which in France produced the revolution, came to England as a literary influence, chiefly embodied in Blake, Godwin, and Shelley. Even Keats wrote *Hyperion* as an allegory of the progress of human intellect from trust in brute force to the godlike wisdom of intuitive understanding. It is true that Rousseau believed in man's original perfection, to which the golden age would be a return; but the idea of progress carried another and more logical implication—that if the race was advancing toward higher stages of development, it must have already advanced from lower stages. Thus the Rousseau ideal of progress joined itself with the general current which was setting toward the concept of evolution, and his glorification of the laws of nature also contributed its share.

Meanwhile, the natural scientists were working toward the same conclusion. As early as the end of the seventeenth century Thomas Burnet and other theologians were striving to reconcile the findings of geology with the Book of Genesis. Soon afterward Diderot and other rationalists opposed the teleological doctrine, and advanced views not unlike those of Empedocles. Contemporary with these theorists were the botanists and zoölogists, Linnaeus and Buffon. The former, although explicitly upholding the separate creation of all species, made the zoölogical and botanical classifications on which those modern sciences are based. Although Buffon, too, was never completely won away from the Genesis story, he found much in comparative anatomy that was irreconcilable with special creation, and his "inspired guesses" regarding the mutability of species caused by environment were developed by Lamarck, Goethe, and Erasmus Darwin.

Lamarck sketched his theory in 1802 in three axioms: that species vary under changing external influences, that there is a fundamental unity in the animal kingdom, and that there is a progressive and perfecting development. He believed that we see in nature a certain order originally imposed by its Author, which is manifested in the successive development of life; we thus study natural forces and nature abandoned to its laws. Instead of suggesting that animals had been created for a certain mode of life, he supposed that their mode of life had created them. The method of this adaptation he held to be "use and disuse"—the frequent and sustained employment of any organ develops it, whereas neglect produces atrophy.

In this belief, he is nearer to the modern theory of "creative evolution" than to the Darwinian theory of entirely accidental adaptation. At the same time as Lamarck, but independently, Goethe also hypothesized the development of organs, in an essay on *The Metamorphosis of Plants* in 1790 and in an almost equally ponderous poem in 1806 on *The Metamorphosis of Animals*. Elsewhere in his work the idea of development appears in more imaginative guise, particularly in the second part of *Faust*, where the classical Walpurgis-Night is a fantasia upon the theme of evolution in three aspects: the evolution of the artistic sense of beauty, portrayed in the course of Greek art; the evolution of the surface of the habitable earth, portrayed in the controversy between Vulcanists and Neptunists; and the evolution of man, portrayed in Homunculus' quest of corporeal existence.

While Lamarck and Goethe were working out their theories, an English physician, Erasmus Darwin, published similar speculations in *Zoönomia* (1794) and in his poems *The Botanic Garden* (1788–92) and *The Temple of Nature* (1802). The chapter on "Generation" in the prose work suggested that all warm-blooded animals may have descended from a single ancestral filament endowed by the First-Cause with powers of expansion; and the copious notes appended to the poems suggest similar ideas of evolution in geology and botany as well as biology. His instances from paleontology and other sources are so clearly presented that we are astonished, with our knowledge of subsequent developments, that he was so unsuccessful in convincing others; but the eccentric poetic imagery which accompanied his arguments evoked nothing but ridicule, and the whole weight of orthodox thought, not only in religion but in science also, was flatly contradictory to his views, and so he was dismissed as a fantastic visionary and was probably more hurtful than helpful to the serious acceptance of the evolutionary concept.

Another theory of the early nineteenth century which strongly implied evolution was Laplace's nebular hypothesis, which declared that the whole universe had been developed by slow natural processes. But even this corroboration of Lamarck, Goethe, and Dr. Darwin failed to shake the vigorous opposition of the conservative scientists, led by Cuvier, whose theory of catastrophism was accepted by geologists in contradiction of the theory of gradual change—known as "uniformitism"—which Lamarck and Goethe upheld. This controversy appears in the *Faust* scene already cited: the Vulcanists held that the surface of the earth was molded by subterranean fire, acting through abrupt cataclysms; the Neptunists, with Goethe, attributed the changes to the agency of water, and regarded them as essentially gradual. The subject reappears in the fourth act, where Mephistopheles is the advocate of the volcanic theory, while Faust is all for gradual development. For a generation the evolutionary idea was suppressed by Cuvier's dogmatic assertion: "All the beings belonging to one of these forms (perpetuated since the beginning of all things, that is, the Creation) constitute what we call species." In 1830 Cuvier's prestige was maintained by his successful controversy with the leader of the evolutionists, Geoffroy Saint-Hilaire.

It was in England that the immediate forebears of the Darwinian theory emerged. Lyell published his *Principles of Geology* in 1830–33, based on the uniformitist hypothesis and accepting the evolutionary principle in many details. In 1844 appeared an anonymous volume (usually attributed to Robert Chambers) entitled *The Vestiges of the Natural History of Creation*, a strong presentation of the scientific evidences for cosmic evolution versus special creation. The writer considered these natural laws to be instruments in working out all the forms of being according to an impulse imparted by God. After being violently assailed as infidel, the book was very widely read and passed through many editions.

The publication of *The Origin of Species* in November, 1859, brought the whole question to a head. Within a month Huxley had supported the theory in a letter to the *Times*, and Wilberforce soon brought it into the current religious controversy by attacking it at the British Association and in the *Quarterly Review*. Darwin received the Royal Society medal in 1864, and Lyell publicly accepted the theory in 1867. Herbert Spencer had long ago made the evolutionary principle the basis of his system and welcomed the corroboration. When Darwin completed the presentation of his theory with *The Descent of Man* in 1871, his hypothesis was firmly established in the scientific world. Since then, his statements of the precise methods of evolution have been questioned, and new theories have been advanced; but the general principle which he enunciated has prevailed and become the basis of all modern science.

EARLY EVOLUTIONARY POEMS

The infrequency with which the pre-Darwinian ideas of evolution found their way into poetry is proof of how abstruse and unfamiliar they always were to the public at large. The few definite appearances are so isolated that one has difficulty in deciding their sources and significance, and they are interesting rather as curiosities than for any influence they exerted on the subsequent relationship of evolution and poetry.

At the beginning of the eighteenth century the conflict between scientific rationalism and dogmatic religion, which is not yet appeased, was initiated by the freethinkers or deists with their disbelief in divine revelation and their dependence on the laws of nature. Pope's *Essay on Man*, which contains many traces of the deism of Shaftesbury and his friends in its logical exposition of the universe, shows how great a change in considering "the ways of God to man" had taken place since Milton. The modern reader finds himself perpetually expecting the next line to express an ex-

plicit evolutionary view, but the poet remains blind
to such implications and restricts himself to the
"argument from design" and the fixed "chain of being"

> which from God began,
> Natures ethereal, human; angel, man;
> Beast, bird, fish, insect which no eye can see,
> No glass can reach; from infinite to thee,
> From thee to nothing.—On superior powers
> Were we to press, inferior might on ours;
> Or in the full creation leave a void,
> Where, one step broken, the great scale's destroyed . . . .
> What if the foot, ordained the dust to tread,
> Or hand, to toil, aspired to be the head?
> Just as absurd for any part to claim
> To be another in this general frame.

This is so direct a rebuttal of evolution that one would
think that Pope was aware of the theory. Similarly,
the mechanistic and atomic cosmology of the Greeks
was attacked with the violence of personal controversy in many poems, such as Sir Richard Blackmore's
incredibly prosy poem *The Creation*, Henry Brooke's
Universal Beauty, and Dr. Arbuthnot's ΓΝΩΘΙ ΣΕ'
ΑΥΤΟΝ, *Know Thyself*. Not only does the ferocity
of these arguments reveal that a materialistic interpretation of science was appearing, but also the de-
fenses of God's existence were very largely made up
of scientific information adduced as proofs of divine
artistry. In presenting these instances, and in stating
the materialistic hypotheses in order to controvert
them, the poets occasionally came close to modern
scientific doctrines without intending it.

Near the end of the eighteenth century, Erasmus

Darwin used poetry as the medium for his evolutionary views; but he was a mediocre poet at best, and besides, the popularity of versified treatises was on the wane; so he evoked only ridicule. The clever parody of James and Horace Smith, *The Loves of the Triangles*, stripped him of any vestige of public respect. Darwin's accounts of the development of life from "the first specks of animated earth" by the gradual acquisition of "new powers" and "larger limbs," of the fierce struggle for survival, and of mankind's eventual rise from some simian family, are startling to the modern reader; but his influence in the uniting of evolutionary science with poetry was wholly deterrent.

The consequent disrepute of metrical scientific expositions did not preclude the growth in English poetry of those more general evolutionary ideas which sprang from the notion of progress. As already remarked, Blake and Shelley and even Keats were attracted by the vision of eventual perfection replacing the present unsatisfactory form of human society, and it was only deficiency of logical thoroughness which prevented them from seeing the corollary that similar progress must have occurred in the past. Coleridge, although better trained in philosophic method, was equally obtuse: the passage already quoted from *Religious Musings* shows that he could regard man occasionally as a "thinking animal" molded by environment; yet in his letters and critical comments he unequivocally scouted Erasmus Darwin's hypothesis and affirmed his belief in a fall from original excellence. Many of his incidental remarks show how close he came to the central principle of evolution, but he stopped short where orthodox faith supervened. When so inexhaustibly speculative a thinker, familiar not only with Erasmus Darwin but also with Goethe, Saint-Hilaire, and Oken, was baffled by the antilogy of evolution and orthodoxy before it even reached the level of conscious recognition, it is not surprising that the more conventionally minded people of his day were entirely oblivious of it.

Among the poets, Byron alone was sufficiently worldly to pay any heed to current science. In *Cain* he was dissatisfied with the Miltonic cosmology, and introduced that of the cataclysmal hypothesis, as he explains in the Preface:

> The author has partly adopted in this poem the notion of Cuvier, that the world had been destroyed several times before the creation of man. This speculation, derived from the different strata and the bones of enormous and unknown animals found in them, is not contrary to the Mosaic account, but rather confirms it; as no human bones have yet been discovered in those strata, although those of many known animals are found near the remains of the unknown.

Byron had enough of the journalistic flair to be attracted by such topical discussions. He returns to the catastrophists more flippantly in *Don Juan* (canto ix):

XXXVII

But let that go:—it will one day be found
With other relics of "a former World,"

When this World shall be *former*, underground,
  Thrown topsy-turvy, twisted, crisp'd, and curl'd,
Baked, fried, or burnt, turn'd inside-out, or drown'd,
  Like all the worlds before, which have been hurl'd
First out of, and then back again to chaos,
The superstratum which will overlay us.

XXXVIII

So Cuvier says:—and then shall come again
  Unto the new creation, rising out
From our old crash, some mystic, ancient strain
  Of things destroy'd and left in airy doubt;
Like to the notions we now entertain
  Of Titans, giants, fellows of about
Some hundred feet in height, *not* to say *miles*,
And mammoths, and your winged crocodiles.

XXXIX

Think if then George the Fourth should be dug up,
  How the new worldlings of the then new East
Will wonder where such animals could sup!
  (For they themselves will be but of the least:
Even worlds miscarry, when too oft they pup,
  And every new creation has decreased
In size, from overworking the material—
Men are but maggots of some huge Earth's burial.)

XL

How will—to these young people, just thrust out
  From some fresh Paradise, and set to plough,
And dig, and sweat, and turn themselves about,
  And plant, and reap, and spin, and grind, and sow,
Till all the arts at length are brought about,
  Especially of war and taxing,—how
I say, will these great relics, when they see 'em,
Look like the monsters of a new museum!

Characteristically, Byron does not undertake to reason the merits of the theory; he pretends to accept it, but with an attitude of irony which leaves his real opinion unrevealed.

As regards the romantic generation, then, the idea of evolution was only just out of sight. Coleridge, Shelley, Keats, and the rest tended toward vague doctrines of development but failed to see that they were incompatible with special creation; Byron had the cultivated man's polite interest in the peculiar geological theory which was midway between the Book of Genesis and the book of Charles Darwin. It is not surprising that the next generation of poets, being of a less emotional and more analytic type, soon attempted to piece out the puzzle; and in so doing, they caught the prevailing mood of their time. The two who recognized the problem at the very beginning of their careers, forestalling scientists and theologians alike, were the two who later dominated their whole era as the Gog and Magog of poetry. Utterly diverse though they were in interest and outlook, Alfred Tennyson and Robert Browning both showed in their earliest poetic experiments that they were already facing the questions which soon demanded universal notice. Only one among their contemporaries gave any evidence of similar precocity, and his restricted fame, resulting from his misanthropy and early death, reduces the importance of his contribution. This was Thomas Lovell Beddoes, whose profession of anatomy brought him into contact with scientific concepts. In addition to passing references in various poems to pre-Adamite creatures and the unity of animal organization, he wrote a remarkable passage which forms a speech of Isbrand, the ambitious and morbid jester in *Death's Jest Book:*

> I have a bit of FIAT in my soul
> And can create myself my little world.
> Had I been born a four-legged child, methinks
> I might have found the steps from dog to man
> And crept into his nature. . . . .
>   It was ever
> My study to find out a way to godhead,
> And on reflection soon I found that first
> I was but half-created; that a power
> Was wanting in my soul to be its soul,
> And this was mine to make. Therefore I fashioned
> A will above my will, that plays upon it,
> As the first soul doth use in men and cattle.
> There's lifeless matter; add the power of shaping,
> And you've the crystal; add again the organs
> Wherewith to subdue sustenance to the form
> And manner of one's self, and you've the plant:
> Add power of motion, senses, and so forth
> And you've all kinds of beasts; suppose a pig:
> To pig add reason, foresight, and such stuff,
> Then you have man. What shall we add to man
> To bring him higher? I begin to think
> That's a discovery I soon shall make.
> Thus, owing nought to books, but being read
> In the odd nature of much fish and fowl,
> And cabbages and beasts, I've raised myself.

This seems too precisely like evolution to be merely an imaginative excursion. The phraseology recalls the writings of the alchemists, and Beddoes may have borrowed the whole notion from them just because it suited his dramatic atmosphere. But the resemblance to those passages in *Faust* wherein Goethe used similar alchemical figures for conveying his evolutionary belief strengthens the probability that Beddoes was aware of the new significance of the idea. This is particularly important because of the close parallel of Beddoes' passage with a longer and more explicit one in Browning's *Paracelsus*, which will be discussed in a later chapter. Browning's poem appeared in 1835; Beddoes' was commenced in 1825, but underwent revision for many years and remained unpublished until 1851. As the two poets had acquaintances in common, Browning may possibly have seen *Death's Jest Book* in manuscript. On the other hand, it is conceivable that Beddoes added the soliloquy after *Paracelsus* appeared. But the resemblance might well have resulted merely from similarity of sources and interests, and from the fact that the idea of evolution was by that time prevalent in many directions. Its contact with poetry was passing from a confused and occasional convergence to a process of assimilation which continued until the end of the century.

DARWINISM AND NINETEENTH-CENTURY THOUGHT

Any discussion of the relationship between the evolutionary theory and nineteenth-century poetry must go far beyond the strictly scientific hypothesis which Darwin propounded. The Darwinian hypothesis itself suffered varying interpretations, ranging down to the vulgar belief that it meant man's descent from monkeys; the poets, if they did not quite agree with that simplification, were all inclined to emphasize particular aspects of the idea which happened to impress them. Then to these selected— and inevitably distorted—elements of Darwinism they added mystical and philosophical ingredients of all sorts, invented by themselves or derived from diverse sources, ancient and modern. Furthermore, no one could estimate the scientific theory dispassionately, because it had promptly entangled itself inextricably with a widespread theological battle.

Whether *The Origin of Species* precipitated the crisis in the religious situation or merely happened to occur simultaneously with it cannot be determined. When the conflict of faith and reason began to stir at the beginning of the eighteenth century, the cause of faith was supported by the whole panoply of established tradition, to which the unaided common sense of the freethinkers was a feeble antagonist. The next hundred years, however, brought more serious assailants, more subtle than the frenzies of the professed atheists like Shelley. Religious precepts were entirely disregarded by the utilitarians when they based ethics on considerations of material welfare; and the Malthusian doctrine of population was scarcely consistent with dependence on the benevolent foresight of the deity. Later came a still more menacing heresy in the form of positivism, which dismissed all metaphysical speculation as meaningless, and respected natural laws as the only certainties. Harriet Martineau, who translated Comte's works in 1853, scandalized the public by her frank profession of infidelity.

Closely related to this rejection of supernaturalism was the progress of "higher criticism," the free analysis of the Bible. It was an adherent of positivism, George Eliot, who translated Strauss's *Leben Jesus* into English in 1846; this book, and its successor, Renan's *Vie de Jésus* (1863), constituted the most noteworthy documents in the rationalistic challenging of the scriptures. When the public realized that the sacred book was being treated as an anthology of Hebrew literature and history, the ascendancy of revealed religion was seriously affected. Most significant of all, the new spirit was taking effect within the Church of England; already disrupted by the reactionary tenets of the Oxford movement, the church was now further beset by the Broad Church movement. These acrimonious disputes aroused a public interest in sectarian affairs unparalleled since the Reformation. The Broad Church party, which strove to admit more liberal speculation into ecclesiastical studies, culminated in the publication in 1860 of *Essays and Reviews*, a group of historical studies in the Scriptures, by eminent churchmen. The seven contributors were met by a storm of contumely, and two of them were suspended by the Court of Arches; the verdict was set aside, however, by the judicial committee, and a similar victory for the liberal cause occurred three years later, when Colenso, Bishop of Natal, was reinstated after being expelled for opposing scriptural authority.

Thus the period from 1860 to 1865 was distinguished by a particularly vicious controversy over biblical authenticity, with the wide circulation of Renan's book, and the excitement caused by *Essays and Reviews* and Colenso's statements, producing a general uneasiness which threatened revolt against the authority of the church. Coming at this moment, the theory of evolution, by immediately reducing the Book of Genesis to the level of primitive mythology, seemed to complete the discrediting of the Bible as a supernatural revelation. Furthermore, by concentrating attention upon the physical basis of life and the identity of man with the lower orders of nature, it appeared to obviate the possibility of a spiritual element in man and of a supernatural creator of the universe. Darwin's emphasis on the struggle for survival suggested a wastefulness and cruelty in nature, incompatible with divine beneficence. The idea of man as the accidental product of blind physical processes encouraged fatalistic and hedonistic philosophies. Hence the impact of the Darwinian theory on English thought is indissolubly connected with the whole trend of rationalism and infidelity.

Certain efforts at compromise were made. Darwin and other scientists disclaimed any antagonism toward religion. Herbert Spencer, seeing that science did not penetrate to first principles, postulated "the Unknowable" behind phenomena, declaring that both science and religion must recognize the impossibility of defining that power. Matthew Arnold, in *Literature and Dogma* (1873), after surveying the rational objec-

tions to miracle and revelation, defined God as "a
stream of tendency that makes for righteousness."
But in spite of these attempts, the great mass of people considered the antagonism to be more extreme:
on the one hand the orthodox utterly condemned science as impious and opposed to God's will; on the
other hand the radical proclaimed entire materialism,
refusing to see any power transcending physical
forces. In 1869 Huxley adopted the word "agnosticism" to signify his inability either to affirm or to deny
any existence beyond the physical, and the term was
widely accepted. Tyndall's famous "Belfast address"
in 1874 declared the independence of scientific speculation from any dominance of theology.

The new science of ethnology showed that Christianity was but one manifestation of a human instinct
which was responsible for all forms of religion. As a
result the non-Christian creeds that had hitherto been
disdained as "heathen" assumed a measure of re-
spectability. In revulsion from the strict dogma
which had prevailed for so many centuries, men turned
with relief to fresh faiths. Somehow the newly re-
habilitated creeds seemed more easily reconcilable
with modern science than the familiar and tradition-
bound tenets of Christianity. Classic mythology
ceased to be a collection of fairy tales, and Swinburne
was able to hymn the Greek divinities with a fervor
that to previous generations would have appeared
factitious. A little later the mystical religions of the
Orient came into prominence: the founding of the

Theosophical Society in 1875 and the popularity of Sir Edwin Arnold's poem *The Light of Asia* (1879) indicate the growing interest in Buddhism and kindred creeds. Their concepts of a universal soul and a spiritual evolution by means of reincarnation were elaborately interpreted as being consistent with the principle of physical evolution. Such mysticism, although unpopular with both ecclesiasts and scientists, continued to gain many adherents and exercised considerable influence, especially on the poets.

In social ideas also the Darwinian theory identified itself very closely with the various tendencies of the period. The material prosperity of England during the nineteenth century produced the optimism and self-satisfaction which Arnold satirized as Philistinism. The idea of progress being paramount, men drew an encouraging vision of potential improvement from the record of the race's emergence from primitive barbarism. The increase in the comforts of civilization appeared to be continuous, and the bourgeois mind enjoyed the pleasant prospect of science rapidly extending the boundaries of man's control. The suggestion of simian ancestry in the evolutionary theory was certainly undignified, but it was an indirect compliment to man's innate abilities; and besides, the theory soon showed its value in advancing the sciences which improved human health and happiness. Moreover, the doctrine of "the survival of the fittest" was complacently adopted by the successful business men of the time in self-justification. In the prevailing optimism Darwin's theory seemed to encourage laissez faire policies and individualism. Carlyle's doctrines of work and leadership, although intended to oppose the bourgeois materialism, were likewise individualistic. The whole spirit of the age, being hopeful and strenuous, extracted from the evolutionary theory the idea of progress and self-confidence.

There was, however, a darker side to the picture. Intensified industrialism had produced serious social problems. To some thinkers it seemed clear that the progress in material prosperity was more than offset by the miseries of the workers in an industrial system. The "struggle for survival" identified itself only too obviously with the depressing population theory of Malthus. Indirectly, the idea of evolution was inimical to the caste system in society and the national system in government: the brotherhood of humanity, which had been an ideal of visionaries at the time of the French Revolution, derived a new significance from the idea that the whole race was striving upward from mean beginnings toward a goal as yet unrealized. Service to the cause of human progress became the highest ideal; the utilitarian doctrine of "the greatest happiness of the greatest number" and the positivist "religion of humanity" assumed deeper meaning. In other words, the evolutionary theory proved the universality of its influence by providing arguments to the socialists and the individualists alike.

These are but a few of the ripples which radiated in

every direction from the impact of the Darwinian hypothesis. Every department of human thought was affected. New sciences came into being—not only the physical and biological sciences depending on the evolutionary principle, but also psychology, sociology, economics. The treatment of history was revolutionized. Ethics was put upon a new basis, and all the topics of religion and metaphysics were disturbed. Probably many people were unconscious of the magnitude of the change, and certainly a vigorous reactionary party flatly opposed it; but these facts are really additional evidence of its thorough pervasion. And even if the general public ignored the extent and gravity of the new theory's implications, and the dogmatists rejected it, there was one group possessed of the wide range of interest and the imaginative penetration to be aware that all intellectual and spiritual values were irrevocably altered. These were the poets.

WHAT THE POETS THOUGHT OF DARWINISM

In its simplest terms, the result of the evolutionary theory was the supplanting of the idea of permanence by the idea of relativity. Of course, the change had been imminent ever since science began to investigate the universe; but so long as the doctrines of orthodox religion were formally respected, most people rested secure. All the evil in the world was attributed to the original sin by which man had forfeited his primal perfection. One had only to live according to the precepts of religion and one could be confident of eternal happiness. Good or wicked deeds would be suitably rewarded or punished in the next world, and self-denial in earthly desires led to compensation by heavenly luxuries. On this solid basis of accepted fact, men established their view of life in which the human race was the pivot of the universe. When microscope and telescope began to reveal infinities surpassing the powers of imagination, man for a time tried to accept them as showing that God had been all the more generous in providing a wonderland for human occupancy; but more and more he became aware of his own insignificance, bounded by inefficient senses and "moving about in worlds not realized." And then the evolutionary theory completed the disruption of the old order. The definite act of creation was replaced by indeterminately long natural processes; the intelligent controlling deity succumbed to blind forces functioning mechanically. Since man was of one essence with the beasts, how could he have an immortal soul, destined for reward or punishment? Human life became a mysterious and melancholy thing, a brief struggle of consciousness against overwhelming and irrational external forces. Mankind appeared as an incidental and fortuitous episode in the age-long history of the stars.

This was the vast shift in human values which gradually revealed itself to the poets. Tennyson, a keen amateur of science, began to perceive the problem about 1830; he recognized the immediate necessity of adapting the idea of God to keep pace with the new outlook. *In Memoriam,* written between 1833 and 1850, is a discussion of the doubts and difficulties involved, an exaltation of human intuition as transcending rational science, and—on that basis—a definition of God as a loving being who directs evolution toward beneficent ends. The other leading poet of the time, Browning, with less attention to scientific arguments, also preached a God of Love, and aligned himself with evolution by finding in human imperfection a promise of development still to come.

The appearance of the Darwinian theory made the problem acute. One of the most painful elements to the poetic mind was the revelation of cruelty in nature. The ruthless struggle for survival, the wasteful fecundity that entailed inevitable destruction, went counter to the belief in beneficence which had colored all previous poetry about nature. If any god existed, he could not be endowed with both omnipotence and benevolence—one or other attribute must be discarded. And if no god existed, nature was but a vast machine indifferent to the sufferings of living beings. Tennyson had to be content with the unsatisfactory conclusion that the world is as yet in the "red dawn" which will eventually develop into a golden noon. Browning dismissed the dilemma more summarily by declaring that suffering and dissatisfaction are necessary concomitants of progress: "Irks care the crop-full bird, frets doubt the maw-crammed beast?" Both Tennyson and Browning were convinced that progress was primarily a matter of the soul, in which earthly life was but an episode.

There were other poets who could not convince themselves of this encouraging possibility. In particular, Matthew Arnold and his friend Arthur Hugh Clough perceived the depressing aspect, and their work was colored with a melancholy fatalistic mood. In *Dover Beach* and *Stanzas in Memory of the Author of Obermann* Arnold spoke regretfully of the loss of faith which left the human spirit unsheltered and oppressed; he looked back to the period when Christianity was unquestioningly accepted, as to a golden age of security and happiness which was irrevocably fled. The fullest expression of his opinions is to be seen in *Empedocles on Etna* (1852)—it is significant that he took the first evolutionist as a mouthpiece to express the fatalism of the nineteenth-century rationalists. He preaches acquiescent endurance of fate and self-reliant defiance of weakness. After surveying the decay of orthodox belief in a benevolent deity who has prearranged man's happiness, he declares that man is conditioned by environment and heredity; his life is but a trivial repetition of an endless recurrent process; he deceives himself with illusions about life, while the world moves on indifferently. Nature has no special regard for humankind:

> Nature, with equal mind,
> Sees all her sons at play;
> Sees man control the wind,
> The wind sweep man away;
> Allows the proudly riding and the founder'd bark.

Whether a man be good or evil, he is similarly the prey to fate; but instead of facing his lot fairly, "to fight as best he can," he has invented supernatural forces, finding it easier to suffer when he can rail at God and Fate for his ills. If any invisible power exists at all, it must be essentially identical with the phenomena and forces of nature, and therefore cannot be omnipotent:

> All things the world which fill
> Of but one stuff are spun,
> That we who rail are still
> With what we rail at, one;
> One with the o'erlabour'd power that through the breadth
> and length
>
> Of earth, and air, and sea,
> In men, and plants, and stones,
> Hath toil perpetually,
> And travails, pants, and moans;
> Fain would do all things well, but sometimes fails in
> strength.

This immanent life-force, creating and sustaining all nature with incomplete success, is the only God and Fate that can be rationally conceived, "this only *is*— is everywhere"; but man insisted on originating a more personal power to blame for his suffering. The next step of the anthropomorphic process comes when man believes that the gods, whom he first created to curse, are beneficent and will "perfect what man vainly tries." As man comes to realize his insignificance, he tends to impute to God the omniscience which he lacks in himself; but Empedocles scorns the argument as illogical. He sees the dream of immortality as a cowardly pretext by which men comfort themselves in the disappointments of life, and he declares that the only true and certain bliss is in making the most of what earthly life offers:

> Is it so small a thing
> To have enjoy'd the sun . . . .
>
> That we must fain a bliss
> Of doubtful future date,
> And, while we dream on this,
> Lose all our present state,
> And relegate to worlds yet distant our repose?

In closing, Empedocles counsels a temperate happiness, neither despair because the orthodox faith is discountenanced by reason nor extravagant hope, but a determination to make the best of life.

This poem expresses all that was abhorrent to Tennyson and Browning. Its materialistic disbelief in a beneficent God and an immortal life, its fatalistic hedonism, are typical of what the new generation was deducing from the evolutionary theory. In Arnold an innate ethical tendency fostered the austere creed of defying fate's blows; but other poets were more blatantly materialistic. In the very year of *The Origin of Species*, Edward Fitzgerald published his version of the *Rubaiyat*. Although the poem did not refer directly to modern science, it won its popularity because it voiced exactly the pessimistic hedonism that so many people drew from evolution. Since an after-life was uncertain, and since man was powerless to overcome the blind fate in which he was enmeshed, life seemed to offer nothing better than self-indulgence.

Fitzgerald displayed this mood as world-weary and disillusioned; Swinburne, a few years later, endowed it with more virility. He combined it with praises of the Greek pantheon, and derived immense glee from his assaults upon the anthropocentric Christian god and the orthodox morality. However, he was not always the epicurean. His most significant evolutionary poems are the *Hymn of Man* and *Hertha,* in which a new creed is shaped—a pantheistic creed in which the human race is deified as the highest manifestation of nature. In the *Hymn of Man* he arraigns the orthodox creed for its selfishness:

Therefore the God that ye made you is grievous, and gives not aid,
Because it is but for your sake that the God of your making is made.
Thou and I and he are not gods made man for a span,
But God, if a God there be, is the substance of men, which is man.
Our lives are as pulses or pores of his manifold body and breath;
As waves of his sea on the shores where birth is the beacon of death.

He goes on to elaborate this concept of a god who is the sum total of mankind, "A God with the world inwound whose clay to his footsole clings." The evolutionary source of such an idea is obvious: man, as the final result of the creative process, is the most perfect embodiment of the life-force; the only spiritual element in the universe is that which has developed within the human species; and religion should be serv-

ice to the cause of the race's further development
rather than the selfish hope of individual salvation.
It is true, Swinburne admits, that man is physically
helpless and vulnerable, a servant of Change, but the
spirit can overcome the cruel blind forces which
hinder him. Man has made himself chains and blinded himself by creating an external God, thereby in-
curring the evils of dogma and priestcraft. As a result, man has suffered dread and doubt and contri-
tion, has delayed his progress, and only now awakens
to the tyranny he suffered. Man's mind has conquered space and comprehended the law of the universe; though the individual perish, the race is immortal:

Men perish, but Man shall endure; lives die, but the life is not
dead.
He hath sight of the secrets of season, the roots of the years and
the fruits,
His soul is at one with the reason of things that is sap to the roots.
He can hear in their changes a sound as the conscience of con-
sonant spheres.
He can see through the years flowing round him the law lying
under the years.

Exulting that man is free from superstition, Swinburne proclaims that the anthropomorphic God is
dead, and the poem closes with "the love-song of
earth": "Glory to man in the highest! for Man is the
master of things."

This is the positivist "religion of humanity" im-
bued with the fervor of a fanatic. Translated into
analytic prose, it is unmistakably derived from scien-

tific rationalism; but Swinburne's abundant emotion and imagery endow it with prophetic extravagance. *Hertha* is in the same mood, using the Teutonic earth-goddess as a symbol of the primordial force whence all life flows:

> I am that which began;
>> Out of me the years roll;
> Out of me God and man;
>> I am equal and whole;
> God changes, and man, and the form of them bodily;
>>> I am the soul.

> First life on my sources
>> First drifted and swam;
> Out of me are the forces
>> That save it or damn;
> Out of me man and woman, and wild-beast and bird;
>>> before God was, I am.

The poem goes on to illustrate the ubiquity of the force, after the usual mystical manner. Then we are told that men are reaching "the morning of manhood" and casting off "the Gods of their fashion"; being responsible for all things, it was this life-spirit that "set the shadow called God in your skies to give light," but now man is evolving beyond it. As component parts of the great life-tree, men are immortal; but the gods are worms in the bark, and perish. The great process of growth, going on eternally, is the sole "guerdon" of existence. Man's part is to further this growth by independence: "the lives of my children made perfect with freedom of soul were my fruits." Man need not pray to Hertha, he need only be free.

The parasitic God that man made is stricken, and truth and love prevail. Man is at one with the universal spirit that brought him forth.

Inspired by precisely the same fact, Arnold and Swinburne reacted in diametrically opposite manners. In the discarding of orthodox faith, Arnold saw uncertainty, futility, and loss of confidence in supernatural protection; Swinburne saw progress, emancipation, and escape from fear of supernatural vengeance. Science had set the mind free in the vastitudes of space; Arnold felt that it revealed man's impotence, and Swinburne that it revealed his omnipotence. Both conclusions, being based on materialistic assumptions, were unsatisfactory to Tennyson and Browning, who clung to belief in God and immortality.

In the foregoing poems of Arnold and Swinburne may be found seminally most of the ideas which were expanded by the next important poets of the evolutionary theme, George Meredith and Thomas Hardy. As in the case of Arnold and Swinburne, the two poets, owing to temperamental differences, move from identical premises to incompatible conclusions. Both saw that the old supernaturalism was inadequate to explain evolution, and both saw that some metaphysical system of explanation was necessary. Meredith agreed with Arnold that the orthodox God was a product of man's selfish desire for an external power to blame or entreat; Hardy agreed with Swinburne that the orthodox God was defunct. To replace him, they both undertook to develop a system out of the evolutionary theory itself. Meredith accepted the idea of *Hertha*, that the cause of the human race is the highest thing in life, and that in the survival of the race the individual finds his immortality. Being essentially a nature poet, Meredith believed in an indwelling power in nature which made for progress, with man's assistance. Hardy accepted the idea of *Empedocles on Etna*, that if there is an invisible power it is a blind and limited one which cannot successfully carry out its designs. Being essentially a poet of fatalism, Hardy believed that progress was an illusion and that the primal force was merely a ceaseless craving for change in manifestation, unconscious of direction. Thus the two moods of Arnold and Swinburne, loosely labeled "pessimism" and "optimism," are reproduced in Hardy and Meredith.

By the nineties the period of evolutionary excitement in English poetry was at an end. Tennyson's late poems expressed a pantheistic creed in which the fact of evolution was accepted, with the corollary that its cruelties would be recompensed in a future spiritual development, and that progress was directed by God. Browning had died in his belief that the onward struggle was the greatest thing in this life and would continue in the next. Arnold had long abandoned poetry, and Swinburne had gradually modified the violence of his opinions until they practically vanished. Meredith and Hardy had given definite form to their systems in which the evolutionary theory was fundamental, and were merely elaborating them. The younger poets either adopted the Tennysonian pantheism or took the evolutionary principle for granted as an accepted phenomenon needing no discussion. The great shift in poetic outlook had been accomplished, and the poets were free to go back to some of the other topics of poetry which had been virtually neglected for a season. The mantle of prophecy and exegesis was laid aside, and the confraternity rather ostentatiously returned to the cultivation of its garden.

Thus the assimilating of the evolutionary idea appears as one of the chief currents of poetic thought during the Victorian era. Nowhere else, probably, can be found a more interesting illustration of the connection between poetic thought and contemporaneous developments in other spheres. Nevertheless, the subject has never been isolated from the general movements of the century and studied by itself. Critics have remarked, in passing, that Tennyson anticipated the Darwinian hypothesis, or that Meredith's philosophy was closely connected with it; but no one has examined and correlated the exact evidence for such statements regarding individual poets, much less traced a definite development in which the various poets marked certain stages, from attempted compromise through extreme discipleship to final tacit acceptance.

Chapter II

ALFRED TENNYSON

THE idea of evolution appeared in Tennyson's poetry not only before the publication of Darwin's theory but even before the *Vestiges of Creation*, which first attracted the English public's attention to the concept. How did a poet come to forestall the scientists in their own game? To admit that in proclaiming his idea boldly as soon as he glimpsed it, on the strength of poetic intuition, instead of spending years in corroborative experiments, he lacked the scientist's caution, does not explain how he got hold of the idea in the first place. The records of his education, reading, hobbies, and friendships show his early contacts with scientific research; special traits of his character and intellect rendered him able to correlate the facts and ideas which he encountered, and to induce the evolutionary theory more promptly than others did; his poems, when studied chronologically, reveal his progress in clarifying the idea and integrating it with his view of life. When Darwin's book gave scientific sanction to the idea, and precipitated terrific discussions of it, Tennyson modified his doctrines in some respects to meet the new views. The poems of his old age gave the most concise expression to the blend of Christianity and evolution which was the ultimate form of his cogitations. Throughout his career, therefore, his utterances on the subject are of importance.

THE YOUNG AMATEUR OF SCIENCE

From boyhood Tennyson evinced a lively interest in scientific studies. His rural surroundings encouraged his keen observation of the habits of birds and beasts and insects, and the rectory library provided books which introduced him to the scientific side of natural history. He was first fascinated by the pictures in Bewick's *British Birds*, and read the accompanying text with tremendous excitement. Thereafter came such books as Sir William Jones's *Eastern Plants* and Baker's *Animalculae*, and, above all, the works of Buffon, wherein the idea of evolution was clearly expounded. The special bent of his early scientific interest, however, was toward astronomy: he used to spend nights with the shepherd on the wold to gaze at the stars, and his advice to his elder brother when, as a schoolboy, he was shy of going to a neighboring dinner-party was: "Think of Herschel's great star-patches, and you will soon get over all that."

This astronomical enthusiasm appeared in his poetry from the very beginning. One of his earliest couplets declared:

> The rays of many a rolling central star,
> Aye flashing earthwards, have not reached us yet.

Another youthful fragment was an attempt to describe the landscape of the moon. These predilections familiarized him with Laplace's nebular theory, which described the development of the existing universe from primordial chaos by a gradual process of nature. In *The Coach of Death*, written when he was about sixteen, there is an imaginative picture of the process:

> That Inn was built at the birth of Time;
> The walls of lava rose,
> Cemented with the burning slime
> That from asphaltus flows.

Several years later he used the same view of the origin of the universe for a simile in the *Supposed Confessions of a Second-Rate Sensitive Mind* (1830):

> .... as from the storm
> Of running fires and fluid range
> Of lawless airs, at last stood out
> This excellence and solid form
> Of constant beauty.

Again, to *The Palace of Art* (1833) Tennyson appended (in the form of a note, since the poem was "already too long") three stanzas "expressive of the joy wherewith the soul contemplated the results of astronomical experiment":

> Regions of lucid matter taking forms,
> Brushes of fire, hazy gleams,
> Clusters and beds of worlds, and bee-like swarms
> Of suns, and starry streams,

proceeding from this general survey of nebular development still in progress to a description of particular constellations.

Later, in *The Princess* (1847) a concise exposition of the nebular hypothesis forms part of the Lady

Psyche's "outline of history," being immediately followed by a statement of evolution in the stricter
sense—that of the human species. In the same poem,
at the expense of a distinctly prosaic effect, Princess
Ida also shows off her knowledge of science:

> There sinks the nebular star we call the Sun,
> If that hypothesis of theirs be sound.

Finally, a less apparent, but perhaps more conclusive,
evidence of Tennyson's thorough assimilation of Laplace's theory is furnished by a metaphor in *In Memoriam* (section lxxxix). The fact that it is so allusive as
to be somewhat obscure to the casual reader suggests
how commonplace the thought had become to the
poet:

> Before the crimson-circled star
> Had fall'n into her father's grave. . . . .

To understand that this means the setting of the
evening star, one must remember Laplace's statement that the planet Venus originated in the sun.

From these evidences of his familiarity with the
nebular hypothesis, it may be concluded that when
Tennyson went to Cambridge in 1828 his scientific
interests had brought him into touch with two of the
special concepts implying evolution—that of Laplace
in astronomy and that of Buffon in biology. At the
university he was stimulated to correlate the idea
with the problems of philosophy; his respected tutor
was William Whewell, historian of the inductive sciences, who would naturally encourage his pupil's in-

ductions, and his associates were the "Apostles,"
thoughtful young men by whom current ideas and
discoveries "on mind and art, and labour, and the
changing mart, and all the framework of the land"
were seriously discussed. When they debated whether
"an intelligible first cause is deducible from the
phenomena of the universe," Tennyson voted in the
negative. In one of these discussions Tennyson advanced the specific theory of human evolution from
rudimentary forms of life, but his colleagues were
unconvinced. "Do you mean," wrote Hallam, "that
the human brain is at first like a madrepore's, then
like a worm's, etc.? but this cannot be for they have
no brains." Yet Hallam knew enough of paleontology
to speak of himself, returning to Cambridge after an
absence, as "a melancholy pterodactyl winging his
lonely flight among the linnets, eagles, and flying
fishes of our degenerate post-Adamic world." Apparently, then, all the members of the group were acquainted with the current interests of science, but
Tennyson alone had made the final inference toward
which the scientists were tending.

After leaving the university he continued to keep in
touch with the investigations of the scientists. He
took every opportunity to look through microscopes
and telescopes, and at the Sterling Club, successor to
the Apostles, he expatiated upon the newest discoveries. A schedule for his studies during the period
1833-35 apportioned the afternoons to languages
and the mornings to science: Tuesday, chemistry;

Wednesday, botany; Thursday, electricity; Friday, animal physiology; Saturday, mechanics. The books which foreshadowed Darwin's hypothesis were frequently in his hands; he read Lyell's *Geology* in 1837, and ordered *Vestiges of the Natural History of Creation* as soon as he saw it advertised, in November, 1844, explaining to his publisher that "it seems to contain many speculations with which I have been familiar for years, and on which I have written more than one poem." In 1855 Herbert Spencer sent him his *Psychology* because of its bearing on the problems discussed in *The Two Voices*. Nor were these interests a side line reserved for his discussions with intellectuals; they invaded his conversations with young ladies, one of whom recorded him in her diary thus:

> He turned to Geology, Weald of Kent, Delta of a great river flowing from as far as Newfoundland. "Conceive," he said, "what an era of the world that must have been, great lizards, marshes, gigantic ferns!" Fancied, standing by a railway at night, the engine must be like some great Ichthyosaurus. . . . . Talked about lower organisms feeling less pain than higher: could not comprehend the feeling of animals with ganglia, little scattered knots of nerves and no brain; spoke of wonderful variety of forms of life, instincts of plants, etc. Told the story of "a Brahmin destroying a microscope because it showed him animals killing each other in a drop of water"; "significant, as if we could destroy facts by refusing to see them."

This substitute for "small talk," unusual as it must have been in early Victorian days, reveals how thoroughly Tennyson was immersed in scientific ideas.

During the same years of early manhood he used his new ideas in poetry with a readiness bespeaking close familiarity, and no misgivings as to their poetic appropriateness. In *Audley Court* (1842) paleontology furnishes a simile in a context by no means dignified:

> . . . . A pasty costly-made,
> Where quail and pigeon, lark and leveret lay,
> Like fossils of the rock.

In *The Epic*, also of 1842, the idea that past events are irrevocable shapes itself as "Nature brings not back the Mastodon." Another simile of this sort occurs in *The Princess* (1847): "Like an old-world mammoth bulk'd in ice. . . . . " In the same poems, as well as these incidental references, there are direct pictures of his own environment and associates which supply similar evidence. As described in the prologue of *The Princess*, the furniture of his friend's manor house included "huge Ammonites and the first bones of Time." The disquietude already affecting orthodox minds is shown in *The Epic* when the Parson's "wider and wider flights" include "hawking at geology and schism." *Edwin Morris* (1851) mentions the talk of a group "who forged a thousand theories of the rock." Thus the poems depicting his everyday life combine with the evidences in his biography to reveal a constant interest in the new discoveries of geology, zoölogy, paleontology, all of which were paving the way for the evolutionary hypothesis; and one realizes the autobiographic element in *Locksley Hall*, the hero of which is described as

> nourishing a youth sublime
> With the fairy tales of science and the long result of Time.

GENERAL IDEAS IMPLYING EVOLUTION

As well as these indications of his approach to the
evolutionary idea through specific scientific data, the
poems of the same earlier period show also a philosophic outlook in which the evolutionary principle
was inherent. A persistent thought which appears
again and again in his work is that of change—the
impermanence of all forms, physical or social. Typical passages from both early and late poems may be
adduced:

> Shadows to which, despite all shocks of Change,
> All onset of capricious Accident,
> Men clung with yearning Hope. . . . .
> —*Timbuctoo*, 1829

> Meet is it changes should control
> Our being, lest we rust in ease.
> We are all changed by still degrees
> All but the basis of the soul. . . . .
>
> Of many changes, aptly joined
> Is bodied forth the second whole.
> —*Love Thou Thy Land* (written 1833)

> The old order changeth, yielding place to new,
> And God fulfils Himself in many ways,
> Lest one good custom should corrupt the world.
> —*Morte d'Arthur*, 1842

Not in vain the distance beacons. Forward, forward let us range,
Let the great world spin forever down the ringing grooves of
change.
—*Locksley Hall*, 1842

Thro' gay quinquenniads would we reap
The flower and quintessence of change.
—*The Day Dream, l'Envoi,* 1842

Then came a change, as all things human change.
—*Enoch Arden,* 1864

Glance at the wheeling orb of change
And greet it with a kindly smile.
—*To Edward Fitzgerald,* 1885

. . . . thy will, a power to make
This ever-changing world of circumstance
In changing, chime with never-changing law.
—*To the Duke of Argyll,* 1885

The idea is, of course, a commonplace; but the very fact that such a commonplace was so often and so emphatically repeated through sixty years is an evidence of its unusual importance to Tennyson. One of its sources was undoubtedly Lucretius, who stressed it as part of his demonstration that all things are mortal; there is a clear echo of the Lucretian manner in the twin poems of the 1830 volume, *Nothing Will Die* and *All Things Will Die.* Tennyson uses Lucretius' images for a lyric theme, with little direct reference to philosophy; yet by contrasting the two antithetical points of view, he seems to hint at a paradox in the philosopher's argument. Lucretius insisted that change is synonymous with death; Tennyson suggests that an opposite conclusion is equally reasonable:

Nothing will die;
All things will change
Thro' eternity. . . . .

> The world was never made;
> It will change, but it will not fade . . . . , etc.

Another philosophic treatment of the subject, that of
Heraclitus, is also the basis of a poem in the 1830
volume, under the title οἱ ρεοντες:

> All thoughts, all creeds, all dreams are true,
>   All visions wild and strange;
> Man is the measure of all truth
>   Unto himself. All truth is change:
> All men do walk in sleep, and all
>   Have faith in what they dream:
> For all things are as they seem to all,
>   And all things flow like a stream.
>
> There is no rest, no calm, no pause,
>   Nor good nor ill, nor light nor shade,
> Nor essence nor eternal laws:
>   For nothing is, but all is made,
> But if I dream that all these are,
>   They are to me for what I dream;
> For all things are as they seem to all,
>   And all things flow like a stream.

"Argal," adds Tennyson in a note, "this very opinion
is only true relatively to the flowing philosophers."
However, in section cxxiii of *In Memoriam* he returns
to the thought more earnestly, opposing his "dream"
of immortality to the physical fluidity of the universe.

Thus an element from classical philosophy is in-
dubitably present in Tennyson's idea, but this does
not explain why he should be attracted to the particular thought again and again. That it was directly

related with his scientific observations is to be seen
in its very earliest appearance, as a fragment surviving from the copious versifying of his boyhood:

> The quick-wing'd gnat doth make a boat
> Of his old husk wherewith to float
> To a new life! all low things range
> To higher! but I cannot change.

As a direct statement of evolution in six words, "All
low things range to higher" might have been spoken
after *The Origin of Species* appeared, instead of half
a century before.

Again, it is the physical universe that supplies the
topic for the *Chorus (in an Unpublished Drama Written
Very Early)* which appeared in the 1830 volume and
in which "change" forms a solemn and impressive
refrain:

> The varied earth, the moving heaven,
>   The rapid waste of roving sea,
> The fountain-pregnant mountains riven
>   To shapes of wildest anarchy
> By secret fire and midnight storms
>   That wander round their windy cones,
> The subtle life, the countless forms
>   Of living things, the wondrous tones
> Of man and beast are full of strange
> Astonishment and boundless change.
>
> Each sun which from the center flings
>   Grand music and redundant fire
> The burning belts, the mighty rings,
>   The murmurous planets' rolling choir,
> The globe-filled arch that, cleaving air,
>   Lost in its effulgence sleeps,

The lawless comets as they glare
    And thunder through the sapphire deeps
In wayward strength are full of strange
    Astonishment and boundless change.

Possibly of a later date, a sonnet which Tennyson gave to his friend C. R. Weld lays more stress on the pleasure derived from the spectacle of perpetual change. There is also one of the paleontological similes to which Tennyson was addicted:

The constant spirit of the world exults
    In fertile change and wide variety,
And this is my delight to live and see
    Old principles still working new results.
Nothing is altogether old or new
    Tho' all things in another form are cast,
And what in human thought is just and true
    Tho' fashioned in a thousand forms will last.

But some high thoughted moods and moulds of mind
    Can never be remodeled or expressed
        Again by any later century,
As in the oldest crusts of Earth we find
    Enormous fossil bones and shapes impressed
        Of ancient races that have ceased to be.

These examples, drawn from his immature and discarded poems, reveal the transition from antique philosophic systems based on the idea of flux to modern scientific theories based on the idea of physical evolution. The two elements are about equally proportioned.

Entirely scientific in character is the application of the idea of change to the human organism. Change is perpetually going on in the tissues of the living body—

"We are all changed by still degrees, all but the basis of the soul," he says in *Love Thou Thy Land*. Also, there is the pre-natal development from a comparatively rudimentary stage to the complexity of function in the living being. This first appears in *The Palace of Art* (1833), when the soul is identifying herself with all the various things she sees:

> "From change to change four times within the womb
> The brain is moulded," she began,
> "So through all phases of all thought I come
> Into the perfect man.
>
> "All nature widens upward: evermore
> The simpler essence lower lies.
> More complex is more perfect, owning more
> Discourse, more widely wise."

Here already the theory of evolution is quite distinct, and although Tennyson did not reprint these stanzas in later editions, he reverted to the same physiological fact, with the evolutionary significance more fully elaborated, in the Epilogue to *In Memoriam*, in *Maud* (1855), and in *De Profundis* (1880).

Having thus convinced himself that perpetual change is an underlying principle of the universe, Tennyson decided that it is beneficial; and hence his idea inevitably became merged with that of progress. It is at the basis of his political principles, his faith in gradual processes "from precedent to precedent." In an early poem (about 1832) entitled *The Statesman* he wrote:

> Knowing those laws are just alone
> That contemplate a mighty plan,
> The frame, the mind, the soul of man,
> Like one that cultivates his own,
>
> He, seeing far an end sublime,
> Contends, despising party-rage,
> To hold the Spirit of the Age
> Against the Spirit of the Time.

The Progress of Spring (about 1836) embodies in the closing stanza the same thought of human development, deriving from the "gradual process" of spring a "simpler saner lesson" analogous to the "larger and fuller" development of the human mind:

> Thy warmths from bud to bud
> Accomplish that blind model in the seed,
> And men have hopes which race the restless blood,
> That after many changes may succeed
> Life, which is Life indeed.

In *The Golden Year* (1846) he echoes Shelley in depicting the future development of civilization in Utopian conditions of life; and the natural corollary of this, that the world is still in a primitive stage, is stated in *The Day Dream, l'Envoi* (1842):

> To sleep thro' terms of mighty wars,
> And wake on science grown to more,
> On secrets of the brain, the stars,
> As wild as aught of fairy lore;
> Titanic forces taking birth
> In divers seasons, divers climes:
> For we are Ancients of the earth,
> And in the morning of the times.

The most concise and definite expression of the thought occurs in *Locksley Hall:*

Yet I doubt not thro' the ages one increasing purpose runs,
And the thoughts of men are widened with the process of the suns.

The idea filled Tennyson with enthusiasm; yet there was a darker implication, which first appears in this same *Locksley Hall*, though not developed to its logical conclusion that was later to rouse such frenzy. If man was on his way to more exalted achievements, he must have already progressed from beginnings which were anything but worthy. The young man in *Locksley Hall* scorns associating with the primitive tribes which retain traces of their kinship with lower animals:

I to herd with narrow foreheads, vacant of our glorious gains,
Like a beast with lower pleasures, like a beast with lower pains!

This was the corollary which evolution appended to the idea of progress; Rousseau and Shelley had dreamed of a return to the pristine virtue in which they imagined the race to have originally lived; but when the nineteenth-century scientists were understood to assert that this pristine condition had been simian in character, attention was shifted from the visionary and uncertain future to the apparently undeniable and shameful past. Even in the forties Tennyson's poetry showed a few hints of man's animal heredity:

For what are men better than sheep or goats
That nourish a blind life within the brain,
If, knowing God, they lift not hands in prayer . . . . ?
                              —Morte d'Arthur

> The blind wildbeast of force
> Whose home is in the sinews of a man. . . . .
>   —*The Princess*

But these suggestions were still few and vague. The optimistic attitude predominated.

DEFINITE COMMITMENT TO EVOLUTION

On coming to write *The Princess*, Tennyson had to face more directly the question of the race's potential development and to adopt a consistent standpoint. The whole fabric of his poem rested on the assumption that the education of women might lead to a more perfect type of humanity in the future. The princess uses the figure of streams floating the thrones of tradition like icebergs to their melting, "for all things serve their time toward that great year of equal mights and rights"; she refuses to fight against the immutable laws of progress, recognizing that their apparent harshness is all for the best; and she disregards the "cancelled Babels" and "monstrous idols" of the past, so long as she hears

> A trumpet in the distance pealing news
> Of better, and Hope, a poising eagle, burns
> Above the unrisen morrow.

It is clear that Tennyson does not mean this to be merely a part of the impractical vision of a manless commonwealth, for after the fallacies of Princess Ida's scheme have been revealed, the idea of woman's essential progress is reiterated as the lesson of the events:

> The woman's cause is man's, they rise or sink
> Together, dwarfed or godlike, bond or free:
> For she that out of Lethe scales with man
> The shining steps of Nature, shares with man
> His nights, his days, moves with him to one goal,
> Stays all the fair young planet in her hands—
> If she be small, slight-natured, miserable,
> How shall man grow?

Whereas, through proper co-operation of the sexes, future perfection will be attained:

> And so these twain, upon the skirts of Time,
> Sit side by side, full-summed in all their powers,
> Dispensing harvest, sowing the To-be . . . .
> Then comes the statelier Eden back to men:
> Then reigns the world's great bridals, chaste and calm,
> Then springs the crowning race of humankind.

And to emphasize still further the fact that this future evolution of the race is the serious argument of the poem, Tennyson upholds it *in propria persona* in the Epilogue:

> "Have patience," I replied, "ourselves are full
> Of social wrong; and maybe wildest dreams
> Are but the needful preludes of the truth:
> This fine old world of ours is but a child
> Yet in the go-cart. Patience! give it time
> To learn its limbs. There is a hand that guides."

In spite of his inclusion of the guiding hand, Tennyson saw that these theories ran counter to orthodox belief, since progress toward a "crowning race" nullified man's creation "in God's image"; so in the early parts of the poem he prepared the way rather skilfully for justifying them. Through the lips of Lady Psyche he presented briefly, and without comment, a

statement of the world's origin as Laplace had described it, proceeding to mention the origin of man in
phrases that might be interpreted without too much
difficulty in accordance with the Genesis story, although the biological interpretation was implied by
the device of *post hoc ergo propter hoc:*

> This world was once a fluid haze of light
> Till toward the centre set the starry tides,
> And eddied into suns, that wheeling cast
> The planets: then the monster, then the man;
> Tatooed or woaded, winter clad in skins,
> Raw from the prime and crushing down his mate;
> As yet we find in barbarous isles, and here
> Among the lowest.

Thus the evolutionary concept of the scientists is
introduced, clear enough for the initiated, but not so
explicit as to force itself on the attention of the orthodox reader as a startling heresy. A little later the
question is taken up again from a different point of
view: the scientific arguments are entirely ignored,
and the possibility of progress is defended on the purely metaphysical grounds that time and succession are
but illusions of the finite mind. Princess Ida demon-
strates that in an eternal "now" the evolutionary
idea does not seem incompatible with the history of
creation in the Book of Genesis:

> Below stuck out
> The bones of some vast bulk that lived and roared
> Before man was. She gazed a while and said
> "As these rude bones to us, are we to her
> That will be." "Dare we dream of that," I ask'd,
> "Which wrought us as the workman and his work,

That practise betters?" "How," she cried, "you love
The metaphysics! . . . .
Let there be light and there was light: 'tis so:
For was, and is, and will be, are but is;
And all creation is one act at once,
The birth of light: but we that are not all,
As parts, can see but parts, now this, now that,
And live, perforce, from thought to thought, and make
One act a phantom of succession: thus
Our weakness somehow shapes the shadow, Time;
But in the shadow will we work, and mould
The woman to the fuller day."

Despite the admirable philosophic panoply, the conclusion reveals feminine logic in evading the original
question of whether human beings have a right to
question God's creative method. Moreover, Ida's
grasp of evolution is not consistently maintained, for
shortly afterward she is to be found adhering to
Archbishop Ussher's chronology:

Six thousand years of fear have made you that
From which I would redeem you.

But considering that the poem appeared twelve years
before *The Origin of Species*, the prevailing assumption of the evolutionary principle is remarkable.
Tennyson intentionally cast over the whole poem an
air of fantasy, but beneath all anachronisms and ex-
travagances lay a serious purpose. Placing the Shel-
leyan view of progress and emancipation against a
new scientific background, he depicted the optimistic
view of evolution with a whole-heartedness to which
he never attained again. More depressing aspects
were already usurping his attention.

EARLY POEMS OF DOUBT

In the foregoing poems, the subject of evolution was secondary to the narrative or descriptive purpose, so that the poet could not digress to discuss all the implications of the idea; he touched upon it casually and linked it with current ideas by stressing the material advantages of progress and the guidance of God as the motive force. But he had not been un- aware of the more serious problem arising from the basic discrepancy between the scientific and the dog- matic views of life. He saw that the rapid spread of scientific incredulity would soon enforce an entire reconstruction of religious faith, and he felt it to be his duty to help in this reconstruction. In 1833 he had resolved to base his poetry on the "broad common interests of the time and of universal humanity," and of such interests the conflict of faith and rationalism was to him the gravest; but during the years from 1833 to 1850 he confined his more serious considera- tions of it to the "short swallow-flights of song" which ultimately assumed the form of *In Memoriam*. After publishing this full and integrated record of his opinions, he began to admit them also into his more objective poems.

Two earlier poems, dealing with the subject of doubt, form a natural prelude to *In Memoriam*. The first, which appeared in 1830, bore the title *Supposed Confessions of a Second-Rate Sensitive Mind*, and thereby betrayed its autobiographic nature by being overanxious to conceal it, since the two protections—

dramatic utterance indicated by the word "supposed" and depreciation by the word "second-rate"— are too conspicuous. But to accept the poem as the record of a state of mind actually experienced by the poet does not oblige us to regard the mood as habitual. Mr. Harold Nicolson, who holds that the tendency toward depression and doubt—although allowed utterance only in these few poems—was the fundamental trait of Tennyson's nature, ranks the *Supposed Confessions* particularly high, as the sole poem in which he did not seek to suppress or disguise his innate pessimism by means of meretricious argument. It is true that science and its resulting materialism are not specifically mentioned as the cause for the loss of faith which is depicted: the speaker's loss of human pride and joy in free will, his fear of what follows death, his conclusion that God is averse to His creatures, are attributed to a vague unrest, and not to any rational cause whatever.

Even if we did not know, however, that at the date of writing the poem Tennyson was already keenly interested in science, we could find within the poem some hint of his mental processes. The speaker says that he had set out confidently to seek truth, holding that "it is man's privilege to doubt" if truth is thereby reached; otherwise he is as the ox and the lamb, unconcerned with their fate.

> Shall we not look into the laws
> Of life and death and things that seem
> And things that be, and analyse

Our double nature, and compare
All creeds till we have found the one,
If one there be?

This clear-cut statement of the scientific point of view hardly conforms with Mr. Nicolson's idea of the poem as the expression of a temperamental mood, unsupported by any process of reasoning. In view of the romantic vagueness of all the poems in the 1830 volume, it is probable that Tennyson preferred the effect of Byronic gloom to the explicit tracing of the scientific arguments with which he was familiar. Three years later, weaned from his immature romanticism by unsympathetic reviews and genuine emotional crises, he handled the subject again, giving the scientific menace to faith its open expression.

The Two Voices is the germ of *In Memoriam*, inspired by the same event—Hallam's death—and introducing the same general idea. It describes a despondent mood, in which the materialistic arguments of science threaten to overcome the orthodox assertions of faith, until an inner intuitive power emerges to triumph over doubt. Whether Mr. Nicolson is right in contending that the sense of confidence is less genuine than the mood of despair, must remain a matter of opinion. It may be admitted that such periods of depression assailed Tennyson at times and that they showed him the "infidel" implications of science which later in the century distressed so many people. But the exact relation of cause and effect between the temperamental liability to doubt and the intellectual promptings of science cannot be defined; the two constantly interact.

Another influence which must be taken into account is that of Lucretius. As the Latin poet was a favorite of Tennyson and Hallam, it is sometimes assumed that Tennyson derived his idea of evolution from the *De Rerum Natura*. Since the Darwinian idea of the development of all species from originals not differentiated is not part of the Lucretian system, it could only have been the atomic theory of matter which was significant. Tennyson paraphrased that particular passage in his dramatic monologue of *Lucretius* (1868):

> I saw the flaring atom-streams
> And torrents of her myriad universe,
> Ruining along the illimitable inane,
> Fly on to clash together again, and make
> Another and another frame of things
> For ever.

Had it not been for the scientific theories of the nineteenth century and Tennyson's interest in them, he would probably have regarded the *De Rerum Natura* as preceding generations had done—as a fantastic nightmare. But as astronomy and physics began to verify Lucretius in the realm of science, Tennyson perceived that there would soon be a revival of his philosophy also. For if Lucretius came so directly and logically to disbelieve in the immortality of the soul and the divine direction of the universe, modern thinkers starting from similar premises would reach the same

conclusion. To oppose such an event became Tennyson's concern; it is the voice of Lucretius which is the
interlocutor in *The Two Voices* and *In Memoriam*,
against whom Tennyson advances all his arguments
on behalf of immortality and a supervising God.
Lucretius, probably owing to a poetic affection for
tradition, did not deny the existence of the gods; but
he depicted them as inaccessibly remote, unconcerned with the destinies of men. Tennyson first
linked this concept with modern skepticism in the
Supposed Confessions:

> Why pray
> To one who heeds not, who can save
> But will not?

In the choric song of *The Lotos Eaters* (1833) the description of the gods is modeled on that of Lucretius
in the third book of *De Rerum Natura:* "They lie beside their nectar, and the bolts are hurled far below
them in the valleys"; and "They smile in secret" at
the panorama of disaster and war and suffering, and
pay no heed to prayers;

> they smile, they find a music centered in a doleful song
> Steaming up, a lamentation and an ancient tale of wrong,
> Like a tale of little meaning tho' the words are strong.

In this particular poem, Tennyson could make the belief appear sufficiently despicable by attributing it to
Ulysses' renegade crew, with the implication that the
poem is an allegory of Epicureanism in general; and
he exaggerated the grimness of the creed by calling

the gods actually cruel, and not, as Lucretius held them, merely indifferent. But he did not rest content with so indirect a condemnation.

The Two Voices is a debate of two opposing forces in the poet's mind—the doubts inspired by science, tending toward depression and suicide, and the faith based on orthodox religion. He does not cling, indeed, to the literal interpretation of the Bible: where the Book of Genesis says that *God* made man on the sixth *day* of creation, Tennyson paraphrases:

> When first the world began
> Young *Nature* thro' five *cycles* ran,
> And in the sixth *she* moulded man.

Despite this modification, however, it is not unjustified to term the positive voice "orthodoxy" and the antagonist "doubt," since the former postulates the immortality of the soul, which the latter denies from a materialistic standpoint.

Orthodoxy claims man to be the final masterpiece of nature because of his "lordliest proportion" of mind, but Doubt says that elsewhere in the universe there may be beings superior to man. When Orthodoxy boasts that science is advancing every month to new discoveries, Doubt dismisses them as infinitesimal in contrast with the endless possibilities untouched. Orthodoxy had hoped "to carve out free space for every human doubt" and to induce the divine secret of life from natural phenomena; Doubt says that such impulses are physiological, a device of nature for enforcing self-preservation by a constant upward struggle toward some vague ideal, though the progress is really imperceptible.

> Thou . . . . owning but a little more
> Than beasts, abidest lame and poor,
> Calling thyself a little lower
> Than angels.

In counseling suicide, Doubt argues that a dead man is enviable in that he enjoys rest from the disappointments of the world—a reminiscence of Lucretius and an anticipation of Thomas Hardy.

Orthodoxy, getting the worst of the argument, shifts to a ground where materialism is at a disadvantage. He adopts the mystical attitude which boldly contradicts the evidence of the senses. (Tennyson had already published a poem on *The Mystic* in the 1830 volume.) Orthodoxy points out that, since it is as impossible to disprove as to prove a life after death, the heart's instinctive conviction of immortality indicates an unseen influence fostering it. With an idea of perfection which is not based on experience, man seems

> through thick veils to apprehend
> A labour working to an end.

He feels, also, an instinctive morality holding the lower impulses in check:

> He knows a baseness in his blood
> At such strange war with something good
> He may not do the thing he would.

In other words, evolution from primitive sensuality is accomplished by this strange divine element which must be on a higher plane than the physical. When Doubt asks whether the soul exists before birth as well as after death, Orthodoxy advances a significant idea—the possibility of reincarnation. Tennyson had already mentioned it in his *Mystic* of 1830:

> His spirit and his secret heart
> The stern experience of converse lives,
> The linked woes of many a fiery change
> Hath purified, and chastened, and made free.

Orthodoxy suggests that life may be an endless cycle with a draught of Lethe to attend "the slipping through from state to state." If the soul has "lapsed from nobler place," it may feel vague emotions and aspirations belonging to that plane; or, on the other hand,

> if through lower lives I came—
> Tho' all experience past became
> Consolidate in mind and frame—

(the last word a clear reference to the organic evidences of evolution), the memory, dealing with time and matter, would not record it.

> Moreover, something is or seems,
> That touches me with mystic gleams,
> Like glimpses of forgotten dreams—
>
> Of something felt, like something here;
> Of something done, I know not where.

Although Doubt says scornfully that such dreams of pre-existence have no tangible proof, Orthodoxy declares that for such a rash act as suicide he might suffer "with this old soul in organs new" and that what he wants, on the contrary, is "more life and fuller." Doubt retires from the contest, and Orthodoxy, after watching a family going to church, concludes that the beauty of the world is a token of "a hidden hope."

The whole poem sets forth, with a conciseness verging on the prosaic, Tennyson's clear recognition of the materialistic pessimism inspired by the scientific view of the universe, and his determination to oppose it by a mysticism not inconsistent with the evolutionary principle. From this nucleus he developed all his later expositions of the subject; and his method, which remained in its essentials identical, was epitomized in his retort to a scientist who was arguing against religion: "T——," said the laureate, bringing down his fist with tremendous force upon the table at which they were sitting, "there *is* a God."

THE STRUGGLE OF SCIENCE AND FAITH

The problems discussed in *The Two Voices* are approached in *In Memoriam* from various angles, with interpolations of lyric and descriptive passages. As the poem was written in diverse moods, over a period of seventeen years, it is impossible to restore the original chronology of the parts. His son's statement that "the sections about evolution had been read by his friends some years before 1844" does not necessarily apply to all the passages in which the influence of the evolutionary idea is latent. In considering the evolutionary sections, therefore, we can only follow the order which Tennyson finally gave to the poem for publication in 1850.

Of course, Tennyson would never have written or thought of writing this elaborate defense of immortality if he had not felt the menace to such a faith implicit in any theory of evolution. His first impulse may have been to clarify his own rather contradictory ideas and emotions, but this soon merged into the mission of helping other people to a reconciliation of science and faith. He ran the risk of inculcating, in the process, the disease as well as the serum, for in the years prior to 1850 the public still regarded scientific discoveries in a mood of militant optimism, interested only in the material benefits to be gained. Tennyson reflected glimpses of this early in *The Two Voices* and recurrently in *In Memoriam*, for example in section xxi (still with the predilection for astronomy):

> Science reaches forth her arms
> To feel from world to world, and charms
> Her secret from the latest moon.

To this popular enthusiasm, *In Memoriam* must have been more significant for the doubts which it expressed than for the rather metaphysical and involved refutations of them. Tennyson was too much of a scientist to deny evolution as a physical principle, but his strong instinct of faith insisted that it should somehow be reconciled with the belief in God which is independent of rationalistic proof. In conversation he said that men could never learn morality and the higher attributes of God from nature even with the aid of science, and that—although scientific truth can never be really at variance with divine truth—men are too apt to mistake what they personally hold to be true for the absolute truth. Not observing that this assertion was double-edged, he wrote *In Memoriam* to show the superiority of the unscientific or intuitive view.

The opening stanza, which must be taken to set the keynote of the poem, expresses the idea of what may be called "spiritual evolution" in the well-known lines:

> I hold it truth with him who sings . . . .
> That men may rise on stepping-stones
> Of their dead selves to higher things.

The reference is to Goethe's "Von Aenderungen zu höheren Aenderungen," which suggests another contributory source for Tennyson's evolutionary idea; but the connection is very secondary, a recognition of kinship in their doctrine rather than a derivative relationship.

In section iii Tennyson introduces the "pessimistic" theme, the sense of a blind and destructive power in nature against which the puny efforts and hopes of mankind are vain. This thought, which has been developed in full by later poets, notably Thomas Hardy, as an immediate deduction from the evidences of evolution, is expressed by Tennyson several times, but always with the emphatic assertion that it is instinctive reaction to sudden grief or to depression of mood, to be uttered merely to be denied. It is the "lying lip" of Sorrow, he explains, which speaks:

> "The stars," she whispers, "blindly run;
> A web is wov'n across the sky;
> From out waste places comes a cry
> And murmurs from the dying sun:
>
> "And all the phantom, Nature, stands
> With all the music in her tone
> A hollow echo of my own,—
> A hollow form with empty hands."

To these thoughts that the universe has passed its period of vitality and is approaching dissolution, and that all man's effort to read purpose or even beauty in Nature is a "pathetic fallacy," Tennyson immediately appends an emphatic rejection of "a thing so blind" to be crushed "like a vice of blood."

Again, in section xxxiv he asserts, as in *The Two Voices*, that self-destruction would follow his loss of belief in immortality:

> My own dim life should teach me this,
> That life shall live for evermore,
> Else earth is darkness to the core,
> And dust and ashes all that is;
>
> This round of green, this orb of flame,
> Fantastic beauty; such as lurks
> In some wild Poet, when he works
> Without a conscience or an aim.

Any such faith in what Thomas Hardy later accepted, with stronger stoicism, as the "Vast Imbecility" would compel Tennyson, he declares, to "drop headforemost in the jaws of vacant darkness." In section 1 he ascribes such horrid suspicions to wholly physiological causes:

> Be near me when the sensuous frame
> Is racked with pangs that conquer trust:
> And Time, a maniac scattering dust,
> And Life, a Fury flinging flame.
>
> Be near me when my faith is dry,
> And men the flies of later spring,
> That lay their eggs, and sting and sing
> And weave their petty cells and die.

Since it was the discoveries of science about the origin of the universe and of man that prompted the distressing materialistic misgivings, Tennyson saw that his belief in the immortal soul could best be defended by adopting those same new discoveries. He says in section xxxv that the conception of the world which science has given has made impossible the hedonistic creed of ignoring an uncertain after-life and seeking present happiness in self-indulgence; such a creed fades into insignificance when compared to

> The sound of streams that swift or slow
> Draw down Æonian hills, and sow
> The dust of continents to be.

He reiterates that the idea of immortality has raised man from his primitive sensual state: if death had been considered the end of all, love would have been

> Mere fellowship of sluggish moods,
> Or in his coarsest Satyr-shape
> Had bruised the herb and crushed the grape,
> And basked and battened in the woods.

In short, we should never have evolved from the brutes.

Assuming, then, as his premise the existence of an immortal soul, Tennyson had to consider its relation to the product of physical evolution—the body. In sections xli and xlii he deals again with the idea of reincarnations by which the soul, like the body, may pass through an evolutionary process. The thought occurs to him that Hallam may be a more highly evolved soul than himself, with whom he can never draw even; their contact was due to the accident of simultaneous incarnation, but Hallam's superior gifts were proof that Tennyson was, and must remain evermore, "a life behind," while "the much-beloved, a lord of large experience," may resume the task of training "to riper growth the mind and will." Tennyson affirms throughout his belief in the survival of personality, and in section xlvii rejects the idea of Nirvana, in which the culmination of spiritual evolution is "remerging in the general Soul."

The most explicit discussions of the scientific hypothesis of evolution appear in two extensive passages, the first embracing sections liv, lv, and lvi. He admits that belief in God and a future life can be defended only on the ground that empirical evidence is transcended by the irrational intuition which promotes the belief. It is his trust "that somehow good will be the final goal of ill" and that all the apparent aimlessness and destruction of nature has some part in the divine plan of progress toward eventual perfec-

tion. The wish for immortality being the most Godlike quality within us, can it be that God and Nature
are at strife, since Nature seems "so careful of the
type, so careless of the single life . . . . that of fifty
seeds she often brings but one to bear?" And even
this is a modified statement of Nature's wastefulness,
since paleontology proves how many whole types have
vanished utterly. So far as natural phenomena go,
the spirit means no more than the breath, and nothing survives. On this basis, man also, "her last work,
who seemed so fair" and who sacrificed himself for
ideals of truth and justice, is doomed to mere extinction. There is intolerable irony in the contrast of
man's religious faith, based on love as "Creation's
final law," and the cruelty of the "struggle for survival"—

> Nature, red in tooth and claw
> With ravine, shriek'd against his creed.

If human life is so futile and frail, man is "a monster,
a dream, a discord," more terrible than the prehistoric
dinosaurs:

> Dragons of the prime
> That tare each other in their slime
> Were mellow music matched with him.

Horrified by the ruthlessness implied in this grim doctrine of "the survival of the fittest," with its special
implication that man, along with all other living
creatures, is but a chance product of blind natural
processes, doomed to extinction as previous types
have been, Tennyson upholds the metaphysical view,

that all the experiences of earthly life are to bear
their fruit in ultimate perfection, bodily incarnation
being but a stage in the soul's development (section
lxxxii):

> Eternal process moving on,
>   From state to state the spirit walks
>   And these are but the shattered stalks,
> Or ruined chrysalis of one.

Thus the concept of evolution is transubstantiated
into a spiritual principle.

The doubts having been conquered, Tennyson proceeds in sections cxviii, cxx, and cxxiii to show that his
faith does not contradict scientific theories but merely
displaces materialistic applications of them. Accepting the evolution of the earth from nebulous matter
and of man from lower prototypes, he proclaims that
the spiritual side of man is not merely a chemical action of the body, that the evolutionary process is still
bearing man upward, and that his inward sense of
immortality is stronger and truer than the inconstant
physical forms of the universe. The history of evolution, "the giant labouring in his youth," shows the
necessity of spiritual faith:

> They say
> The solid earth whereon we tread
>
> In tracts of fluent heat began,
>   And grew to seeming-random forms,
>   The seeming prey of cyclic storms,
> Till at the last arose the man;

Who throve and branched from clime to clime
    The herald of a higher race,
    And of himself in higher place
If so he type this work of time

Within himself, from more to more;
    Or, crowned with attributes of woe
    Like glories, move his course, and show
That life is not as idle ore,

But iron dug from central gloom,
    And heated hot with burning fears,
    And dipt in baths of hissing tears,
And battered with the shocks of doom

To shape and use. Arise and fly
    The reeling Faun, the sensual feast;
    Move upward, working out the beast,
And let the ape and tiger die.

There seems to be a certain confusion between the idea of a racial evolution to which the efforts of each individual contribute (an idea later developed by George Meredith) and the evolution of the individual soul through experience of suffering. But the general argument is clear enough, that the evolutionary process has a spiritual side, and that it is yet to elevate mankind completely above his atavistic traits—a process in which suffering is essential. Tennyson realizes that his early training is responsible for his certainty: if science should ever prove men to be "magnetic mockeries, cunning casts in clay," he would leave the world to the new generation of materialists:

> Let him, the wiser man who springs
> Hereafter, up from childhood shape
> His action like the greater ape,
> But I was born to other things.

Meanwhile, science has only succeeded in showing that all the earth's topography has been transient, trees and cities replacing oceans; and in contrast with this universal inconstancy he is satisfied with his intuitive sense of immortality.

Finally, the Epilogue, written for his sister's marriage in 1842, reviews in a tone of confident serenity the concept of racial evolution, as God's method of developing His creation harmoniously toward perfection. A description of the process of birth, by which the soul animates the unborn infant to pass through the various stages of evolution in the ante-natal period, is followed by the assertion that the next generation, profiting by the efforts of the present, will be nearer to that future perfected race of which Hallam was a forerunner:

> A soul shall draw from out the vast
> And strike his being into bounds,
>
> And, moved thro' life of lower phase,
> Result in man, be born and think,
> And act and love, a closer link
> Between us and the crowning race
>
> Of those that, eye to eye, shall look
> On knowledge; under whose command
> Is Earth and Earth's, and in their hand
> Is Nature like an open book;

No longer half-akin to brute,
    For all we thought and loved and did,
    And hoped, and suffered, is but seed
Of what in them is flower and fruit;

Whereof this man, that with me trod
    This planet, was a nobler type
    Appearing ere the times were ripe,
This friend of mine who lives in God,

That God, which ever lives and loves,
    One God, one law, one element,
    And one far-off divine event
To which the whole creation moves.

Thus the poem ends with a note of assurance in the future of the race and the divine control of evolution.

In Memoriam was welcomed by the leading scientists and philosophers as the first significant effort to give the new problems serious poetic treatment. Herschel, Owen, Sedgwick, Tyndall, and Huxley were among those who admired Tennyson's scientific method and his desire to champion truth. They encouraged him to continue his reconciliation of genuine scientific interest with sincere and independent religious conviction.

TENNYSON'S OPINION OF DARWINISM

For Tennyson, *In Memoriam* had appeased his grief and vanquished his miserable attacks of doubt by confirming his belief in immortality despite all the allowances demanded by science; for the public, it had solaced many similarly afflicted and had aroused serious constructive discussion; for the scientists, it had established Tennyson's right to utter authoritative comments on scientific theories from the metaphysical point of view. For nearly thirty years thereafter, he touched the subject only in incidental and allusive passages, and with the two conflicting elements isolated. In some poems he implied plainly his belief in the truth and spiritual significance of the evolutionary principle; in others, he showed his hatred for the prevalent materialistic interpretation of it by displaying in dramatic form the various types of reaction which this interpretation produced in minds not powerful enough to oppose it.

Maud (1855), the first of these dramatic expositions, was intended to be "the history of a morbid poetic soul under the blighting influence of a recklessly speculative age." The contribution of the evolutionary theory to the blighting process was hopeless despair and a quietism approaching agnosticism. Like Tennyson himself in section lvi of *In Memoriam*, he is obsessed with the cruelty of nature revealed by the "struggle for survival":

For nature is one with rapine, a harm no preacher can heal;
The Mayfly is torn by the swallow, the sparrow is speared by the shrike,
And the whole little wood where I sit is a world of plunder and prey.

He feels that, despite all our pride and beauty, we are puppets, helpless in the unseen hand that perpetually pushes us aside in favor of successors, yet even our ephemeral life is devoted to cruelty and conflict. He feels that man is too despicable to be the final goal of evolution, and may be doomed to the same extinction as the primitive monsters:

A monstrous eft was of old the Lord and Master of Earth,
For him did the high sun flame, and his river billowing ran,
And he felt himself in his force to be Nature's crowning race.
As nine months go to the shaping of an infant ripe for his birth,
So many a million ages have gone to the making of man:
He now is first, but is he the last? is he not too base?

Hence he derives a sense of man's impotence and God's callousness: the world is but one of infinite planets and suns, and the Maker's purpose is "an Isis hid by the veil"; so how can an individual mind fathom it? This passive fatalism (already sketched as early as the *Sensitive Mind* of 1830) is largely responsible for the tragedy of the man whom Tennyson intended to be a modern Hamlet.

Maud was attacked by many critics on the ground that the topical passages were unsuited for poetic treatment. During the next twenty-five years he was occupied with the *Idylls of the King*, the tales of humble life, and the historical dramas, into none of which could contemporary problems readily intrude. While Darwin's theory was the battlefield of the scientific, theological, and public controversy, Tennyson's poetry was less concerned with the matter than it had been during the preceding quarter-century. Having made clear his attitude, he preferred to avoid the stress and uncertainty of the discussion at its height. Besides, much of it followed a line which did not closely concern him, pursuing such quarry as

Christian dogma and the inspiration of Scripture, the struggle to liberate thought from the trammels of historic religion. This problem, vital to Arnold and Clough, serious even to Browning, appears scarcely at all in Tennyson's opinions, for the reason that, whether he was aware of it or not, he was a deist rather than a Christian.

Having formed his own evolutionary theory so many years before, he was naturally interested in *The Origin of Species*, and ordered a copy in advance that he might read it as soon as it appeared; but on the whole he seems to have been disappointed. Instead of welcoming its confirmation of his beliefs, he felt that it encouraged the materialistic viewpoint which he abhorred; so he spoke slightingly of it and stressed his mystical creed more than ever. Of the hypothesis he said, "That makes no difference to me, even if the Darwinians did not, as they do, exaggerate Darwinism. To God all is present. He sees present, past, and future as one." Again, he remarked to Tyndall, "No evolutionist is able to explain the mind of man or how any possible physiological change of tissue can produce conscious thought." He even tended to adopt the popular fallacy that Darwinism implied merely the descent of man from monkeys, remarking to Allingham and Barnes in 1863: "Darwinism, Man from Ape, would that really make any difference? . . . . Time is nothing, are we not all part of Deity?" In short, Darwin's theory served only to force him to a more explicit pantheism.

Nevertheless, he was for a while deeply distressed by the problem of life's meaning. Allingham records his frequent expressions of unhappiness, aroused by man's pettiness, and above all by the apparent profusion and waste of life and the universality of pain and suffering. He would say, "An Omnipotent Creator who could make such a painful world is to me *sometimes* as hard to believe in as to believe in blind matter behind everything. The lavish profusion too in the natural world appals me, from the growths of the tropical forest to the capacity of man to multiply, the torrent of babies." His only escape from such woes was in asserting that the faith in a God of love, since it comes from within us, in direct contradiction to the evidences of nature, must be divinely inspired. It was the problem he had fought out years before, but the Darwinian theory revived it by emphasizing the elements of cruelty and chance.

In his constant effort to gain "some real insight," as Allingham says, "into the nature and prospects of the Human Race," he read every pertinent book with trembling eagerness and questioned everyone who might conceivably help him. His quest kept him in touch with the scientific leaders: he had long chats with Tyndall on mind and matter; Darwin visited him (impressing Mrs. Tennyson as "very kindly, unworldly and agreeable") and to Tennyson's remark, "Your theory of evolution does not make against Christianity," replied "No, certainly not"; and in 1869 he was instrumental in forming the Metaphysi-

cal Society for the full discussion of such topics. All
of these contacts, while winning his respect for "the
earnestness and lofty aims of many agnostics," merely reinforced his conviction that pure materialism was
irrational.

He ended by drawing a faint satisfaction from Darwinism. Holding that the theory "in a modified form
was partially true, although some of Darwin's disciples had drawn unwarrantable inferences," he was inclined to think that the theory helped to teach that
the "Life of Nature is a lower stage in the manifestation of a principle which is more fully manifested in
the spiritual life of man, with the idea that in this
process of evolution the lower is to be regarded as a
means to the higher"; and furthermore, that "mankind is as yet on one of the lowest rungs of the ladder,
although every man has had from everlasting his true
and perfect being in the Divine Consciousness."

His disturbed state of mind at this period is revealed by a couple of unpublished epigrams. A comment on human pettiness (1868) is entitled *By a Darwinian:*

> How is it that men have so little grace,
> When a great man's found to be bad and base,
>   That they chuckle and chatter and mock?
> We come from apes—and are far removed—
> But rejoice when a bigger brother has proved
>   That he springs from the common stock.

Equally cynical is *Fame* (1874), which deduces a less
comforting thought from geological changes than he
uttered in section cxxiii of *In Memoriam:*

> This London once was middle sea,
>   These hills were plains within the past,
>   They will be plains again, and we,
>   Poor devils, babble "we shall last."

In his published work, however, such gloomy comments were excluded. The only traces of evolutionary thought are in the general allegory of the *Idylls of the King*, wherein is shadowed forth the spiritual progress of the world, the gradual advance—despite temporary setbacks—toward the highest ideal mankind can conceive. It was the history, said Tennyson, "not of one man or of one generation, but of a whole cycle of generations." Arthur symbolizes the rational soul, defeating all the brutal and sensual powers in human nature.

Leaving the thankless task of interpreting allegory, one finds the first specific response to *The Origin of Species* to be tiny but suggestive. In the early editions of *In Memoriam* a line in section xxiv had been, "Since Adam left his garden yet"; but in 1860 the line was changed to the form which it has since retained, "Since our first sun arose and set." Tennyson had decided that the almost simultaneous publication of *The Origin of Species* and *Essays and Reviews* had invalidated the Genesis creation-myth even for incidental figurative allusions. Otherwise, the reaction to Darwinism appears only in utterances of increasingly dogmatic pantheism. For the first Metaphysical Society meeting he wrote *The Higher Pantheism*, giving concisely the mystical view of the universe by which he could reconcile physical principles with a pervading spiritual purpose.

It was not till 1880 that he published a poem explicitly discussing evolution. *De Profundis* is a not altogether successful attempt to embody in a short poem the whole range of man's relation to the universe, entailing the use of vague metaphysical phrases. Although the poem is said to have been begun at the birth of Tennyson's eldest son in 1852, internal evidence suggests that it received most of its form later when the Metaphysical Society had affected his vocabulary and the scientific system of evolution had forced him to attempt an equally organized system of his ideas on reincarnation and spiritual development. The doubts and contradictions of the earlier discussions have given place to a didactic certainty. The chief part of the poem is "The Two Greetings" to a new-born infant, stating in two parallel sections the dual development of the individual. First is the physical evolution:

> Out of the deep, my child, out of the deep,
> Where all that was to be, and all that was,
> Whirled for a million aeons thro' the vast
> Waste dawn of multitudinous-eddying light—
> Out of the deep, my child, out of the deep,
> Thro' all this changing world of changeless law,
> And every phase of ever-heightening life,
> And nine long months of ante-natal gloom. . . . .

Then follows Tennyson's idea of the spiritual evolution by which the soul emerges from the divine unity and assumes personality, "from that true world within the world we see, whereof our world is but the bounding shore." When the creation of an individual is willed, the spirit has to suffer banishment into mystery "and the pain of this divisible-indivisible world," half-losing itself in "this fleshly sign that thou art thou" and assuming

> our mortal veil
> And shattered phantom of that infinite One
> Who made thee unconceivably Thyself
> Out of his whole World-self and all in all.

After unhappy attempts to convey his dualistic theory of the universe by such phrases as "finite-infinite space and time," Tennyson sums up his belief in spiritual progress by successive incarnations:

> and still depart
> From death to death thro' life to life, and find
> Nearer and ever nearer Him, who wrought
> Not Matter, not the finite-infinite,
> But this main-miracle, that thou art thou,
> With power on thine own act and on the world.

His opposition to materialism and determinism is now completely systematized and completely metaphysical.

DRAMATIC REPRESENTATIONS OF THE CONTROVERSY

As well as giving ex cathedra statements of his opinions, Tennyson frequently sought to convey them indirectly through dramatic characters. Even in some of the historical monologues we can find a contemporary application, countenanced by Tennyson's own comment, "When I write an antique like this I must put it into a frame—something modern about it. It is no use giving a mere réchauffé of old legends." In *Sir John Oldcastle, Tiresias,* and *Columbus,* which showed enlightened thought struggling against rigid dogma, intelligent readers could scarcely fail to see the parallel with controversies of their own day. *Columbus,* particularly, was significant in its treatment of so-called "heresy" that really produced deeper and truer religious feeling than the dogmatic sects opposing it. Columbus, pioneer of a new hypothesis which was held to contradict scriptural authority, was in a position startlingly like the evolutionist's.

On the other hand, the evils of scientific materialism were also represented. In the monologue *Lucretius* the protagonist is drawn as the noblest of Epicureans, driven to suicide despite his philosophic panoply by his uncomprising materialism:

> Let her that is the womb and tomb of all,
> Great Nature, take, and forcing far apart
> These blind beginnings that have made me man
> Dash them anew together at her will
> Thro' all her cycles—into man once more
> Or beast, or bird or fish, or opulent flower.

In these closing words the similarity of his theory to Darwinism is plainly shown. Tennyson makes Lucretius the spokesman of modern pessimism just as Arnold chose his predecessor Empedocles for the same purpose.

The poem *Lucretius* thus forms one of the series initiated in *Maud,* in which the evil effects of materialism are studied through various dramatic types. The hero of *Maud* assumed passive agnosticism; Edgar, in *The Promise of May* (1882), being a man of more positive character, derived from the same scientific doctrines a thoroughgoing hedonism which makes him an adequate villain for the three-act play in which he is dissected. Tennyson's hatred for the materialist was given such free rein that the Marquis of Queensberry interrupted a performance of the play to protest on behalf of his fellow-freethinkers. Edgar is introduced as a student of scientific works:

> This author . . . . all but proving man
> An automatic series of sensations,
> Has often numbed me into apathy
> Against the unpleasant jolts of this rough road
> That breaks off short into the abysses—made me
> A quietist taking all things easily.

He has, accordingly, no scruples about indulging his lusts at the expense of the innocent country-folk. The cruelty of the struggle for survival provides him with an excuse for his own ruthlessness:

> 'What are we,' says the blind old man in Lear?
> 'As flies to the Gods; they kill us for their sport.'
> The Gods! but they, the shadows of ourselves,
> Have past for ever. It is Nature kills,
> And not for *her* sport either. She knows nothing.
> Man only knows, the worse for him! for why
> Cannot *he* take his pastime like the flies?
> And if my pleasure breed another's pain,
> Well—is not that the course of Nature too,
> From the dim dawn of Being—her main law
> Whereby she grows in beauty—that her flies
> Must massacre each other?

As Edgar's character is revealed, he appears as the exponent of all the social theories that Tennyson most hated and dreaded. He proclaims the downfall of all traditions—marriage, religion, royalty—as directly consequent upon loss of faith in the immortality of the soul:

> When .... man perceives that
> The lost gleam of an after-life but leaves him
> A beast of prey in the dark ..... When the man
> The child of evolution, flings aside
> The swaddling-bands, the morals of the tribe,
> He, following his own instincts as his God,
> Will enter on the larger golden age.

This prospect of self-indulgence and anarchy is the very antithesis of Tennyson's own earlier visions of a golden age, as shown in *The Princess;* his youthful timid radicalism had been routed by the disquieting thoroughness of later apostles of progress.

When Edgar begins to suffer the unhappy consequences of his self-indulgence, he expresses fatalism, in the new scientific guise of heredity:

> Oh my God, if man be only
> A willy-nilly current of sensations—
> Reaction needs must follow revel—yet—
> Why feel remorse, he, knowing that he *must* have
> Moved in the iron grooves of Destiny?
> Remorse is then a part of Destiny,
> Nature a liar, making us feel guilty
> Of her own faults. .... O this mortal house,
> Which we were born into, is haunted by
> The ghosts of the dead passions of dead men;
> And these take flesh again with our own flesh,
> And bring us to confusion.

> He was only
> A poor philosopher who called the mind
> Of children a blank page, a *tabula rasa*,
> There, there is written in invisible inks
> 'Lust, Prodigality, Covetousness, Craft,
> Cowardice, Murder,'—and the heat and fire
> Of life will bring them out.

He tends to conclude that life is not worth living on such conditions, foreseeing the possibility of universal self-destruction—rendered easy by scientific devices—as a result of the general loss of man's "old-world faith" producing a fierce passion "not so much for Death as against Life." But he is not serious enough to put his convictions into practice, and the end of the play finds him embittered by the tragic outcome of his actions, but still defiantly materialistic. He declares himself more tolerant and forgiving than the orthodox clergy because of his recognition of all men as "poor earth worms crawling in this boundless Nature"; and his last words, in reply to the withering contempt addressed to him by the righteous rustics, are his curse on

> This world of mud, with all its idiot gleams
> Of pleasure, all the foul fatalities
> That blast our natural passions into pains.

Tennyson thus renders despicable the sensualist who uses the evolutionary idea as a justification for abandoning moral inhibitions.

Edgar was described as a person of culture and sophistication, "a surface man of theories, true to none." In the dramatic monologue *Despair* (1885)

the speaker is of a different type, a man of passionate
conviction and narrow outlook, who has rebelled violently against the dismal Calvinism of his upbringing,
under the influence of materialistic science. His new
vision of the world as a soulless mechanism and God
as an anthropomorphic fable has driven him to attempt suicide, but even in his misery he prefers the
idea of Nature as an emotionless power to the positive cruelty implied by the Calvinistic creed of a
vengeful deity. The poem points to the danger of
destroying a faith when there is no other to replace it;
but at the same time the too-strict adherence to dogma is shown as sharing the responsibility by ignoring
progress. The speaker had found temporary inspiration in the "growing dawn" which had seemed to
promise escape from "the cramping creeds that had
maddened the people," but now the pessimistic aspect
has conquered. He reads no hope nor deity in "the
suns of the limitless Universe," believing that "the
dark little worlds running round them were worlds of
woe like our own." God has been reduced to man's
vain desire for compensation:

The guess of a worm in the dust and the shadow of its desire—
Of a worm as it writhes in a world of the weak trodden down by
    the strong,
Of a dying worm in a world, all massacre, murder, and wrong.

No longer sustained by the prospect of reward in an
after-life—since, having "come from the brute," man
can have no soul, and must "die with the brute"—he
feels utterly alone, "born of the brainless Nature who

knew not that which she bore," and filled with "pity
for all that aches in the grasp of an idiot power." If
all our earthly sufferings end merely in eternal death,
he sees no reason to endure them; he foresees the
earth eventually depopulated:

When the worm shall have writhed its last, and its last brother
    worm will have fled
From the dead fossil skull that is left in the rocks of an earth
    that is dead.

He attributes his opinions to the "knowing and know-
nothing" books of popular science, which have produced "the new dark-ages" by disseminating doubt,
and reiterates his suicidal intention. When *Despair*
was written, Tennyson's younger contemporaries
were at their heyday; and the laureate was plainly
seeking to discredit Arnold, Fitzgerald, Swinburne,
and Hardy, by the same indirect method which he
had used long before in *The Lotos Eaters* for discrediting Lucretius.

IMMORTALITY REAFFIRMED

Fully convinced that the prevalent agnosticism
must be combated by some form of faith, preferably
his own particular blending of mysticism and evolution, Tennyson repeated in his final poems his favorite arguments that belief in immortality is the only
thing to make life on earth endurable, and that the
inner conviction of immortality outweighs all rational
disputation. The latter appears in *Vastness*, a cumu-
lative series of stanzas describing all the woe and
apparent futility of the world, the insignificance of

human affairs when compared with the universe, until the last line converts the voice of Thomas Hardy into that of Tennyson by interrupting its talk of ants and gnats to proclaim, "Peace, let it be! for I loved him, and love him forever; the dead are not dead, but alive." The Epilogue to *The Charge of the Heavy Brigade* treats the same theme in a less grandiloquent manner: Tennyson compares the task of the modern poet with that of Horace, who could not envisage "the man in Space and Time" and was therefore happier than those who must reconcile "our brief humanities" with the infinite wonders of astronomy; the scientists foresee the world's future as "sun-flame or sunless frost," and all human effort is vain unless man somehow survives:

> And tho', in this lean age forlorn,
>   Too many a voice may cry
> That man can have no after-morn,
>   Not yet of these am I.
> The man remains, and whatsoe'er
>   He wrought of good or brave
> Will mould him thro' the cycle year
>   That dawns beyond the grave.

Thus Tennyson still emphasizes spiritual evolution beyond the physical; and in this poem he ingeniously attempts to reconcile his system with the scriptural story of the fall of man by suggesting that "our mortal shadow, Ill" is punishment for some sin committed early in the evolutionary process—"some abuse of Will in worlds before the man involving ours."

An important poem of the closing years is *The Ancient Sage*, a recension of *The Two Voices* in a slightly more objective form, the dialogue of an old mystic and a young hedonist. Although to this extent dramatic in form, it is so intimately a picture of Tennyson's own ideas and era that he attributed it vaguely to a philosopher living "a thousand summers ere the birth of Christ," instead of specifically to Lao Tse, by whom it was partly suggested. The situation and presentation are strongly reminiscent of Arnold's *Empedocles on Etna*, but the relation of the two people is reversed: it is the young lyrist who denies immortality and the old philosopher who maintains it. The lyrical passages which form the argument of the epicurean, if detached from the blank-verse context, would constitute a complete poem in the Omar Khayyam vein easily attributable to some *fin de siècle* pessimist molded by Clough and Swinburne. But it is chopped up and imbedded in the sermon of the sage, who reviews all Tennyson's favorite contentions based on intuition and mystical visions and the illusion of Time. The youth utters in a light and trivial measure his disdain for the superstitions of religion, and his cynical view of life as a doomed progress toward extinction; the Sage replies with a mixture of rational argument and mystical exaltation, seeing beneath apparent confusion the hidden pattern of evolution and declaring the divine power (which he calls the "Nameless") to be the immanent principle which keeps our so-called "realities" in existence. There is

an unexpected appearance of Browning's favorite doctrine when the Sage says that the very defects of the
earth indicate that "that which knows" shall some-
time

> descend
> On this half-deed, and shape it at the last
> According to the Highest in the Highest.

After producing various subtle metaphysical theories
of unity and relativity and illusion, and a more practical defense of faith on the basis that, since logic can
establish neither immortality nor the contrary with
finality, it is more comfortable to retain faith as "the
sunnier side of doubt," the Sage ends by paternally
recommending the youth to live virtuously for posterity's sake:

> In the fatal sequence of this world
> An evil thought may soil thy children's blood;
> But curb the beast would cast thee in the mire.

The poem shows clearly the many elements which
united to form Tennyson's philosophy—Plato and
Berkeley and the newly-imported oriental mystics
reconciled with physical principles of heredity and
"creative evolution." Although the argument has not
essentially changed in the fifty years since *The Two
Voices*, the cause of intuitive faith has been reinforced
with much metaphysical ammunition, while Doubt
has waned from the stature of Giant Despair to that
of a shallow and ineffectual trifler.

Tennyson summed up his denunciation of contemporary ideas in *Locksley Hall Sixty Years After*.

Realism in art, pessimism in philosophy, socialism in politics, utilitarianism in morals, are lashed furiously, and the representative of the "younger generation" is not given even the perfunctory hearing allowed to the hedonist in *The Ancient Sage;* the old man holds the floor unopposed. Although Tennyson insisted that this poem was not to be regarded as a self-portrait, nevertheless beneath the exaggerated tone of bitterness and disillusionment there are the familiar Tennyson traits—passionate belief in an after-life, in the divine guidance of evolution, and in the higher development toward which man is advancing. A fact which was implicit in several of his poems of this period is here admitted: the ideas which he himself was among the first to formulate and encourage have been perverted by the popular mind toward conclusions which are abhorrent to him. The enthusiasm with which he had greeted scientific progress in the thirties was sadly dimmed by the trend of later thought toward materialism, vivisection, and kindred abominations:

Gone the cry of 'Forward, Forward,' lost within a growing gloom;
Lost, or only heard in silence from the silence of the tomb.

Half the marvels of my morning, triumphs over time and space,
Staled by frequence, shrunk by usage, into commonest commonplace.

Modern vivisection seems to him in some respects worse than the brutal "passions of the primal clan." He blames the leaders of contemporary thought, with their pandering to the lower elements, as lowering "the rising race of men" and turning backward to the beast from which we have risen. He gives a summary of the optimistic evolutionary vision which had glowed in the earlier *Locksley Hall*:

Stronger ever born of weaker, lustier body, larger mind,

Earth at last a warless world, a single race, a single tongue—
I have seen her far away—for is not Earth as yet so young?—

Every tiger madness muzzled, every serpent passion killed. . . . .

But now this Utopian chimera has been blighted by two of the most depressing theories of the period, the Malthusian doctrine and the Darwinian "struggle for survival":

Warless? when her tens are thousands, and her thousands millions, then—
All her harvests all too narrow—who can fancy warless men?

Is there evil but on earth? or pain in every peopled sphere?
Well be grateful for the sounding watchword 'Evolution' here,

Evolution ever climbing after some ideal good,
And reversion ever dragging Evolution in the mud.

What are men that He should heed us? cried the king in sacred song;
Insects of an hour, that hourly work their brother insect wrong,

While the silent Heavens roll, and Suns along their fiery way,
All their planets whirling round them, flash a million miles a day.

Many an Aeon moulded earth before her highest, man, was born,
Many an Aeon too may pass when earth is manless and forlorn.

Only That which made us, meant us to be mightier by and by,
Set the sphere of all the boundless Heavens within the human eye,

Sent the shadow of Himself, the boundless, thro' the human soul;
Boundless inward, in the atom, boundless outward, in the whole.

He resorts to compromise, allowing uncertainty and admitting that progress is not constant:

Far away beyond her myriad coming changes earth will be
Something other than the wildest modern guess of you and me.

Earth may reach her earthly-worst, or if she gain her earthly-best,
Would she find her human offspring this ideal man at rest?

Forward then, but still remember how the course of Time will
    swerve,
Crook and turn upon itself in many a backward streaming curve.

The poem is a strange confusion of contradictory views—condemnation of his contemporaries for thwarting evolution, realization that dreams of progress toward a golden age are impractical, assertions that the Creator is somehow guiding human evolution in spite of man's insignificance in the cosmos. One has a glimpse of how close Tennyson could come to the fatalism and agnosticism which he condemned.

As the best expression of this belief that evolution is God's plan by which He intends man to develop toward perfection, Tennyson used to quote a passage from *The Ring* (1889):

No sudden heaven, nor sudden hell, for man,
But thro' the Will of One who knows and rules—
And utter knowledge is but utter love—

Aeonian evolution, swift or slow,
Through all the Spheres—an ever opening height,
An ever lessening earth.

The poem entitled *By an Evolutionist*, written in 1888
when he was dangerously ill, puts more stress on the
duty of the individual in the evolutionary plan.
Knowledge of his kinship with the brutes should not
make a man give way to sensual instincts, but should
make him more determined to exercise his control
over them; for even if the physical part has been
evolved from lower forms, the spiritual part origi-
nates in the divine, and is temporarily incarnated in
the physical in order to improve it. The record of a
man's life should be the starvation of the wild beast
that was linked with him at birth; and if the soul has
fulfilled this duty, it will inhabit a finer form next
time.

Tennyson's book of 1892, which he felt to be his
final testament to the world, gives a definite summary of his principal opinions. *Kapiolani* and *Akbar*
are further objective representations of people who
defied priestcraft and superstition in the cause of true
religion and human progress. Akbar, particularly, is
for Tennyson a sympathetic figure, with his tolerance
and his vague platonic pantheism. *Crossing the Bar*
repeats his belief in the survival of personality. Two
short poems give final dismissal to the darkest doubts
that had assailed him throughout his career. *God and
the Universe* dismisses the sense of human annihilation arising from the vastness of the physical uni-

verse, and *Faith* dismisses the doubt arising from the apparent ruthless cruelty of nature; both are in the mood of intuitive certainty, seeking no rational support. Finally, two other poems summarize very succinctly his opinions on the actual theme of evolution. *The Dawn* points out that human evolution is only beginning: men have already made admirable progress "from the dens below" in being "no slaves of a four-footed will," and in the millions of years to come we may "lay the Ghost of the Brute that is haunting us yet" and reach unimaginable perfection. The same thought, with more emphasis on the divine guidance of the process, is voiced in *The Making of Man:* no one has yet wholly risen above "the lower world within him, moods of tiger or of ape," but he has far to go, and "prophet-eyes may catch a glory slowly gaining on the shade." Thus sixty years after his pioneer experiments with the theme, Tennyson still maintains that the principle of evolution is genuine and encouraging, but that our inner intuition of immortality and deity must be given precedence over the materialism of physical science.

By making personal intuition his final arbiter, he could escape the charge of inconsistency. His natural interest in science, which had early led him to perceive the evolutionary principle, tempted him to undertake rational analysis, but he always desisted whenever his cherished faith was endangered. His recognition of this peril within his own mind gave him warning of its menace to the public; and when the

Darwinian theory fulfilled his forebodings by promoting agnosticism and hedonism, he strenuously opposed it. In particular, its attention to the cruelty and waste in natural processes distressed him; but he gradually decided that God intends all such apparent suffering as contributing to progress. His original sketchy reconciliation of faith and evolution, in *In Memoriam*, was insufficient to withstand the generation of determinists and materialists which derived from Darwinism and ensconced itself in literature in the sixties. Not satisfied with depicting dramatically the shocking effects of such views on moral and intellectual fiber, he felt that he must oppose the organized evidence of the physical scientists with an equally systematic creed; so he studied metaphysics and equipped evolution with a spiritual counterpart. Using a pantheistic conception of the universe as an embodiment of God, he suggested that time may be an illusion due to the limitations of the human mind, in which case evolution and creation need not be contradictory. The soul, he held, evolves both before and after its span of life in the body. He frequently implied that this evolution entails repeated incarnation in physical form, but at other times he seemed to think that the development is upon other planes of existence. In any case, he held that the experiences of life are but preparation for the future development. Although never explaining how the evolving soul forms its contact with the evolving body, he assumed the two processes to be consistent; and in his later poems, oracular as befitted his age and repute, he proclaimed that present imperfections are due to the lingering remnants of "the ape and tiger" which will be eliminated as mankind continues to advance under God's guidance. Having satisfied himself that evolution does not necessarily imply the soul to be a chemical process and belief in God a physiological impulse, he felt justified in accepting the principle without relinquishing his intuitive faith. Throughout the period of fiercest controversy between "science" and "religion" Tennyson retained and elaborated his compromise between the two which he had constructed before the general engagement began.

Chapter III
ROBERT BROWNING

ALTHOUGH Browning, like Tennyson, prophetically stated the idea of evolution a quarter-century before Darwin, the two poets were entirely dissimilar in their approach to the subject, in the form of their statement, and in the subsequent development of their opinions. Tennyson made constant references to contemporary science, revealing in scattered passages his gradual perception of evolution by distinct processes of thought and from definite sources of information. Browning's statement of the idea appeared in a single passage of considerable length, setting forth the concept extensively as a philosophical theory, with no indications of the grounds on which he formulated it. The passage occurs in *Paracelsus* (1835), and Browning did not again explicitly refer to evolution until after the Darwinian theory had become a topic of general discussion. The problem, therefore, is whether the concept was to any extent an integral part of his thought or was merely placed dramatically in the mouth of Paracelsus and thereafter abandoned. Where he got hold of the idea must also be considered, since his life, letters, and poems show nothing like Tennyson's numerous scientific contacts.

Browning's education was less systematic than Tennyson's, though in some directions undoubtedly more extensive. It depended chiefly on his father's well-stocked and very miscellaneous library. The elder Browning was notable for an inexhaustible store of information, but his chief interests were Greek literature and medieval occultism, so that his intimacy with modern science is problematical, except that he knew enough of anatomy to teach it in his old age to his grandson in comic illustrated rhymes. The future poet's favorite book was *The Wonders of the Little World* by the seventeenth-century divine, Nathaniel Wanley, with its thousands of anecdotes illustrating the prodigies of human nature, and anything but scientific in its attitude. His only university training was a few weeks of Greek and German at the newly established university of London. The obviously autobiographical passages in *Pauline*, wherein the speaker describes his intellectual development, mention only imaginative books.

William Sharp includes in Browning's education "occasionally various experimental studies in technical science," but gives no instances. It is known that he attended some lectures by the abdominal expert, Dr. Blundell, which aroused in him a considerable interest in the sciences connected with medicine. Later, in Italy, he assiduously studied anatomy as a preparation for drawing. But these facts indicate a casual and intermittent interest rather than any strong enthusiasm.

Nor do the friends of his early manhood appear to have had much concern with science. The letters exchanged by Browning, Dommett, and Arnould are innocent of any reference to it; and *Waring*, the only poem in which he depicts the social life he was leading at that time, fails to reveal anything like Tennyson's interests. Browning writes of the year 1842—the year of *Locksley Hall* with its feverish excitement over contemporary advances:

> Someone shall somehow run amuck
> With this old world for want of strife
> Sound asleep. Contrive, contrive
> To rouse us, Waring! Who's alive?
> Our men scarce seem in earnest now.
> Distinguished names!—but 'tis, somehow,
> As if they played at being names
> Still more distinguished, like the games
> Of children. Turn our sport to earnest
> With a visage of the sternest!
> Bring the real times back, confessed
> Still better than our very best.

Nowhere in Browning's recorded conversations can his view of contemporary science be discovered. Indeed, nearly everyone who talked with him was struck with his earnest avoidance of serious and debated subjects. Consistent with the general impression, though expressed less temperately, is Robert Buchanan's account of his

dilettante omniscience. Many of his opinions seemed narrow, some of them even childish. They seemed to me essentially the opinions of a man in good society, less concerned with the great movements of Humanity than with the fleeting artistic phenomena of the hour. On some of the great subjects which concern our happiness as conditioned beings, he scarcely seemed to have thought at all.

It is true that this refers to the dining-out Browning of the seventies; but contrast it with Tennyson's preoccupation at all ages, and in every company, with the problems of science and faith.

The letters to Elizabeth Barrett contain very occasional allusions to science, generally disparaging to its methods. As sundry poems show, he was strongly opposed to vivisection, and in the same vein remarks, "How different that is from lying to be dried and pressed flat, and prized highly, and put in a book with a proper account at top and bottom, and shut up and put away . . . . and the book called a 'Flora' besides." And again, "All which pieces of instinct I could detect, and catch struggling and pin to death in a moment, and put a label on, with name, genus, and species, just like a horrible entomologist." And showing a less antagonistic view, but still that of an utterly uninitiated layman, "as the fine French analysts bring themselves to appreciate matter in its refined stages by *millionths*."

It would be rash to assume from such negative evidence that he was entirely unfamiliar with scientific ideas. His alert mind, wide reading, and retentive memory must have given him some knowledge of the current discussions. Mrs. Orr says: "He absorbed almost unconsciously every item which added

itself to the sum of general knowledge. . . . . His
mind was made up on the chief subjects of contemporary thought, and what was novel or controversial
in the proceeding had no attraction for him." Another admirer, Dr. Berdoe, has collected an assort-
ment of passages which are intended to prove that
Browning's poetry reveals a minute acquaintance
with many sciences, though Browning himself mod-
estly wrote of them as "my attempts to make use of
the few materials of a scientific nature which I have
had any opportunity of collecting—would they were
of more importance." Of these citations, only some
twenty-four occur in poems written earlier than 1859.
Certain of them contain mere commonplaces of information, such as "this moon's control over the sea's
depths," which is neither abstruse nor modern. Most
of the others are so vague or allusive that their scientific traits would never be observed without Berdoe's
insistence. A line in *Easter Day*, for instance, "flesh
refine to nerve beneath the spirit's play," evokes
from Berdoe an enthusiastic paragraph on this "precise statement of the origin of the nervous system"
which forestalls the investigations of Herbert Spencer, Romanes, and Eimer in "the evolution of the
first rudiments of a nervous system in Medusae and
other low types of animal life." Similarly, Berdoe
interprets a description of the ear as "hungry for
music": "here, of course, the reference is to the organ of Corti in the internal ear. . . . ." But in spite
of this elaborate special pleading, the learned doctor

fails to convince us that Browning was "intimately acquainted with the physical sciences." A smattering of popular science must inevitably have merged into his general view of the world, but his interests did not lie in that direction, and he clearly made little effort to examine or correlate the chance data that he picked up.

THE EVOLUTIONARY PASSAGE IN "PARACELSUS"

In spite of his apparent remoteness from the scientific theories which were already afoot, Browning published in 1835, in his dramatic poem *Paracelsus*, a statement of the evolutionary principle more extensive and coherent than anything which Tennyson had said about it by that date. Nor was the passage an accidental or equivocal allusion; it stands as the very climax and message of the poem. Paracelsus, after all his failures and false aims, rises from his deathbed to utter the vision of life's meaning that has finally been revealed to him. The more strongly to emphasize its significance, the section is entitled *Paracelsus Attains*.

Naturally, the sixteenth-century philosopher cannot be expected to base his exposition on the researches of nineteenth-century science; but, as a matter of fact, Paracelsus was the pioneer of modern scientific methods, as Browning knew—referring to him in the notes as the father of modern chemistry—so the restrictions of dramatic utterance cannot be held wholly responsible for the absence of allusions to his scientific work. His belief in transmutation, his search for the artificial propagation of life, and other of his theories might plausibly have been adduced as contributing to the theory of evolution which he expounds in the poem; but Browning was apparently determined to avoid all processes of induction and all contacts with the physical plane, for he does not present the theory till Paracelsus has relinquished his scientific ambitions in disgust at their futility, and the conception of it is clearly shown to be wholly intuitive.

The idea resembles the recent theories of "creative evolution" rather than Darwin's "natural selection." God is perceived as the life-force and as identical with joy, existing in all the manifestations of life, from the lowest to the highest, wherever the joy of living exists; and always in this enjoyment of life there is an element of dissatisfaction, a longing toward fresh happiness beyond. It appears in the geological changes of the earth (and this is the only scientific reference in the poem):

> The centre-fire heaves underneath the earth,
> And the earth changes like a human face;
> The molten ore bursts up among the rocks,
> Winds into the stone's heart, outbranches bright
> In hidden mines, spots barren river-beds,
> Crumbled into fine sand where sunbeams bask.....

Still in the springtime's recrudescence of life "God renews his ancient rapture," i.e., the process of creation is repeated. Paracelsus goes on to state definitely that all the early strivings of the life-force through

the various primitive forms reached their eventual
fulfilment in man:

> Thus he dwells
> From life's minute beginnings, up at last
> To man—the consummation of this scheme
> Of being, the completion of this sphere
> Of life: whose attributes had here and there
> Been scattered o'er the visible world before,
> Asking to be combined, dim fragments meant
> To be united in some wondrous whole,
> Imperfect qualities throughout creation
> Suggesting some one creature yet to make,
> Some point where all those scattered rays should meet
> Convergent in the faculties of man. . . . .
> Hints and previsions of which faculties
> Are strewn confusedly everywhere about
> The inferior natures, and all lead up higher,
> All shape out dimly the superior race,
> The heir of hopes too fair to turn out false,
> And man appears at last. So far the seal
> Is put on life; one stage of being complete,
> One scheme wound up: and from the grand result
> A supplementary reflux of light
> Illustrates all the inferior grades, explains
> Each back step in the circle.

These last lines apparently mean that the anatomy
of man reveals his relationship to the lower orders
through which he has evolved—which is, of course,
one of the scientific demonstrations of evolution.

Immediately he proceeds to the thought which
Tennyson also stressed as a corollary of evolution—
that the future of the race will continue the process
of development:

> For these things tend still upward, progress is
> The law of life, man is not Man as yet.

> Nor shall I deem his object served, his end
> Attained, his genuine strength put fairly forth,
> While only here and there a star dispels
> The darkness, here and there a towering mind
> O'erlooks its prostrate fellows: when the host
> Is out at once to the despair of night,
> When all mankind at once is perfected,
> Equal in full-blown powers—then, not till then,
> I say, begins man's general infancy.

Thus the full development of intellect, the completion of the present cycle of evolution, will be but the starting-point of a new cycle:

> all tended to mankind,
> And, man produced, all has its end thus far:
> But in completed man begins anew
> A tendency to God. Prognostics told
> Man's near approach; so in man's self arise
> August anticipations, symbols, types
> Of a dim splendor ever on before
> In that eternal cycle life pursues.

Paracelsus realizes that the service of mankind, which will help toward the advance of the race, is the highest task. He had formerly wished to ignore man's ignominious past, and had dreamed of a sudden millennium:

> I would have had one day, one moment's space
> Change man's condition, push each slumbering claim
> Of mastery o'er the elemental world
> At once to full maturity, then roll
> Oblivion o'er the work, and hide from man
> What night had ushered morn.

But he sees, now, that love of man's imperfections and recognition of the struggle through which he has risen are necessary in anyone who hopes to serve him:

> To see a good in evil, and a hope
> In ill-success; to sympathize, be proud
> Of their half-reasons, faint aspirings, dim
> Struggles for truth, their poorest fallacies,
> Their prejudice and fears and cares and doubts;
> All with a touch of nobleness, despite
> Their error, upward tending all though weak,
> Like plants in mines which never saw the sun,
> But dream of him, and guess where he may be,
> And do their best to climb and get to him.

All this is like enough to *The Princess*, save that the emphasis is on the spiritual rather than the social aspect of progress, a difference typical of the diverse interests of the two poets. In both poems, the exposition of evolution is climactic. The whole four thousand lines of *Paracelsus* must have been written in order to prepare the way thoroughly for this concluding evangel, since it alone gives unity to the poem. Since Browning obviously considered it a topic of such high importance, we may infer that Paracelsus is being used as a spokesman for the poet himself. The first question, then, is how much—if any—of the idea was expressed by the Paracelsus of actual history. Browning insisted that the poem was simply a revitalizing of the available data and did not depart from the recorded facts to any serious degree. Paracelsus was one of the people that the poet's father used to discuss with such intimacy that he seemed to be a personal crony; and in addition to the three folio volumes of Paracelsus' works in the paternal library, Browning consulted the material in the British

Museum. So the poem's claim to authenticity may be taken seriously.

The strange admixture of mysticism and science entertained by the medieval alchemists reached in Paracelsus its highest development. On the mystical side, he was a student of the Kabbala and similar esoteric works: on the scientific side, he was an enthusiastic exponent of inductive method, agog to investigate everything that came within his ken. In his works, amid vast masses of solemnly recorded superstitions and alchemical calculations, it is possible to unearth statements which indicate, in the light of modern scientific research, that Paracelsus had stumbled, through his maze of occult theories, on ideas far in advance of his age. Baas in his *History of Medicine* writes:

> A striking similarity with the doctrines of Darwin is found in the view of Paracelsus that the origin of everything is simply the transformation of germs always existing (and therefore is a metamorphosis), as well as in the fact that he maintained that every object and being originated at the expense of, and through the destruction of, another—a doctrine in which we see already developed the war of individual against individual, and the struggle for existence.

This doctrine of the real Paracelsus—which is, of course, the atomic theory of Epicurus—resembles Darwin's more closely than it resembles the high idealism of Browning's poem. Throughout his works, however, Paracelsus was intensely religious, as he is depicted in the poem, seeing all the processes of nature as the actions of God. He based his medical lore

on the relationship which man the microcosm bears
to nature the macrocosm. "There is nothing in heav-
en and earth," he says, "which is not in man, and
God who is in heaven is also in man." He insists on
the single mystical "spirit of truth," "soul of the
world," and so on, underlying all things, restoring
"the destructible things of nature" and identical with
the creative force "which in the Beginning filled the
earth and brooded over the waters."

Coming down to the material plane, he clearly perceives the planet's geological evolution: "The whole
ball of the earth is only something thrown off, concrete, mixed, corrupted, ground, and again coagulat-
ed, and gradually liquefied into one mass, into a stony
work, which has its seat and its rest in the midst of
the firmamental sphere." The origin of man, however, was Paracelsus' particular concern. He tells us
that after God had created all the elements, stars, and
all other physical phenomena, and had disposed them
according to his will, he proceeded lastly to the forming of man. He extracted the essence out of the four
elements into one mass; he extracted also the essence
of wisdom, art, and reason out of the stars, and this
twofold essence he congested into one mass—what
the Bible calls the slime of the earth. All potency,
all property, all essence of the superior and inferior
globe God joined in his hand, and from these he
formed man according to his image.

Finally, Paracelsus gives clear hints of man's future

development. After discussing the transmutation of minerals, he adds:

> So also man must become that which he is not. In a word, whatever is to pass into its ultimate matter must become something different from what its origin was—varied and diverse, though from one mother. Thus God willed to be One in all, that is, to be the one primal and ultimate matter of all things.

Thus one can pick out from Paracelsus' alchemical jargon the main points which Browning developed in his poem; but it is a physical rather than a humanistic theory. Browning subtly modified it all, raising it from the level of the superstitious charlatan to that of the philosophic visionary by making love of mankind the spur. As Tennyson recognized that the science of Lucretius had enough in common with that of his own day to make him a pertinent type of scientific pessimism, so Browning recognized that the science of Paracelsus had enough in common with that of his own day to make him a pertinent type of scientific optimism. Browning must have known something of the incipient evolutionary theory or he would not have observed the resemblances to it in the obscure doctrines of a medieval hermetic philosopher, which three centuries had dismissed as fantastic.

FIRST GLIMPSES OF EVOLUTION

In search of possible sources for Browning's evolutionary idea, we must turn to the poem which is the spiritual autobiography of his adolescence, *Pauline*. This intimate piece of introspection, colored by the somewhat morbid fancy of youth, was given a flimsy veil of imaginary circumstances, just as Tennyson's similar poem, the *Supposed Confessions of a Second-Rate Sensitive Mind*, was feebly protected by pretenses of dramatic utterance. Browning's friends recognized *Pauline* as an authentic, though romanticized, record; and the very fact that he prevented its republication for many years is further evidence. Moreover, its general ideas are wholly consistent with those later expressed in *Paracelsus* and *Sordello*.

Browning had met and dismissed his problems of faith and doubt at an earlier age than Tennyson. At fifteen he read Voltaire, and in the next year Shelley, with the result that he became a professing atheist and, for two years, a practicing vegetarian. His brief atheism was potent enough to disturb seriously the faith of the devout Sarah Flower, and to be still associated with his name by gossip fifteen years later, when he was wooing Elizabeth Barrett. By the time he came to write *Pauline*, however, at the age of twenty, he was already able to look back on his doubts as conquered. It must be remembered that, growing up among Unitarians, he imbibed a much more liberal spirit than his orthodox contemporaries, such as Tennyson, and so was not so profoundly agitated by any sudden discovery of rationalism.

Among the causes for doubt which are described in *Pauline*, the findings of physical science are not included. The speaker is "the scoffer who has probed life's vanity," but his divagations do not extend to dabbling in scientific theories. Indeed, he has always

had "a yearning after God," and sees him everywhere,
even while professing doubt of his existence. In the
first liberation of his mental powers he had "dreamed
not of restraint, but gazed on all things," surveying
various systems with the vanity of weakness to choose
his prize. Influenced by Plato and Shelley, he formed
a high dream of future perfection for the race:

> I was vowed to liberty,
> Men were to be as gods and earth as heaven.

But when he set out to test this theory by contact
with real life, he suddenly lost his faith in any power
higher than the human mind, and became a hedonist.
No rational cause is stated; just as in the Sensitive
Mind of Tennyson's poem, it is shown as a mere
mood. Browning's speaker, however, formulates a
dualistic faith, holding that the soul has

> floated from its sphere
> Of wide dominion into the dim orb
> Of self . . . .

(compare Tennyson's *De Profundis*) and that the
sensual instincts of the flesh strive to debase it. But
the soul asserts itself:

> Souls alter not, and mine must still advance. . . . .
> I cannot chain my soul: it will not rest
> In its clay prison, this most narrow sphere:
> It has strange impulse, tendency, desire,
> Which nowise I account for nor explain,
> But cannot stifle, being bound to trust
> All feelings equally, to hear all sides:
> How can my life indulge them? yet they live
> Referring to some state of life unknown.

He is consumed with an excruciating desire to experience all pleasure and master all knowledge: but the latter craving he keeps resolutely in check, feeling that he would perish if he were to forego "all happy ignorant doubts and fears."

The same impulses characterize Paracelsus, freed from such nullifying infirmity of purpose. He finds justification for his effort to master all the secrets of life in the fact that the impulse exists so strongly within him. He believes that in obeying it he is obeying the intention of God: "Is it for human will to institute such impulses?" God would not give the energy if it were not to be utilized. Thus, as with Tennyson, intuition is exalted as the criterion of truth; and Paracelsus explains it by the dualistic concept already noted in *Pauline:*

> Truth is within ourselves. . . . .
> Wall upon wall, the gross flesh hems it in,
> This perfect, clear perception—which is truth,
> A blinding and perverting carnal mesh
> Binds it and makes all error.

Still paralleling Tennyson, Browning makes Paracelsus suggest the possibility of reincarnation as explaining the evolution of the soul:

> At times I almost dream
> I too have spent a life the sages' way,
> And tread once more familiar paths. Perchance
> I perished in an arrogant self-reliance
> Ages ago; and in that act a prayer
> For one more chance went up so earnest, so
> Instinct with better light led in by death

> That life was blotted out not so completely
> But scattered wrecks of it enough remain
> Dim memories, as now. . . . .

As well as having this belief in the development of the individual soul, Paracelsus sought—like the hero of *Pauline*—the prompt improvement of the race:

>   'tis time
> New hopes should animate the world, new light
> Should dawn from new revealings to a race
> Weighed down so long, forgotten so long: thus shall
> The heaven reserved for us at last receive
> Creatures whom no unwonted splendours blind.

And again, he prays God to "set free the soul alike in all," so that all human beings may be equal to those who are now exceptional:

>   Make no more giants, God,
> But elevate the race at once! we ask
> To put forth just our strength, our human strength,
> All starting fairly, all equipped alike,
> Gifted alike, all eagle-eyed, true-hearted—
> See if we cannot beat thine angels yet!

At the end of the poem his doctrine of evolution is based on this same confidence in man's potentialities:

> So glorious our nature, so august
> Man's inborn uninstructed impulses,
> His naked spirit so majestical . . . .
>   . . . . still seizing fresh pretense
> To turn the knowledge and the rapture wrung
> As an extreme last boon from destiny
> Into occasion for new covetings,
> New strifes, new triumphs.

Evolution will continue as long as human ambition remains insatiable.

Browning's three early heroes—Pauline's lover, Paracelsus, and Sordello—are alike in their intense desire for contact with life, for a most varied experience, and for a channel of self-expression to relieve them of the intolerable inward urge to do something for the race's advance. The speaker in *Pauline* declares,

> I have gone in thought
> Through all conjuncture, I have lived all life
> When it is most alive, where strangest fate
> New shapes it past surmise.

Paracelsus states his quest to be "the secret of the world, of man, and man's true purpose, path and fate." Sordello is equally universal in his range. We may venture, therefore, to attribute to the youthful Browning this restless quest for some theory of existence that might link the infinitely numerous manifestations of life into a coherent synthesis. This was the first stage of his preparation for perceiving the evolutionary idea. Inspired by Plato and Shelley, he shaped his ambitions into grandiose schemes for the future development of the race, and felt that this innate ambition was the most immediate proof that such progressive development was intended by the Creator. Then his special interest in psychological processes—the chief topic of all his poetry—revealed to him the inward development of the individual soul. In the three early poems there is this double conception of human development—the spiritual progress of the protagonist toward enlightenment and the ideal of racial progress which that enlightenment brings. The final corollary, that humanity has already advanced from lower origins, might easily have been suggested by the pseudo-scientific talk of transmutation and the microcosm and the limbus containing "the potency and nature of all creatures," in his father's three folio volumes of Paracelsus.

In comparing the early poems of Tennyson and Browning, we find a striking contrast in mental processes. Tennyson derived his evolutionary idea from science, but opposed the materialism of the scientists by the proof of God and immortality supplied by intuition, whereas Browning derived his evolutionary idea directly from that intuition itself. Tennyson proceeded from the physical to the spiritual; Browning from the spiritual to the physical. From scattered scientific facts and philosophic hints Tennyson formed his theory of physical evolution inductively; from a belief in the progress of the soul Browning formed his theory of physical evolution deductively. Both poets, however, countered all the dangers of materialism by glorifying their inherent sense of divinity and immortality. Browning's artistic method makes his references to contemporary problems less explicit, since most of his poems are located in earlier centuries; but this dramatic medium is the natural expression of his mentality, beginning with the subjective—the traits of human nature which are not affected by transient ideas—and working outward until he had attained a contact with current thought.

Tennyson, on the contrary, began with the current thought, and worked inward until he came to the deeper principles; even when he chose the dramatic form, it was with an obvious purpose of reflecting on the contemporary topics. Both Tennyson and Browning encountered the same principle, which a little later became the chief fetish or bugbear of all thinking men; but they approached it from opposite directions.

GENERAL IDEAS IMPLYING EVOLUTION

While it is true that after the extended statement of evolution which he made in *Paracelsus*, Browning did not again refer explicitly to the subject for many years, yet there are recurrent ideas in his poetry which imply that he steadily adhered to the doctrine, though perhaps not in a very coherent form. In particular, there is his idea of what has been termed by George Herbert Palmer "the glory of the imperfect." It was the lesson that Paracelsus finally learned, after his prolonged error of being impatient with the shortcomings of mankind and anxious for sudden perfection. That final message, "to see a hope in ill-success, to be proud of their half-reasons, faint aspirings," and so on, is reiterated at greater length in *Sordello*. Of this poem the theme is the fate of those who, despising "our common nature" because it is "restricted and unfit to bear the burden they impose on it," cannot transcend their restrictions,

> Each a god's germ, doomed to remain a germ
> In unexpanded infancy;

and Sordello, like Paracelsus, finally wins free by rising above self.

The immense value of *Sordello* as a record of Browning's philosophy of life and theory of art has been neglected. Efforts have been made to disentangle the story, whereas the story is a mere pretext for Browning's disquisitions on the evolutionary character of both the race and the individual soul. Imbedded in the poem, at the end of the third book, is a long passage in which Browning speaks in his own person. The narrative has reached a point where Sordello has failed in his first aspirations:

> one round
> Of life was quite accomplished: and he found
> .... that a soul, whate'er its might,
> Is insufficient to its own delight,
> Both in corporeal organs and in skill
> By means of such to body forth its Will—
> And, after, insufficient to apprise
> Men of that Will, oblige them recognize
> the Hid by the Revealed. . . . .

From this illustration of how the ideal ever exceeds the execution, Browning draws a conclusion applicable to himself. It is in the work of the self-satisfied minor poet only, he says, that you find completeness, the writer's purpose wholly fulfilled; whereas "true works," such as Sordello's "dream-performances," even though they never advance from dream to actual existence, yet reveal the latent greatness of the poet, a potential passion and knowledge transcending the imperfect achievement. Browning would rather be the faulty exponent of the high philanthropic aim than the accomplished trifler. Looking at a group of peasant girls, he cannot enjoy their beauty and delight because the thought of sufferers intrudes. He has long ago given up the hope that

> the whole race
> Might add the spirit's to the body's grace,
> And all be dizened out like chiefs and bards.

He has come to see that perfection is incompatible with human life, that it is impracticable to

> hinder Life the evil with the good
> Which make up Living, rightly understood.

He resorts to the more modest ambition that a just meed of happiness, the peasant's endowment of youth, strength, and health, might be the birthright of all. But meanwhile the true lover of humanity must show no disgust toward the existing miseries: personifying his mistress as a pitiable figure "with those thin lips on tremble, lashless eyes inveterately tearshot," he declares that these very defects increase his affection:

> care-bit erased
> Broken-up beauties ever took my taste
> Supremely; and I love her more, far more
> Than her I looked should foot Life's temple floor.

It may be but a slight advance, he admits, to acknowledge his participation in the common woes of humanity, but at least he is better than the complacent poets. While we are all struggling together through the desert, the dilettante poet, with his superficial accomplishments, does little good by asserting that there are lots of springs about: the real hero is the Moses who, awkwardly enough, smites the rock, though thereby he foregoes the Promised Land and is stigmatized as a "metaphysical poet." In other words, Browning has dedicated himself to the service of the race, and is willing to suffer the censure of critics if he can further the onward struggle.

Proceeding to a new metaphor, he says we are watching the construction of an engine, which in this lifetime is incomplete, "yet in probation"; therefore we can only guess at its ultimate function; at death the whole thing is dismantled "to be set up anew elsewhere," and to work in "a clearer clime than the murk lodgment" in which it was built. In short, Browning holds that earth-life is the constructive period in which the soul is developing toward its future efficiency. So, he says, in this life we cannot consider man as a perfect entity; but the province of the poet—the man of abnormal insight—is to help the general public toward the vision of life's purpose. At present there are the two types: men of vision, who make no practical use of what they perceive; and men of action,

> Who, seeing just as little as you please,
> Yet turn that little to account,—engage
> With, do not gaze at,—carry on a stage
> The work o' the world, not merely make report
> The work existed ere their day!

Like Carlyle, Browning prefers the worker to the visionary; but the ideal he would strive for is a union of vision with action.

The most important idea underlying this passage is Browning's sense that it is his mission to reveal the potential greatness of man, not by reviling his present imperfection, but by sympathetically analyzing it. This is the antithesis of the ideal poet of previous ages, dwelling aloof in an ivory tower, exemplified by Wordsworth, who isolated himself from the stress of the conflict, and in another aspect by Shelley, whose visions for mankind were apt to overleap the immediate present and its practical obstacles. The doctrine of evolution is a great leveler, and it was that principle of a common cause in which all mankind is striving to transcend its humble physical origin and attain eventual spiritual perfection, which brought Browning down from the pinnacle where his romantic forebears ensconced themselves.

At the opening of the fifth book there is another long discussion of development and progress. Sordello is now possessed of the ambition to restore Rome's ancient glory, which typifies "the scheme to put mankind once more in full possession of their right." In commenting on the impossibility of this desire, Browning uses as his text the adage "Rome was not built in a day." When Sordello realizes that his squalid comrades are scarcely the "shining ones meet for the Shining City," his visionary Rome tumbles in ruins. But, Browning suggests, why not re-

tain a certain ambition, though a more practicable
one?

> Study mere shelter, now, for him, for him,
> Nay, even the worst,—just house them! any cave
> Suffices.

Thence the poet embarks on a sketch of man's gradual advance from the primitive cave dwelling to modern houses. One generation makes loopholes in its
cave to admit the sunlight. The next

>   fells
> Oak and devises rafters, dreams and shapes
> His dream into a door-post, just escapes
> The mystery of hinges.

Passing over another era we come to brick and stone,
and equivalent progress in the other arts. After a further interval we find the city with all its elaborate
architecture, and the skill of man is then turned toward sculpture. This gradual progress, each individual contributing his tiny quota to the total, is prefer-
able to a sudden improvement which would leave the
spiritual standard of the race far below its material
benefits:

> The work marched: step by step,—a workman fit
> Took each, nor too fit—to one task, one time,—
> No leaping o'er the petty to the prime. . . . .
> That way was Rome built. "Better" (say you) "merge
> At once all workmen in the demiurge,
> All epochs in a lifetime, every task
> In one!" So should the sudden city bask
> I' the day—while those we'd feast there, want the knack
> Of keeping fresh-chalked gowns from speck and brack,
> Distinguish not rare peacock from vile swan,
> Nor Mareotic juice from Cæcuban.

So Sordello recognizes that he had begun at the wrong end. God concedes two sights to man—the vision of the total achievement of the race, and the single specific action by which the individual can initiate the movement. The former, descried first, is simply an incentive "only to give you heart to take your first step, and there stay." The hope of taking the final step first is absurd; so, after proving one's kinship with God by perceiving the remote ideal, one must prove one's self a man by taking the initial step which is within one's power. "Collective man outstrips the individual." Any art can be traced back through a gradual lineage till it is lost in "a forgotten yesterday." Each man is but the product and epitome of all who went before him; even the outstanding figures, such as Charlemagne and Hildebrand, are merely the culmination of infinite work by other men, summarized and named in the individual.

In essence, Browning's theory of gradual development is almost identical with Tennyson's insistence on caution, his dread of "raw haste, half-sister to delay"; but in effect the two doctrines seem very different—Tennyson's reads like conservatism, Browning's like Fabian socialism. Once more we find Tennyson never far from the contemporary incident, the current political or philosophical movement, while Browning formulates his doctrine in universal terms, even for the purpose of illustration using such expansive things as the building of Rome, rather than more modern instances.

Once again, at the close of the poem, when Sordello looks back over his apparently ineffectual life, the ideas of Browning upon perfection and imperfection, good and evil, are set forth extensively. Men of less ability than Sordello, by keeping to some single aim persistently, have fulfilled their task in life and thus advanced in their evolution:

> To each who lives must be a certain fruit
> Of having lived in his degree,—a stage,
> Earlier or later in men's pilgrimage
> To stop at.

Everyone forms an ideal for himself, which continually remains out of reach, "a progress pursued through all existence," since the achievement of a "widened range" reveals a fresh objective. But having advanced so far, why should we doubt eventual achievement? Since Good is already manifest, will "only the Best break faith?" Just as we cannot create gems at will, although the component elements are all around us, so the elements of life are in nature everywhere, and one might hope therefore to produce "men beyond these actual men." Is it a fallacy, he wonders, thus to argue from the existence of Good the necessary consequence of the Best?

Turning from theory to experience, Sordello sees that service in the cause of human progress is heartbreaking work. A youth who catches a glimpse of a new truth cannot advance straightway to the next, which seems to him twice as important, but must spend a lifetime imparting the first to the crowd.

Thus the glimpses of truth are so limited and infrequent that "the prime of truth, the very truth which, loosed, had hurled the world's course right," is invisible, only the accidental striking of "mean sparks" occasionally indicating its buried existence. This fact is likely to dishearten idealists, since it means countenancing much present error and evil while preparing the way for future good. To alienate men by condemning their present shortcomings does not promote progress, since it is merely destroying "an orb half done" in favor of "a new segment." Facing the problem of good and evil, Browning sees the fact which so distressed Tennyson—the apparent cruelty of nature; "the seasons' strife with tree and flower, the hideous animal life," as well as the bad elements in average human beings, suggest that evil is not "a result less natural than Good." It is the common bond of sorrow that promotes sympathy and brotherhood. Furthermore, even for man's benefit evil is essential, for joy depends on the overcoming of obstacles, and therefore is constantly destroying itself— "a partial death is every joy." For when we escape from one limitation, change vexation to contentment, complete the growing circle,

> All's to begin again—some novel bound
> To break, some new enlargement to entreat;
> The sphere though larger is not more complete.

"Salvation for Mankind springs by each hindrance interposed." Evil is essential for progress; we are not able to see the whole of life's purpose, as if we were

on a summit gazing at heaven but bereft of wings;
we are at the foot of the mountain and therefore have
a chance to climb. If we ever achieved the perfection we dream of, could we revert to enjoy the efforts
by which we gained it? From all these and many
other cogitations of the problems of progress and
service, Sordello—like Paracelsus—in the last moments of his life attains illumination, seeing that ill
and well, virtue and vice, may be

> but modes of Time and this one sphere,
> Urgent on these, but not of force to bind
> Eternity;

and that therefore the soul, in order to be complete
and satisfactory for the whole series of spheres—i.e.,
eternity—must necessarily exceed each single sphere
and therefore seem incomplete for it.

This doctrine of gradual development and the necessary imperfection of finite life—implying some larger completeness of which it is a fragment—which is
woven into the whole fabric of *Sordello*, became the
credo which Browning obeyed in framing his outstanding contribution to English poetry. His gallery
of self-revealed rogues and sinners, fanatics and cas-
uists, is his vindication of man's imperfection: his
Lippo, his Sludge, show how there are incipient elements of good admixed with characters that are conventionally dismissed as despicable. That from the
worldly point of view so many of his more admirable
protagonists, such as Paracelsus, Sordello, the Gram-
marian, Pippa, Childe Roland, are failures—idealists

who find that the actual world falls short of their visionary hopes—is another result of the same doctrine. These poems do not indicate, as some recent critics have argued, that Browning was at heart a pessimist; he intended rather to convey that these people are in themselves testimonies to the race's high destiny; that their self-sacrifice for their ideals was not failure, but success, in the larger cycle of existence; and that the only hope for the race as a whole lies in a gradual evolution under the stimulus of ideals which are necessarily impracticable.

This conception also explains the puzzling ethics of *The Statue and the Bust*, which declares that the only sin is the evasion of life, "the unlit lamp and the ungirt loin." The responsibilities and stresses of life must be encountered honestly if the soul is to be developed; unless everyone "contend to the uttermost for his life's set prize, be it what it will," evolution is retarded. Similarly in *By the Fireside* it is pointed out that the decisive deed at the opportune moment is the supreme event of each life; and whether the immediate effect be apparently good or evil, the eventual result is the progress of the race; whenever a soul declares itself "by its fruit, the thing it does,"

> Be hate that fruit or love that fruit,
>   It forwards the general deed of man,
> And each of the Many helps to recruit
>   The life of the race by a general plan;
> Each living his own, to boot.

This stanza sums up tersely the double concept of evolution which was constantly in Browning's the-

ory: the progress of the race through the accumulated contributions of individuals, and the progress of
the individual soul by its experiences in mortal life.
So in *The Lost Leader*, the man who fails in his duty
to the cause of progress is stigmatized as a "lost soul,"
"one more task declined, one more footpath untrod."
And, to cite one more example, there is a long passage
in *Old Pictures in Florence*, comparing Greek art,
which portrays a static ideal, with Renaissance art
of the realistic and analytical type—the pictorial
counterpart of Browning's own poetry—which, by
showing man's imperfections, implies his potentialities. Feeling insignificant beside the perfection of the
Greek statues, men remained content in their poor
degree, with their little power and knowledge, and
learned that "to submit is a mortal's duty." The
poet adds explicitly that he is referring to "the common soul, the collective,"

> the race of Man
> That receives life in parts to live in a whole,
> And grow here according to God's clear plan.

Progress did not come till men turned their eyes inward and discovered the possibility that mortals,
with all their blemishes, may be greater and grander
than the Greek divinities,

> Precisely because of our wider nature;
> For time, theirs—ours, for eternity.
>
> Today's brief passion limits their range;
> It seethes with the morrow for us and more.
> They are perfect—how else? they shall never change:
> We are faulty—why not? we have time in store.

The Artificer's hand is not arrested
With us; we are rough-hewn, nowise polished:
They stand for our copy, and, once invested
With all they can teach, we shall see them abolished.

In almost all of the infrequent poems wherein
Browning speaks in his own person, he contrives to
introduce this doctrine of evolution. The best service, he insists, to be performed by artists and others
whose perceptions are more highly evolved than the
average, is to reveal the hope and inspiration latent
in the race's present imperfection. Practicing what
he preaches, he writes his dramatic monologues with
this objective; and so in those poems also, although
indirectly, his doctrine is embodied.

ATTITUDE TOWARD RELIGION AND SCIENCE

Browning's theory of evolution, far from entailing
any religious doubts, was mentioned repeatedly as
"God's plan." His Unitarian background had protected him from servility to the letter of the Scripture; and besides, his theory was not imposed on him
by external arguments, but emerged as a consistent
part of his own metaphysical system. So his interest
in the conflict of science and religion was not dictated
by personal concern: secure in his self-generated
faith, he studied churches and creeds for their dramatic possibilities alone. A group of his poems is devoted to representing the bigotry and inconsistence
of various dogmatic creeds, particularly those which
encourage men to be self-centered and intolerant,
qualities antithetical to Browning's creed of service

and love. *Johannes Agricola in Meditation* displays the irrational and barbaric selfishness which may result from belief in predestination. The *Soliloquy of the Spanish Cloister* reveals another result of religious selfishness—ritualistic formality concealing un-Christian traits of hate and revenge. The *Bishop Orders His Tomb in St. Praxed's Church* depicts the absurd anthropomorphism of the Renaissance ecclesiast, his sensuality, his fundamental inability to imagine an after-life divorced from the flesh.

After Browning's marriage, however, this rather aloof and satiric treatment of ecclesiastical themes gave place to more serious efforts to analyze the religious instincts. The first evidence of the change was the long double poem *Christmas Eve and Easter Day*, appearing almost simultaneously with *In Memoriam*, in 1850. Although a few perfunctory lines seek to imply that the poem is spoken by a dramatic personage, the consensus of critical opinion attributes the views expressed to Browning himself. The first section, *Christmas Eve*, is a general survey of current religious conditions, typified by a dissenting chapel in London, St. Peter's in Rome, and the lecture hall of a German professor who is demolishing the "Christ-myth." The latter figure is the most significant, being a composite of Comte and Strauss (whose *Leben Jesus* had appeared just before Browning left England). He embodies the rationalistic tendency of the time; and while Browning is not blind to the merits of the professor's point of view—the figure is not drawn unsympathetically—he condemns this scientific analyzing of Christianity as he condemned in his letters the scientific vivisection and classification of nature. He emphasizes the essential part played by love in the relationship of God and man, through which man intuitively recognizes his own importance despite his apparent insignificance in the cosmos: the skies reveal God's power, but the human heart gives equally convincing evidence of "the nobler dower," His love,

> For the loving worm within its clod
> Were diviner than a loveless god
> Amid his worlds, I will dare to say.

God, after creating man with the potential faculty of love in him, leaves it to man whether he shall exercise that faculty. In his intellectual endowments, which Browning designates as "power," man can make progress, though he can never reach omnipotence. Love, however, is in a different category: man may develop or reduce his capacity for entertaining it, he may profit by it or abuse it, but the total remains the same, and God is still solicitous for man's best interests as He is for the leaf or the stone. All of this the speaker has felt instinctively in his youth, and the vision which he is shown confirms his faith.

In the sequel, *Easter Day*, the speaker goes deeper into the obstacles which beset intelligent faith, and asserts the folly of the commonplace temporizing style of belief which simply ignores everything that menaces it. Dismissing such a faith as "blind hopes," he insists that faith must be something more than a condiment to heighten the flavors of worldly experiences. In view of nature's cruelty, belief cannot be based on a mere acceptance that all's for the best in a perfect world: "No. The creation travails, groans," and one must reconcile that fact with one's creed as best one may. Some people, while admitting that a scientifically proved faith is an absurd contradiction in terms, yet seek a plausible explanation for their religious beliefs; but the speaker brands as valueless a faith which justifies itself by finding a rational explanation of Jonah's whale or even attributing the religious impulse to a psychological source. After explaining that from childhood he has preferred certainty to the fallacious security of ignorance, he describes the vision which converted him from an insincere compromise of laissez faire religion and worldly indulgence. He was shown that the beauty of nature, the skill of art, the exercise of intellect, are all alike unprofitable if they are considered as sufficient in themselves; their virtue lies in their incompleteness.

Browning's poem resembles Tennyson's almost coincident *In Memoriam* in examining at some length the problems of contemporary religion, the difficulty of reconciling faith with an intelligent interest in philosophy and science. Each believes that such a reconciliation is possible, since faith depends on an intuitive sense transcending reason. And in each poem the argument is based largely on the author's particular metaphysical interpretation of evolution. The differences are in treatment and mental processes: Tennyson uses the didactic method and Browning the dramatic; Tennyson proceeds from the individual problems to the general theory, Browning applies the revealed vision to the individual problems.

After this analysis of doubt and faith and religious experience, Browning resumed, in the collection of *Men and Women* (1855), his study of the religious element in various types of character. He also added a second section to *Saul*, enforcing his doctrine of love's omnipotence and the all-pervading presence of God, the contrast of human knowledge and imagination with the revelation of divine power "in the star, in the stone, in the flesh, in the soul and the clod." It is at some expense of verisimilitude that the shepherd boy of Judah is made to utter such metaphysical doctrines and to deduce by analogy that the failures of this life are but probation for future achievements. There is an even more obvious modern application in the *Epistle of Karshish*, which presents the impact of Christ's personality on the world, as it affected an impartial and enlightened outsider. Karshish is the ideal scientist, open-minded and skeptical, seeking the rational explanation of the so-called "miracle," yet subconsciously disturbed by the challenge to his conventional creed.

Of particular importance is *Bishop Blougram's Apology*, an expansion of the study of modern Roman Catholicism which figured in *Christmas Eve*. Blougram, modeled somewhat on the famous Cardinal Wiseman, discusses freely the objections which were being hurled against established religion. He admits that there are many difficulties which he cannot solve, so he gives up hope of solving them. He holds that doubt is necessary for faith's existence, that the mere desire for faith is its sufficient apology. Although the argument is ostensibly a masterpiece of casuistry, and admits materialistic considerations which Browning despises in such poems as *Easter Day*, yet at bottom Blougram's justification of faith rests on the same foundations as Browning's own. Indeed, the poet explicitly comments, "He said true things, but called them by wrong names." The Bishop's adroit reasoning as a man of the world does not entirely discredit his moments of deeper seriousness, when he points out that unfaith has no stronger rational support than faith, that the unbeliever cannot exclude qualms of belief when beauty appeals to mystical instincts. The Bishop is alert to modern discussions: he deals with Strauss, in much the same way that Browning dealt with his prototype in *Christmas Eve*, emphasizing the uselessness of such destructive arguments, which are of no real use even if they are right, and positively harmful if they are wrong. Similarly, he dismisses "Fichte's clever cut at God Himself." He is familiar enough with scientific works to quote a recent "French book" which explains the origin of chastity on ethnological grounds, as the primitive man's necessary caution among enemies:

indeed, he is not opposed to science, since it promotes
the doubt which "occasions still more faith":

> How you'd exult if I could put you back
> Six hundred years, blot out cosmogony,
> Geology, ethnology, what not
> (Greek endings, each the little passing bell
> That signifies some faith's about to die)
> And set you right with Genesis again.

In such an age of unmenaced faith, says Blougram,
morality was at a low ebb; it is the strife of faith and
doubt that promotes spiritual growth. Blougram
even uses the word "evolution," applying it to an
idea of his own:

> Do you know, I have often had a dream
> Of man's poor spirit in its progress, still
> Losing true life forever and a day
> Through ever trying to be and ever being—
> In the evolution of successive spheres—
> *Before* its actual sphere and place of life,
> Halfway into the next, which having reached,
> It shoots with corresponding foolery
> Halfway into the next still, on and off.

This is really a repetition, in a satiric tone, of Browning's own theory of the necessary discontent which
produces progress.

It is in *Cleon*, however, that Browning, for the first
time in the twenty years since *Paracelsus*, gives an
explicit statement of evolution. Cleon, the classical
philosopher, untroubled by the bonds of dogmatic
religion, summarizes the evolutionary theory concisely, but he infers only discouragement; Browning
means to show that Cleon, for all his enlightenment,

lacked the spirituality that was given to the world by the Christian concept of a future life. Like Tennyson in *Lucretius*, Browning is depicting a refined and pessimistic materialist in order to discredit the revival of such opinions in his own time. Cleon holds that the expansion of culture, which has made the mind more complex and the interests more eclectic, is fulfilling a harmonious scheme. He believes that "this sequence of the soul's achievement" in human life is to be viewed as a great whole, in which all the parts are synthesized, and

> How shall a certain part, pronounced complete,
> Endure effacement by another part?

Progress, therefore, is the gradual combining of the original "separate perfect forms," and the eventual result is "mankind, made up of all the single men." Growth is the only reason for staying on earth, and Cleon prefers his civilized mind to the cruder genius of his predecessors, as he prefers the cultivated flower or fruit to its wild forebears. His argument that "imperfection means perfection hid," he illustrates from physical evolution:

> If, in the morning of philosophy,
> Ere aught had been recorded, nay perceived,
> Thou, with the light now in thee, couldst have looked
> On all earth's tenantry, from worm to bird,
> Ere man, her last, appeared upon the stage,
> Thou wouldst have seen them perfect, and deduced
> The perfectness of others yet unseen.

The final endowment possessed by man alone is self-consciousness, for the brute creation represents the

perfection of "life's mechanics," mere matter inspired
with the "joy in natural life," whereas man has
an intro-active quality within his soul which enables
him to observe and analyze his own behavior. But instead of making man happier, as one might have expected, this power is responsible for his misery, because it makes him conscious that there is "a world
of capability for joy" all around him which he cannot
attain owing to the restrictions of the flesh: "life's
inadequate to joy as the soul sees joy." Therefore
it would have been better if the race had never progressed beyond "the natural man, the better beast,
using his senses, not the sense of sense."

> In man there's failure, only since he left
> The lower and inconscious forms of life.
> We call it an advance, the rendering plain
> Man's spirit might grow conscious of man's life,
> And, by new lore so added to the old,
> Take each step higher over the brute's head.

So Cleon concludes in "profound discouragement"
that "most progress is most failure." He flatly dismisses, in confident rationalism, the unfounded vision
of "some future state unlimited in capability for joy,
as this is in desire for joy." Thus Browning makes
clear that, without the belief in immortality, the very
argument which is to himself a proof of man's potentialities produces only despair. He depicts the
same contrast between the Hellenic discouraging emphasis on perfection and the Christian promise of development as in the earlier poem *Old Pictures in
Florence*.

POEMS CONTEMPORANEOUS WITH "THE ORIGIN
OF SPECIES"

Darwin's book appeared midway between Browning's *Men and Women* and its successor, *Dramatis Personae* (1864), and in the latter volume there is unmistakably an added seriousness in his proclamations of immortality and divine love. His wife's death in 1861 had naturally brought him face to face with grave spiritual problems, as shown, for example, in *Prospice;* but his sorrow, taken by itself, might be expected to turn his attention inward and deter him from addressing the world, whereas, on the contrary, there is a distinct tendency toward evangelizing. One no longer feels Browning's enjoyment of objective historical accuracy and local color: John, in *A Death in the Desert*, is explicitly addressing the age of doubt which he foresees; and Rabbi Ben Ezra is not equipped with any circumstantial details of his period, race, or profession.

There are signs that Browning was in touch with both the scientific and the theological events of the day. In *Mr. Sludge, "the Medium"* it is pointed out that the new microscopic knowledge of animalculae demands a fresh concept of God as the life-force inhabiting them all:

> The world wears another aspect now:
> Somebody turns our spyglass round, or else
> Puts a new lens in it: grass, worm, fly grow big:
> We find great things are made of little things,
> And little things go lessening till at last
> Comes God behind them. Talk of mountains now?

We talk of mould that heaps the mountain, mites
That throng the mould, and God that makes the mites.
The Name comes close behind a stomach-cyst,
The simplest of creations, just a sac
That's mouth, heart, legs and belly at once, yet lives
And feels, and could do neither, we conclude,
If simplified still further one degree.

Even through the mouth of the egregious casuist
Sludge, Browning gives a religious twist to the new
evolutionary biology.

The religious controversy appears at the end of
Gold Hair:

The candid incline to surmise of late
    That the Christian faith proves false, I find;
For our Essays-and-Reviews debate
    Begins to tell on the public mind,
    And Colenso's words have weight.

The disrespectful tone suggests that Browning does
not take the affair very seriously; but the Epilogue
of the volume shows a more active concern. As fifteen
years before he had been impressed by Strauss's
Leben Jesus, so he read Renan's *Vie de Jésus* promptly on its appearance in 1863; and in this Epilogue,
published next year, Renan is made the mouthpiece
of the current skepticism. The epilogue opens with
an ecstatic chant typical of Old Testament theism,
uttered by David, and describing "the presence of
the Lord" in the Temple. The second speaker, as
Renan, sketches the decline of belief in divinity, in
words reminiscent of Arnold's lament for "the sea of
faith." God being dispossessed, man succeeds to the

rank of master of things; but he has no joy in the
dignity, and curses the "dread succession to a dizzy
post." Finally the poet speaks in his own person and
affirms that the miracle of personality, produced by
mysterious forces of nature, inspires a faith quite as
strong as that of the Old Testament, and merely replaces anthropomorphic belief with pantheism.

Several poems reiterate the familiar doctrine of the
glory of the imperfect, such as the conclusion of *Dis
Aliter Visum:*

> The mere star-shell in its vault
> . . . . whole in body and soul, outstrips
> Man, found with either in default.
>
> But what's whole can increase no more,
> Is dwarfed and dies, since here's its sphere.

The same thought is set to more solemn music in
Abt Vogler, and echoes through other poems also.

The relationship of science and faith figures most
prominently, however, in the three principal poems
of the volume. *Caliban upon Setebos* is a product of
modern anthropology, a study of the first incipient
religious ideas of the human mind emerging from the
mere animal life of instincts. Naturally, the anthropomorphic deity envisaged by this primitive intelligence is as cruel and capricious as himself. Moreover,
Caliban expressly states his unbelief in the two ideas
which Browning himself held particularly important
—immortality and development. Unlike the evolutionists, Caliban holds that his deity created the

world as it is, and only a complete fresh start could
alter it:

> 'Conceiveth all things will continue thus,
> And we shall have to live in fear of Him
> So long as He lives, keeps His strength: no change,
> If He hath done His best, make no new world
> To please Him more. . . . .

As a contrast to this primitive superstition, *A
Death in the Desert* sets forth a theory of religion in
which development is admitted. The dying apostle
has a prevision of the materialistic age which discred-
its Christianity because of its element of miracle.
His vindication of his creed follows a line similar to
that laid down by Matthew Arnold in *Literature and
Dogma* nine years later.

It is made clear that John's idea of evolution does
not extend to the physical plane: "The body sprang
at once to the height, and stayed: but the soul,—
no!" In spiritual matters, he holds, the race will ever
progress, and therefore doubt is necessary, since certainty would mean a static condition of perfection.
"Were this gift of truth once grasped, why, man's
probation would conclude, his earth crumble," and
"therefore, to test man, the proofs shift." John foresees the doubters who will explain Christ as a mere
fiction created by the instinct which seeks something
to worship:

> " 'Tis mere projection from man's inward mind,
> And, what he loves, thus falls reflected back,
> Becomes accounted somewhat out of him."

Similarly, the power ruling the universe will be explained as force or law, the last stage in man's progressive conception of deity, which began with the ancient gods of human forms and human passions, and advanced through the Christian idea still including human attributes of will, power, and love. To the nineteenth-century mechanistic concept thus prophesied, John replies,

> I say that man was made to grow, not stop;
> That help, he needed once, and needs no more,
> Having grown but an inch by, is withdrawn:
> For he hath new needs, and new helps to these.
> This imports solely, man should mount on each
> New height in view; the help whereby he mounts,
> The ladder-rung his foot has left, may fall,
> Since all things suffer change save God the Truth.

Thus miracles, when they have outlived their purpose, become a tyranny instead of a help. To the challenge that the gospels are misleading and inaccurate, John retorts that "man is not God, but hath God's end to serve," his duty being "something to cast off, somewhat to become"; if man must advance from error to fact, he must first have "what seemed good" in order to discard it for "what now proves best." When man takes unto himself the title "first, last, and best of things," he has come to believe in a ruling power with neither will nor love, though he recognizes these elements in himself. If it be proved that they combine nowhere else but in man, then he is, indeed, the highest being, he is God himself—and with this perfection "his life becomes impossible, which is death." Man's rightful rôle is one of imperfection: lower than God, who is perfect, and higher than the beasts, which are also perfect in their mechanical limits. Progress is "man's distinctive mark alone, not God's and not the beast's." At first man was compelled to learn as the brutes do, by compulsion of external facts; but afterward his mind assumed the control, and it is this yearning for truth, approached through endless mistakes, that is God's gift to man.

The foregoing Epistle to the Infidels, as well as controverting the naturalism and rationalism of the nineteenth century, is emphatic in denying the identity of man with the lower orders of creation, inclusively termed "the brutes." Clearly Browning's purpose in the poem was not merely to support man's kinship with God—impugned by contemporary materialists—but also to impugn man's kinship with the monkeys, which was the popular version of Darwinism. The same purpose is obvious in *Rabbi Ben Ezra*, in which even the device of prophecy is discarded; although bearing the name of an historic personage, it savors wholly of the nineteenth century, just as Fitzgerald had used a contemporary of Ben Ezra's to express a very modern mood; indeed, the application of Browning's poem to the hedonism of the *Rubaiyat* is explicit:

> Aye, note that Potter's wheel,
> That metaphor! and feel

Why time spins fast, why passive lies our clay,—
Thou, to whom fools propound
When the wine makes its round,
"Since life fleets, all is change; the Past gone, seize
to-day!"

Almost equally pointed are the references to the other book of 1859, *The Origin of Species*. Attacking the problem of man's relation to the beasts and to God, he states first the advantage of having the doubt which is absent in "low kinds," "finished and finite clods, untroubled by a spark." If man lived for mere sensual gratification as animals do, his would be a "poor vaunt of life"; but the spark proves him nearer allied to "God who gives than his tribes that take." Here recurs the glory of the imperfect, the necessity of life's rebuffs and stings for progress. Paradoxically, life succeeds "in that it seems to fail":

What I aspired to be
And was not, comforts me:
A brute I might have been, but would not sink i' the scale.

Granting that man is to be grateful to God for including in his plan the pleasures of a season of physical enjoyment, "those manifold possessions of the brute," nevertheless, one must not be subservient to the flesh. If life is carried on as an unflinching struggle,

Thence shall I pass, approved
A man, for aye removed
From the developed brute; a God, though in the germ.

Thus the human soul proceeds on its "adventure brave and new," advanced not merely by the actual achievements which all the world can recognize but by the impulses and purposes which never matured in action, the thoughts too vast for expression, "all I could never be." Despite the "dance of plastic circumstance" in which man finds himself, he must exert his will and bear in mind why he is placed there —to develop himself.

The poem is a summary of Browning's doctrines, applied to the questions raised by man's place in the evolutionary scale. Immortality, the freedom of the will to assist or retard development in accord with God's plan, the necessity of doubt for true faith, the divine principle of love, the glory inherent in imperfection—all are reaffirmed in defiance of scientific materialism. The whole volume of 1864 not only assails the science-inspired fatalism of *Empedocles on Etna* and Fitzgerald's *Rubaiyat* but also shows an antagonism—in part, perhaps, subconscious—toward the theory of evolution in its Darwinian form, as emphasizing man's kinship with the lower orders of animal life.

DARWINISM AS SEEN BY TWO MEN
OF THE WORLD

For the next seven years Browning's poetry was restricted to themes which gave him little opportunity for discussing contemporary ideas, but *Prince Hohenstiel-Schwangau*, published in 1871, marks a return to modern topics. Like Blougram and Sludge, the prince is a man of the world, interested in all

current theories and events. It is particularly hard to
determine Browning's own attitude toward the ideas
which he attributes to this protagonist—the critics
termed it variously an "eulogium" and a "scandalous
attack"; but Browning, in a letter concerning the
book, commended the ideals of his model, Napoleon
III, and condemned only his weakness in failing to
carry them out; so we may infer that the poet was in
sympathy with at least much of the apology which
he constructs on behalf of the banished potentate.

Hohenstiel-Schwangau is something of a pragma-
tist and very much of an opportunist. His ideal of
progress does not entail any sudden revolution in
social structure: theories of perfection are long, and
the lifetime of the statesman is short. So he believes
in a gradual adaptation of existing institutions and
has no use for such theorists as Fourier and Comte:

> I find advance i' the main, and notably
> The Present an improvement on the Past,
> And promise for the Future—which shall prove
> Only the Present with the rough made smooth,
> Its indistinctness emphasized. . . . .
> We have toiled so long to gain what gain I find
> I' the Present,—let us keep it! We shall toil
> So long before we gain—if gain God grant—
> A Future with one touch of difference
> I' the heart of things, and not their outside face.

This eminently "practical" view may be more reminiscent of Tennyson's politics than of the liberalism
which Browning professed; nevertheless, it might be
contended that it is merely an application to adminis-

trative problems of Browning's ideas on gradual development and necessary imperfection.

Two important passages deal with scientific concepts. One of them is an extensive simile drawn from the cataclysmic theory of geology, with no recognition of the fact that it had been long ago superseded. The prince affirms that the race progresses by abrupt transformations, instigated by great men (Carlylean heroes):

> And liker, so, the natural process. See!
> Where winter reigned for ages—by a turn
> I' the time, some star-change, (ask geologists)
> The ice tracts split, clash, splinter and disperse,
> And there's an end of immobility. . . . .
> As a fresh sun, wave, spring, and joy outburst.
> Or else the earth it is, time starts from trance,
> Her mountains tremble into fire, her plains
> Heave blinded by confusion: what result?
> New teeming growth, surprises of strange life
> Impossible before, a world broke up
> And remade, order gained by law destroyed.

In contrast with this antiquated theory of geology, the prince's knowledge of Darwinism, shown in another passage, is quite up to the minute. As no reason for this inconsistency appears in the poem, one is left to assume that it represents Browning's own information on the two subjects, which seems therefore to have been picked up in a desultory manner, and never clearly integrated. Many years before, while the cataclysmic theory was still dominant, Tennyson discarded it in favor of the concept of gradual development. If Browning, on the contrary, still adhered to the cataclysmic theory in 1871, it is good proof that his early concept of evolution owed little to physical science, and that he regarded the Darwinian theory as an isolated hypothesis with slight bearing on his own metaphysical system. The Darwinism of Prince Hohenstiel-Schwangau need not be based on anything more profound than current articles in reviews. Founding his theory on belief in divine guidance, the prince sees the tribe-instinct paramount in primitive man:

> I, who trace Providence without a break
> I' the plan of things, drop plumb on this plain print
> Of an intention with a view to good,
> That man is made in sympathy with man
> At the outset of existence, so to speak.

Developing civilization, he holds, entails more and more individualism, until each man is isolated from his fellows, the reason being that man, the only creature bearing "the stamp of God," while feeling his kinship with the race in his more primitive and sensual instincts and emotions, yet "tends to freedom and divergency in the upward progress." Nature prompts man with two contradictory impulses, the social and the individual, and no man has ever followed either exclusively; both are "acknowledged blindly" by everyone. For the explanation, he quotes "modern science":

> "That mass man sprung from was a jelly-lump
> Once on a time; he kept an after course
> Through fish and insect, reptile, bird and beast,

> Till he attained to be an ape at last
> Or last but one. And if this doctrine shock
> In aught the natural pride. . . . . "

The prince deprecates the idea that his natural pride
is shocked. He himself had to gain his experience
through ups and downs, and the ideal potentate
ought to have known the whole social scale; human
life being too short for such first-hand investigation,
the life of the race has to furnish it. So he sees an
advantage in evolution through lower forms, and
finds evidence of it in his sense of identity with Nature:

> God takes time.
> I like the thought he should have lodged me once
> I' the hole, the cave, the hut, the tenement,
> The mansion, and the palace; made me learn
> The feel o' the first, before I found myself
> Loftier i' the last, not more emancipate;
> From first to last of lodging, I was I,
> And not at all the place that harbored me.
> Do I refuse to follow further yet
> I' the backwardness, repine if tree and flower,
> Mountain or streamlet were my dwelling place
> Before I gained enlargement, grew mollusc?
> As well account that way for many a thrill
> Of kinship, I confess to, with the powers
> Called Nature: animate, inanimate,
> In parts or in the whole, there's something there
> Man-like that somehow meets the man in me.
> . . . . Yes, I lodged
> In those successive tenements; perchance
> Taste yet the straitness of them while I stretch
> Limb and enjoy new liberty the more.

So far the speaker is quite ready to accept, and even
to welcome, physical evolution as a hypothesis. But

he is not prepared to admit that it nullifies the idea
of a creating and guiding power. The new theory
shows the past as a series of links instead of an un-
broken bar of identical human beings:

> Yes,—and who welds a lump of ore, suppose
> He likes to make a chain and not a bar,
> And reach by link on link, link small, link large,
> Out to the due length—why, there's forethought still
> Outside o' the series, forging at one end,
> While at the other there's—no matter what
> The kind of critical intelligence
> Believing that last link had last but one
> For parent, and no link was, first of all,
> Fitted for anvil, hammered into shape.
> Else, I accept the doctrine, and deduce
> This duty, that I recognize mankind
> In all its height and depth and length and breadth.

There is no apparent reason why this review of the
Darwinian theory should be introduced as part of the
prince's sophistry; and in spite of his nonchalant
manner and colloquial phrases, one feels real emotion
in the claim to kinship with nature and brotherhood
with all men. It gives, moreover, a serious and reasonable verdict on Darwinism—that it does not de-
grade the human race, and that acceptance of its
principle does not obviate belief in a creating and
guiding God. Beyond question, this is a sensible
compromise between the extreme horror of the orthodox and the extreme enthusiasm of the radical.

If *Prince Hohenstiel-Schwangau* had seemed to its
readers a sufficiently puzzling combination of wisdom
and sophistry, Browning's next poem, *Fifine at the*

Fair, was even more disturbing to their sensibilities. His Don Juan's apology for marital infidelity was embodied in so many of Browning's acknowledged opinions and so much debonnaire aesthetic comment and valid moral argument that Mr. Nettleship felt constrained to publish an analysis definitely labeling each section as truth, sophism, or a mingling of the two. A modern student of sex-psychology might almost prove that Browning anticipated the theories advanced by some recent writers on biological grounds. On the other hand, it might be held that Don Juan, like Edgar in Tennyson's *Promise of May*, is a horrible example of the depravity resulting from freethinking and scientific materialism. The fact lies between these two extremes. The speaker explains lengthily that truth can be perceived only in glimpses, and actually because of error; and this was Browning's theory in writing most of the monologues, including *The Ring and the Book*. The statements which were truth to Don Juan were not necessarily truth to the poet; but apart from the shortish passage defending infidelity, there is little that he would repudiate.

Don Juan's arguments are not founded primarily on biology, or indeed on materialistic reasons at all. The basis of his theory is the development of the soul, and his authority is Plato rather than Darwin. Section xxix repeats Browning's doctrine that every individual, and even the meanest object in creation, must have its moment of supreme glory, fulfilling its place in the plan. Section l affirms that nature "at worst always implies success—however crossed and curst by failure." He goes on to say that the soul, through love, perceives the ideal of which the physical form is but a partially evolved representation. He discusses the soul's growth through experience (sections liv, lv) and speaks of "the eternal progress." As a long passage in *Sordello* elaborated the aphorism that "Rome was not built in a day," so a long passage near the end of *Fifine* elaborates the aphorism that "history repeats itself." The fashion in forms changes, but the essence is the same. Don Juan has an apocalyptic vision of life's imperfection and the endless process of change, affecting all that we imagine to be fixed. He sees the sequence of temples rise and decay, and not only religions but academies (i.e., philosophical systems), which, though based on "steadfast mother earth," with no claim to supernatural sanction, fare worst of all, rising and decaying within a lifetime. Each new theory is acclaimed as final and perfect, and the most recent biological hypothesis may be no more permanent:

> Here gape I, all-agog
> These thirty years, to learn how tadpole turns to frog;
> And thrice at least have gazed with mild astonishment,
> As skyward up and up, some fire-new fabric sent
> Its challenge to mankind, that, clustered underneath
> To hear the word, they straight believe, ay, in the teeth
> O' the Past, clap hands, and hail triumphant Truth's outbreak—
> Tadpole-frog-theory propounded past mistake!

The only truth is that truth seeks to embody herself to each generation, though no form is ever final. History, morals, art, are as ephemeral as the fundamental theories of life and the soul. Change is the only stability, yet there is an ultimate permanence underlying it. The archaeologists cannot explain the druidic monument any more plausibly than the superstitious peasantry, and this symbolizes the permanence that survives theories. By recognizing the hints of truth, the soul can progress "as truth successively takes shape, one grade above its last presentment."

In addition to this disillusioned philosophic view of evolution, there are in the poem several incidental references showing interest in scientific phenomena. The rudimentary form of life—the stomach-cyst which Mr. Sludge mentioned—is described in some detail as it expands and contracts in the water; and another simile refers to the chemist who follows his clues back, "unbinds the composite,"

> And tracing each effect back to its cause, elate,
> Constructs in fancy, from the fewest primitives
> The complex and complete, all diverse life, that lives
> Not only in beast, bird, fish, reptile, insect, but
> The very plants and earths and ores.

An illustration used near the end seems to refer to Lamarck's hypothesis of what is nowadays called "creative evolution":

> Promotion comes to Sense because Sense likes it best;
> For bodies sprouted legs, through a desire to run:
> While hands, when fain to filch, got fingers one by one. . . . .

This seems to take rank with Hohenstiel-Schwangau's catastrophism as revealing the lack of co-ordination in Browning's knowledge: encountering diverse ideas in his wide reading, he apparently stored them in isolation from one another and reverted to them separately; he certainly did not relate them to his original metaphysical system of evolution. They appear in the poems to show the eclectic culture of the speakers rather than to support the basic ideas which are discussed.

FINAL REVIEW AND CONFIRMATION OF FAITH

Interspersing the prolific narrative poems which succeeded the two studies in casuistry, there are a couple of personal reflective pieces which bear directly on the conflict between faith and doubt. The brief *Fears and Scruples* is clearly addressed to the "higher critics" who were questioning the authenticity of Scripture, and in a wider sense to the proponents of a mechanistic universe. God is personified as a friend whom the poet has never seen but whose letters are evidence of his affection. Foolish critics cast doubt on the authenticity of the letters, asserting that they may be assigned to other sources. God makes no sign to refute the criticisms, but perhaps he expects man to recognize his presence even when it is not perceptible to sense or reason. Certainty would obviate the possibility of faith.

A longer and more personal exposition of his creed is given in *La Saisiaz*. The death of a friend leads

him to take stock of his real beliefs on the subject
of God and the soul, since he has been accustomed
to discuss with her the current controversies on the
matter,

> passing lightly in review
> What seemed hits and what seemed misses in a certain fence-play
> —strife
> Sundry minds of mark engaged in "On the Soul and Future Life."

Adopting the Cartesian method, Browning starts with
the premise that God and the individual soul are the
only two realities, for the very fact that they transcend rational proof. Hence he builds up a demonstration of the soul's immortality, considering and dismissing the various usual objections. The faith in a
future life, he asserts, alone raises man above the
brutes. Belief that earth is but a state of pupilage is
the only possible reconciliation of wisdom with "a
world distraught," "goodness with triumphant evil,
power with failure in the aim." Was God so deficient
in power or in will that after making the world to
minister to man's wants he should subject man to
the annihilation of death? Browning takes for granted that a "wise and good" power was at work when
the leaf and the dew came into being for the nourishment of the worm. The poem proceeds with the inevitable exposition of glorious imperfection, the only
reference to evolution being in the tone of Hohenstiel-Schwangau's temperate optimism:

> Life to come will be improvement on the life that's now; destroy
> Body's thwartings, there's no longer screen betwixt soul and
> soul's joy.

Why should we expect new hindrance, novel tether? In this first
Life, I see the good of evil, why our world began at worst:
Since time means amelioration, tardily enough displayed,
Yet a mainly onward moving, never wholly retrograde.
We know more though we know little, we grow stronger though
     still weak,
Partly see though all too purblind, stammer though we cannot
     speak.
There is no such grudge in God as scared the ancient Greek, no
     fresh
Substitute of trap for drag-net, once a breakage in the mesh.
Dragons were, and serpents are, and blindworms will be: ne'er
     emerged
Any new-created python for man's plague since earth was purged.

After this proving of evolution's beneficence by the
disappearance of prehistoric monsters, the end is a
condemnation of Rousseau for his tenet that "all
that's good is gone and past" and of Byron for his
that "of all objects found on earth, man is meanest."

The poem shows that Browning's ideas were really
not affected at all by the new vision of the universe
which the theory of evolution implied. Tennyson,
though as positive as Browning in affirming God's
control and the soul's immortality, made a serious effort to adapt these concepts to the evolutionary
scheme. But Browning's universe is still the old anthropocentric one. There is no hint that man had to
accommodate himself to external conditions: the
world was made for man just as the leaf and the dew
were made for the worm. His theory of development
is exclusively a spiritual matter, more remote from the
idea of physical evolution than it was when he wrote
Paracelsus forty years before.

A positive manifesto was included in his penulti-mate volume, *Parleyings with Certain People of Importance in Their Day*, which was confessed by himself to be more personal in utterance than most of his other work. He chats to his imaginary interlocutors without formality, and by making them shades he gives them licence to forsake their epochs and discuss modern topics. As a mouthpiece for his opinion of evolution he uses the seventeenth-century painter-priest, Francis Furini, who addresses a sermon to the people of modern London, "the cultured, therefore sceptical," who are so respectful to the theories of any scientist,

> the meanest who has racked
> Nature until he gains from her some fact,
> To state what truth is from his point of view,
> Mere pin-point though it be.

Claiming that his point of view has an equal right to be heard, he stresses the fact that the scientists begin with the primordial and work down:

> Evolutionists!
> At truth I glimpse from depths, you glance from heights,
> Our stations for discovery opposites,—
> How should ensue agreement? I explain:
> 'Tis the tip-top of things to which you strain
> Your vision, until atoms, protoplasm,
> And what and whence and how may be the spasm
> Which sets all going, stop you; down perforce
> Needs must your observation take its course,
> Since there's no moving upwards: link by link
> You drop to where the atoms somehow think,
> Feel, know themselves to be: the world's begun
> Such as we recognize it. Have you done

Descending? Here's ourself,—Man, known today
Duly evolved at last, so far, you say,
The sum and seal of being's progress.

Man, according to the evolutionists, has no power or
valid knowledge: he cannot create even the minutest
thing. But in compensation he is deified by righteousness—where else but in man did moral sense begin?
If the "initiator-spasm" had seen fit to endow man
with power to create and understand, the universe
would be better off, since man perceives only faults
and omissions which he would remedy had he the
power and knowledge. As it is, since "mere blind
force, ... undirected in its course by any care for
what is made or marred," cannot logically be awarded
the crown, "Man, nowise loth, accepts pre-eminency,"
as the only being endowed with a righteousness
which "would cure the wide world's ailing" if he
could. The Spasm, they argue, had no moral sense
till man came into being, so man stands supreme,
though impotent; but he is hurled from his pinnacle
by the sense of his own ignorance—his notions are
relative, and he cannot trust his own senses, far less
gain any knowledge of first causes.

Thus Furini summarizes the current ideas evoked
by the evolutionary theory. He includes, not only
the Hardys who attribute creation to a mindless "initiator-spasm" and the Swinburnes who proclaim
"glory to man in the highest," but also such moderate
agnostics as Arnold, with his belief in the "stream of
tendency that makes for righteousness." Furini then

advances his own system, which begins with man instead of with the protoplasm. It is the argument of
La Saisiaz. He postulates his own self-consciousness
and his Cause—God. He knows that the universe
had its rise through causes beyond his comprehension.
Starting with his own soul—or consciousness, if you
will—he finds outside of himself a confusion of ignorance, with evil and good apparently irreconcilable.
But the body's adaptation to the soul's requirements,
and the soul's vision of heaven, are sufficient proof to
him that the First-Cause had a purpose in causing
the strife of fears and hopes to exist. Being "made
to know on, know ever," one must master all that is
offered by each halting-stage of the soul's journey,
such as earth, where the war of evil with good occurs
"just for soul's instruction." To the challenge that
this creed is blindly anthropocentric, causing the
whole world to suffer that the individual may develop, he retorts that all externals may be only illusion;
but if this were known, the test of the individual
would vanish, since no choice between evil and good
would be required. The argument is by no means
clear at this point, but Furini brings it to a conclusion
by reiterating that the proper procedure is to begin
with soul and body, and thence to infer God.

This is the only poem in which Browning openly
comes to grips with the evolutionists, as Tennyson
met them repeatedly. Browning's perception of the
fundamental weakness in the hypothesis is sound
enough—he sees that it shirks accounting for the

cause which sets the process in motion; but when he substitutes his own system, there are weaknesses in that which are equally apparent. The Cartesian method does not gain validity in his hands. The existence of evil and pain, for example, which to Tennyson was the most serious cause for doubt of the divine care, is Browning's most frequent demonstration of it—perhaps through subconscious perception that it was the part of his system least easy to justify.

At the very end of his life, as shown by *Asolando*, he was still proclaiming his familiar doctrines. A counterpart to Tennyson's *Crossing the Bar*, the *Epilogue* affirms his belief in personal immortality. The third of the series called *Bad Dreams* conveys an argument on aesthetics by using an image of the earth in pre-human times, with gigantic vegetation and primitive monsters. In the poem *Rephan* the soul's rebellion against the static perfection of a life free from evil and suffering is compared to the perfect single rose which begins to evolve into the double, the new petals unmaking the disk, spoiling rondure, but eventually producing a thing of higher beauty. The very abstruse poem *Reverie* epitomizes in difficult symbolism of love and power the main points of the Furini sermon and the other later poems—that man's possession of love proves its existence in God, that evil exists to enable the soul to grow and that the speculations of science are vain because they can reach no real explanation of first-causes.

Browning's tenets regarding God, the soul, immortality, and faith necessarily bulk large in any study of his evolutionary ideas, because they are the outcome of his own particular metaphysical theory of evolution and the obstacles to a sympathetic attitude toward Darwin's hypothesis. Although he seldom mentioned the latter specifically in his poems, his suspicion of it is clear in them, and one is not surprised to find him, in asserting to Allingham that "the world is in its dotage," remarking of Darwin, "whatever his merits as an investigator, his philosophy is of little or no importance." But despite this negligent attitude, he was annoyed when it got abroad that "he was strongly against Darwinism, rejecting the truths of science and regretting its advance"; so he wrote a formal rebuttal of the rumor:

It came, I suppose, of Hohenstiel-Schwangau's expressing the notion which was the popular one at the appearance of Darwin's book—and you might as well charge Shakespeare with holding that there were men whose heads grew beneath their shoulders because Othello told Desdemona that he had seen such. In reality, all that seems *proved* in Darwin's scheme was a conception familiar to me from the beginning: see in *Paracelsus* the progressive development from senseless matter to organized until man's appearance. Also in *Cleon* see the order of "life's mechanics"—and I dare say in many passages of my poetry: for how can one look at Nature as a whole and doubt that, whenever there is a gap, a "link" must be "missing"—thro' the limited power and opportunity of the looker? But to go back and back, as you please, *at* the back, as Mr. Sludge is made to insist, you find (*my* faith is a constant) creative intelligence, acting as matter but not resulting from it. Once set the balls rolling, and ball may hit ball and send any number in any direction over the table; but I believe in the cue pushed by the hand. When one is taunted (as I notice is often fancied an easy method with the un-Darwinized)—taunted with thinking successive acts of creation credible, metaphysics have been stopped short at, however physics may fare: time and space being purely conceptions of our own, wholly inapplicable to intelligence of another kind—with whom, as I made Luria say, there is an everlasting moment of creation, if one at all —past, present, and future, one and the same state. This consideration does not affect Darwinism proper to any degree. But I do not consider his case as to the changes in organization, brought about by desire and will in the creature, proved.

It may be noted that the suggestion of an everlasting moment of creation—time and space being illusions of the finite mind—was one of Tennyson's arguments in his reconciliations of evolution with Genesis, first appearing in *The Princess* in 1847, while Browning's parallel passage occurred in *Luria* in 1846. The conclusion of the letter just quoted shows that Browning was by no means clear in his mind regarding the differences between Darwin's hypothesis and that of Lamarck, since it was the latter who postulated "desire and will in the creature" rather than Darwin's "natural selection."

On the whole, the letter forms an apt summary of how Browning's concept of development, though implicit in his poems from the beginning, yet avoided the ideas of science and became more and more confined to spiritual progress. When the physical aspect was brought prominently before the public by Darwin, Browning drew on it desultorily for illustrations, but it is plain that the essentials of it never penetrated to his cherished theories. Instead of trying,

like Tennyson, to make his evolutionary idea keep
pace with science, he withdrew it further from the
risk of contamination, until they did not have enough
in common to be debatable. He insisted that the
soul's sojourn in the body is but a stage in the spiritual development; but how the physical form was developed to accommodate it, was of little importance
to him.

Chapter IV

GEORGE MEREDITH

IN CONTRAST with both Browning and Tennyson, who startlingly anticipated the evolutionary theory in their early poems, only to shrink from its later developments and strive for compromises with traditional faith, George Meredith had little perception of the idea till the scientists announced it; but thereafter he devoted himself to it unstintingly. When he became acquainted with Darwinism, his philosophic system developed promptly and completely; so the stages of its growth cannot be chronicled.

Being primarily a nature poet, he was necessarily concerned in the new theory to a vital extent. Tennyson and Browning wrote chiefly about humanity—the former about the race's intellectual heritage of legends and history and metaphysics, and the latter about the actual psychology of individuals—and the evolutionary theory affected these themes chiefly by implication: religion was still religion, and character still character, although the deductions to be drawn regarding their origin and significance were altered. But the poetry of man's relation to nature was fundamentally transformed, as a comparison of Meredith with Wordsworth can show. Tacitly assuming the evolutionary interpretation of the universe to be fully valid, Meredith did not discuss and expound and revise it as did the transitional poets, but it determined his whole outlook.

THE FORMATIVE YEARS

From his home life and early schooling Meredith probably derived little or no intellectual stimulus. But at the age of fourteen he entered the Moravian school at Neuwied on the Rhine, famous for its liberal outlook and toleration. Among the half-dozen writers whom he later listed as having had a formative influence were Niebuhr—pioneer of the evolutionary view of history, who stressed ethnological distinctions, institutions, tendencies, and social traits to the neglect of individuals—and Goethe, whom he termed "the most enduring." From these two German sources he could easily have derived the general concept of development.

His religious record was the antithesis of Browning's. In adolescence he went through a six-weeks' spasm of active evangelism, resembling Browning's spell of atheism, and never thereafter (to quote his own words) "swallowed the Christian fable." His earliest surviving poetic experiments express a sort of "sentimental spiritualism" fostered by Tennyson and Mary Nicolls, his future wife. Mrs. Nicolls, more mature than he and somewhat talented as a writer, in 1848–49 collaborated with him in a manuscript maga-

zine, the *Monthly Observer;* and in his contributions
the influence of Tennyson is paramount. Twenty
years later he was to confess, "what Ruskin says of
Tennyson I too thought in my boy's days, before I
began to think. Tennyson has many spiritual indications, but no philosophy, and philosophy is the palace
of thought." The vague traces of the evolutionary
idea discernible in Meredith's early work are merely
chance echoes of what Tennyson had been saying
during the previous score of years, tinged with the
mystical predilections of Mrs. Nicolls. He commented
on a poem of hers: "The universe is only a succession
of links, and we are all joined, in nobility, in gener-
osity, in love; all that is bestial is of another nature,
but gentle love unites all beings." He suggested as a
topic for discussion "a philosophic inquiry into the
connection of poetry with general life and the progress of science"; but a dull sonnet of his is definitely
opposed to scientific theory and materialism, using
the typical Tennysonian argument of intuition proving immortality:

> Hateful are those false schemes of speculation
> Goading the wise and harassing the weak—
> This world of ours, so lovely and unique
> Why is it subject to such sad vexation?
> 'Tis all for want of proper occupation
> "Philosophers" become so void and vain;
> With birth, life, death, mind, matter, bone and brain
> Can there be any doubt of our Creation?—
> And of our Spirit early information—
> Intelligence and Action?—chiefly whereby
> Thro' rapid glances of the inner eye

> The Soul is sentient of its own salvation
> And in the Faith that such a knowledge brings
> Feels the great glory of its future wings.

Several poems published two or three years later in *HouseholdWords* are still echoes of Tennyson, but now political and social rather than religious. The year 1851, with its great exposition celebrating international peace, was the climax of the century's militant optimism, and Meredith shared the popular enthusiasm for progress and a dawning golden age. *The Congress of Nations* declares that war belongs to the time "while yet the World was young, ere it drank wisdom from the fount of reason"; that "love of man" and "love of his Creator" are replacing the "Ignorance that mars Heaven's gracious plan"; and that "a glorious epoch brightens history's page." Amid the abstractions one catches a faint foreshadowing of the poet's future opinions in the faith in reason's victory over ignorance and in "the bloodless triumph of the labouring Great"; but they are subordinate to the truisms of progress. Two other poems are still more Tennysonian: *Britain* emphasizes the value of caution and slow broadening from precedent to precedent, while *A Wassail for the New Year*, a direct echo of *Hands All Round*, proclaims the English "the vanguard of advancing men."

The only poem of this group which was republished in Meredith's first book is *The Olive Branch*, proclaiming science's service to progress:

> Now when the ark of human fate,
> Long baffled by the wayward wind,

Is drifting with its peopled freight,
Safe haven on the heights to find;

Safe haven from the drowning slime
Of evil deeds and Deluge wrath;—
To plant again the foot of Time
Upon a purer, firmer path;

'Tis now the hour to probe the ground,
To watch the Heavens, to speak the word,
The fathoms of the deep to sound,
And send abroad the missioned bird.

On strengthened wings for evermore
Let Science, swiftly as she can,
Fly seaward on from shore to shore,
And bind the links of man to man.

These boyish exercises under the aegis of Tennyson show that Meredith was interested in the progress of the race and the contributions of science to that end, but they are simply an embodiment of current popular enthusiasm, with no real grasp of the evolutionary idea.

As clearly as his religious and political views at this time reflected Tennyson, his nature poems were in the tradition of Wordsworth, save that the actual descriptions were perhaps more vivid and precise, displaying that extensive knowledge of natural history which later impressed even such a professional scientist as Grant Allen. In speaking of this first book (1851), Meredith described himself as one of the "earnest students of nature who are determined to persevere until they obtain the wisdom and inspira-

tion and self-possession of the poet"; and it is this
belief in the power to be gained from communion with
nature that links him with Wordsworth. The first
Pastoral declares it:

> No disenchantment follows here,
> For nature's inspiration moves
> The dream which she herself fulfils;
> And he whose heart, like valley warmth,
> Steams up with joy at scenes like this
> Shall never be forlorn.

In the third *Pastoral* he describes fuller subordination
to her power:

> A thing of Nature am I now,
> Abroad, without a sense or feeling
> Born not of her bosom;
> Content with all her truths and fates. . . . .

And again in *South-West Wind in the Woodland* he
proclaims that wisdom is to be learned from "the
voice of nature":

> Who that hears her now and yields
> His being to her yearning tones . . . .
> . . . . will gather in the flight
> More knowledge of her secret, more
> Delight in her beneficence,
> Than hours of musing, or the lore
> That lives with men could ever give!
> Nor will it pass away when morn
> Shall look upon the lulling leaves,
> For every elemental power
> Is kindred to our hearts, and once
> Acknowledged, wedded, once embraced,
> The union is eternal.

As compared with Wordsworth, there is, perhaps, a
deeper submission of the poet's self to nature's con-

trol, but the difference is in degree rather than in kind. In some of the other poems, where he undertakes to define "her truths and fates," the ideas of his own generation and the germ of his future doctrines show more clearly. In *The Wild Rose and the Snowdrop* he writes of the two flowers:

> Each, fulfilling nature's law, fulfils
> Itself and its own aspirations pure;
> Living and dying, letting faith ensure
> New life when deathless Spring shall touch the hills.

The simile of the snowdrop is used again in *The Flower of the Ruins*, an apostrophe to a princess visiting the site of her ancestral castle:

> From the snowdrop learn:
> Not in her pale life lives she,
> But in her blushing prophecy.
> Thus be thy hopes,
> Living yet to yearn
> Upwards to the hidden copes;—
> Even within the urn
> Let them burn!

The maiden is abjured to disregard the ghosts of her melancholy forebears:

> Heed not their despair!—
> Thou art thy future, not thy past.

The same creed of progress and fulfilment is repeated in *Pictures of the Rhine*, in a couplet of which one line recalls a famous one by Tennyson and the other a famous one by Wordsworth:

> Beauty renews itself in many ways;
> The flower is fading while the new bud blows.

At the age of twenty-three, then, Meredith revealed a loving eye for nature, a sense of dependence on her power to sustain and inspire him, and a creed of "looking forward" derived from the processes by which she functions. He had also picked up from Tennyson a belief in the gradual progress of the race toward greater perfection. The idea of evolution was latent here, but he had not consciously grasped it.

THE IMPACT OF THE EVOLUTIONARY IDEA

Little is known of Meredith's life between 1851 and 1859. He produced his first experiments in fiction, *The Shaving of Shagpat* and *Farina*, both remote from contemporary events and ideas. In poetry also, imagining that the failure of his first book had been due to its theorizing, he avoided speculative themes and portrayed the concrete. In a letter at the end of 1861, when his second volume of poetry was in prospect, he wrote: "One result of my hard education since the publication of my boy's book in '51 has been that I rarely write save from the suggestion of something actually observed. I desire to strike the poetic spark out of absolute human clay." Accordingly, the volume of 1862 consisted of *Modern Love*—the outcome of his own domestic difficulties—and *Poems of the English Roadside*, such as *Juggling Jerry*—the outcome of his character studies as a novelist.

It is not to be assumed, however, that he had relaxed his interest in speculative topics. From 1859 to 1866 he was actively engaged in journalism, and his

contribution to the *Ipswich Journal* included a weekly
digest of the leading current events; so even had his
predilections been otherwise he must necessarily have
followed the great controversies of those particular
years. His first long novel, *The Ordeal of Richard
Feverel*, which appeared in the crucial year 1859, con-
tained significant references to the state of English
intellect at the time. Caution is needed, of course, in
attributing to an author the opinions expressed by
his fictitious characters; but one passage is well au-
thenticated on several counts. In the first place, it is
consistent with an earlier poem of Meredith's, *London by Lamplight*, which had figured rather inappro-
priately among the paeans of progress in the 1851
book, being a vigorous condemnation of existing social conditions, as shown in the pitiably degraded life
of the slums and industrial areas:

> O agony of grief! for who
> Less dainty than his race, will do
> Such battle for their human right
> As shall awake this startled night?
>
> Proclaim this evil human page
> Will ever blot the Golden Age
> That poets dream and saints invite,
> If it be unredeemed this night?

In *Richard Feverel*, when this disgust is expressed in
still more extreme terms, Adrian is opposing the self-
satisfied Sir Austin's admiration for the material
prosperity and mental placidity of the period, and one
of his arguments includes the view of comedy which

Meredith repeated *in propria persona* elsewhere: "The stage is the pastime of great minds. That's how it comes that the stage is now down. An age of rampant little minds, my dear Austin! How I hate that cant of yours about an age of Work. . . . . Rank radicals, all of you, base materialists." To sum up this scorn of the age, Adrian quotes a poem attributed to Diaper Sandoe:

> An Age of petty tit for tat,
>   An Age of busy gabble:
> An Age that's like a brewer's vat,
>   Fermenting for the rabble!
>
> An Age that drives an Iron Horse
>   Of Time and Space defiant,
> Exulting in a Giant's force
>   And trembling at the Giant.
>
> An Age of Quaker hue and cut,
>   By Mammon misbegotten,
> See the mad Hamlet mouth and strut!
>   And mark the Kings of Cotton!
>
> From this unrest, lo, early wreck'd,
>   A Future staggers crazy,
> Ophelia of the Ages, deck'd
>   With woeful weed and daisy!

Apart from the exaggerated contempt in its tone, attributable to the aristocratic elegance of its supposed author, the poem accords with Meredith's own views in *London by Lamplight* and with those of his revered preceptor Carlyle. Feeling that the vaunted material progress of civilization was more likely to debase mankind than to foster development, he advanced in opposition his doctrine of communion with nature and reliance on her power to heal and sustain.

Such was the attitude which Meredith brought to the consideration of Darwin's book and the other important documents which succeeded it, a few of which are mentioned in his published letters. He gave some attention to Buckle, who in 1859 inconsistently published an impassioned plea for belief in immortality, only two years after his strongly rationalistic *History of Civilization;* the latter book had advanced several theories which figure later in Meredith's poetry—that the aspects of nature are the primary causes of intellectual progress, that human advancement has been due less to moral agencies which are static than to intellectual activity which is constantly stirring and changing, and that civilization varies directly as "scepticism" or the disposition to doubt and to investigate and inversely as "credulity" or "the protective spirit."

Shortly after his allusion to Buckle, Meredith termed Renan's *Vie de Jésus* "one of the finest works of this generation." In 1862 he was one of the enraptured group of listeners when Swinburne read aloud his recent discovery, the *Omar Khayyam* of Fitzgerald. It is not until 1874, however, that one finds in the letters a definite reference to evolution and its bearing on religion:

Tyndall's Belfast address . . . . has roused the Clergy. *They* warned away from science? *They* excluded from the chief works of

God and told to confine themselves to the field of the emotions! They affirm that Tyndall is an atheist, and would dare to say he is already damned if the age were in a mood to hear that language. The man of the country that fights priestcraft and priests is to my mind striking deeper for freedom than can be struck anywhere at present. I foresee a perilous struggle with them.

In conversation, too, he showed during these years a grave concern over human progress and the power of nature, to the extent of importunity. We hear of him sitting on top of a stile on a raw inclement January day to lecture an uninterested friend at great length "on his views of the future destinies of the human race"; and again, while watching a sunrise with two children, pouring out to their puzzled ears "the most wonderful prose hymn to Nature, Life, and what he called *obligation*."

With matters of theory and doctrine bulking so largely in his consciousness, Meredith could not maintain his resolve to banish speculation from his poetry. He was convinced that his poems formed his most valuable and lasting contribution to literature, and that he had a mission to fulfil in the intellectual "struggle for freedom." He said later in life: "Chiefly by that in my poetry which emphasizes the unity of life, the soul that breathes through the universe, do I wish to be remembered, for the spiritual is the eternal." Even in the 1862 volume he admitted one poem expressing his doctrines—the *Ode to the Spirit of Earth in Autumn*, wherein may be found seminally many elements of his later philosophy; and his preference for this poem is revealed by his specially commending it to his friend Maxse's attention in no less than three letters.

That this first definite appearance of his theories did not antedate the Darwinian hypothesis is proved by the fact that the *Ode* resulted from his taking up residence at Copsham Cottage, in the midst of heaths and commons, in the autumn of 1859. In this environment he inevitably returned to the theme of his pastorals—the love of nature and man's intimate communion with her—now impregnated with a deeper and more independent philosophy as a result of the scientific and religious commotions. By 1871 he had definitely determined to make poetry the vehicle for his theory of man and nature, as he informed John Morley:

> Latterly I have felt poetically weakened by the pressure of philosophical reflection, but this is going, and a fuller strength comes of it, for I believe I am within the shadow of the Truth, and as it's my nature to sing I may now do well.

Accordingly, during the next dozen years he wrote the poems which gave specific form to his philosophy, notably *The Woods of Westermain*, *Earth and Man*, and a number of sonnets, the group being collected in 1883 as *Poems and Lyrics of the Joy of Earth*. Two years later the death of his wife caused the spiritual crisis recorded in *A Faith on Trial*, comparable to *In Memoriam* as an impassioned analysis of the poet's creed. This poem, along with *The Thrush in February*, *Hard Weather*, and shorter pieces, appeared in *A Reading of Earth* (1888). The two books present a consistent expression of Meredith's evolutionary philosophy in its mature form, and can therefore be regarded as a unit for the tracing of his principal tenets.

A CREED BASED ON EVOLUTION

In defining Meredith's interpretation of the evolutionary idea, it will be profitable to compare him with Browning. Between the conclusions of the two poets regarding the conduct of life there is a close similarity, but in the arguments from which the conclusions were drawn there is wide divergence. Both, although discounting the notion of any sudden improvement in mankind, yet held the chief sin to be indolent evasion of vigorous effort, and counseled for every man perpetual and cheerful struggle toward his ideal. Both were confident that the trend of such conflict is toward ultimate perfection. But the two assumptions on which Browning based all his theory—the validity of the Christian creed and the immortality of the individual soul—were the very things which Meredith most vehemently denied. Meredith was not without convictions of his own regarding both the existence of God and the survival of the spiritual part of man, but they were the direct outcome of the evolutionary hypothesis; whereas Browning's assimilation of that hypothesis was prevented by his persistent clinging to preconceived views on those matters. Since Meredith took it for granted without debate, and couched his brief references to it in his particularly cryptic symbolism, his deductions from it cannot be readily

understood until his opinions on religious creeds and
the immortality of the soul are surveyed, preferably
through his informal comments in letters and conversations.

His dissatisfaction with religion was based on its
disregard for nature's pre-eminence. His friend Clodd
says:

> I never heard him apply any other term than "fable" to the
> orthodox creed. "Was there ever," he said, "a more clumsy set
> of thaumaturgic fables made into fundamentals of a revealed re-
> ligion? As for the belief in a future life, directly you try to put
> your ideas into shape, how unreal the thing becomes!"

Preaching contempt of nature, the creeds set up an
artificial supernaturalism. In a letter he remarked,
"Our great error has been (the error of all religion, as
I fancy) to raise a spiritual system in antagonism to
Nature." And again, with emphasis on its primitive
traits: "The ecclesiastical dogma is an instance of the
poverty of humanity's mind hitherto, and has often
in its hideous fangs and claws shown whence we draw
our descent." His principal objection was that in
proclaiming the survival of the personal soul it
truckled to the selfish and sensual instincts, which retard progress. "If I speak of a life that is a lasting
life," he writes, "it is not meant to be the life of the
senses—which is a sensual dream of the creeds—
whereon our good Mother looks her blackest." Another letter expresses his theory more fully:

> I should like to think it a vileness to crave for the happiest
> of renewed existences. The soul's one road is forward. Dreams of
> sensational desires drown it. But as to the soul, we get the con-

ception of that, by contrast with the sensations. We go and are unmade. Could elective reason wish for the reconstruction? And yet it is quite certain that the best of us is in the state of survival. We live in what we have done—in the idea: which seems to me the parent fountain of life, as opposed to that of perishable blood (i.e. sensation). I see all around me how much Idea governs; and therein see the Creator; that other life to which we are drawn, not conscious as our senses demand, but possibly cognizant, as the brain may now sometimes, when the blood is not too forcefully pressing on it, dimly apprehend. Consciousness excites human felicity to kill it. Past consciousness there may be a felicity eternal. These are not words, they are my excruciated thoughts—out of bloody sweat of mind, and now peaceful, imaging life, accepting whatever is there.

One is tempted to think of Tennyson in this exalting of intuition; but one must realize that the ideas of intuition of the two poets have nothing in common. To Tennyson it was a certitude of immortality impugning scientific rationalism; to Meredith it is the highest form of that rationalism, freed from the sensual egotism which is no other than Tennyson's certitude of immortality. Meredith held that the next stage of evolution would make this super-consciousness a general trait.

His idea of immortality is summed up in the words of the passage just quoted, "We live in what we have done." In his letters concerning the death of his wife, and in others to bereaved friends, it is his reiterated consolation:

These men live in us. And more, they are the higher work of Nature, which she will not let pass away. They have the eternal in them. I do not look on death as a victory over us. Death and life are neighbors, each the cause of the other; and the Task for us, under stress of deprivation, is to take our loved ones into the mind, and commune with them spirit to spirit—so will they be wedded to us faster, closer about us, than when we had the voice and eyes.

He makes it quite clear that this surviving spirit has nothing to do with the senses of the former individual: "The thought often uppermost in my mind is in amazement at the importance we attach to our hold of sensation. So much grander, vaster, seems her realm of silence. She is in earth, our mother, and I shall soon follow." The reason for his stress on deeds of service is now apparent: since the only true immortality is in the lives of one's successors, one can only gain it by doing something that will affect the future of the race.

Believing, then, that the selfish love of sensation is the insuperable obstacle to human development, he had no sympathy for the creeds which flatter it. Nevertheless, he was willing to admit that Christianity had served a purpose in the race's progress:

What you say about Christianity arresting sensualism is very well: but the Essenian parentage of Christianity was simply asceticism. Hitherto human nature has marched through the conflict of extremes. With the general growth of reason, it will be possible to choose a path midway. Paganism no doubt deserved the ascetic reproof; but Christianity failed to supply much that it destroyed.

Accordingly, unlike his fellow-heretic Swinburne, he did not counsel immediate iconoclasm and the expulsion of all priestcraft. Like Tennyson and Browning he believed in gradual processes, and to this effect he gave much good advice to his radical friend Maxse, prototype of the impulsive reformer Neville Beauchamp:

You presume to declare yourself as if, perceiving a system to be faulty, it was an imperative duty to explode every shred of it to the winds. You must bear in mind that Christianity will always be one of the great chapters in the History of Humanity: that it fought down brutishness: that it has been the mother of our civilization: that it still supplies for many nourishment that in a certain state of the intelligence is instinctively demanded. I cannot think that men's minds are strong enough, or their sense of virtue secure, to escape from the tutelage of superstition in one form or another, just yet. From the pagan divinity to the Christian, I see an advanced conception, and the nearer they get to a general belief in the abstract Deity—i.e. the more and more abstract—the nearer are men to a comprehension of the principles (morality, virtue, etc.) than which we require nothing further to govern us.

So he counsels sound progress by education rather than the open revolt which extremists were attempting:

Let Philosophy sap the structure and work its way. If in the meantime we alarm such placid fellows as we see in the clerical robes, we are really doing Truth no service. Objectless (that is indistinct, blind) protests are like all unseasonable things, useless, and are shelved as Mother Nature shovels away the dust which does not serve her. . . . . We differ in our spirit of objection to the dominant creed. When the ministers of religion press for an open rupture by attempts at persecution it will be time to take rank under colors; until when, I hold myself in reserve. I don't want the day to be advanced. I think you are altogether too impetuous: five hundred years too fast for the human race.

In these passages Meredith makes it clear that his advocacy of caution is based on his reading of the processes of nature. Evolution cannot be hurried.

In the poem *Foresight and Patience*, written in 1894,
he reviews the existing status of humanity in a dialogue between the two principles. With his usual
symbolism he terms them children of "the father
blood, the mother brain" (i.e., instinct and intellect)
and says that on the rare occasions when they meet,
life becomes inspired. Patience, being blind, requires
to be encouraged by Foresight's vision of future progress, and Foresight, in turn, depends on Patience to
restrain her eagerness. Their union gives reason,
which understands "what cowering angel and what
upright beast make man," and sees the universe in its
true perspective, wherein the stars and the flowers are
of equal importance. Patience insists that her principle is not synonymous with resignation; mere contentment is no better than death, and so long as any
trace of humanity's primal brutality remains, resignation is impossible to her "true pupils." Although man
is the offspring of earth, and must remain loyal to her,
he soon becomes "carrion" if he remains "very earth";
he must exercise the more active principle by striving
to improve conditions; "no home is here for peace
while evil breeds, while error governs."

Foresight, disgruntled with contemporary materialism, complains that, while the senses are being
flattered by prosperity, mankind appears to be advancing; but such an impression is illusory, and, in
fact, men have in one sense retrogressed by losing
"the beauty of frank animals." Patience, however,
appeals to the history of evolution:

Observe them, and down rearward for a term
Gaze to the primal twistings of the worm.
Thence look this way, across the fields that show
Men's early form of speech for Yes and No,—

that is, the instinctive appeal to force, wherein neither
Foresight nor Patience was consulted. When Foresight declares the present age to be equally neglectful
of them, since Science has fostered an attitude of
despair, Patience points out that despair is passive,
whereas the prevalent scorn of happiness is unrest;
the temperate happiness which is not predatory being
still unattained, happiness only signifies "our soul
asleep or body's lust," and so contempt of it is a
promising sign. Foresight, still pessimistic, declares
brains to be subordinated to the brute force of fool
and knave. Patience, while asserting that knave and
fool will vanish with the human lusts and lassitudes
that breed them, yet admits that they may master
and destroy the race unless every man combat them
individually to the utmost, by holding subject the
primitive "traitorous devildom" within himself. All
the faults of the age—its selfish love of creature comforts, disregard for posterity, lack of faith, absurd
blend of cynical skepticism and gross superstition—
are useful as tests "to strengthen our foundations,"
and there is at least an escape from old shackles:

Out of the course of ancient ruts and grooves
It moves: O much for me to say it moves!

Vigor is necessary for progress, though it often appears to be wantonly destructive: the barbarous force

with which the race originated must continue to cause "cancelled blessings" until men learn the need of "shaping strength," a recognition which can come only through warfare and suffering; then at last "of rabble passions may grow the chieftain mind." As final justification of the present age, the utilitarian argument is introduced, that a greater proportion are now finding pleasure in living than was possible under the oppressive systems of the past; and so long as philosophers refrain from emulating Empedocles by plunging into Aetna (i.e., the smoky recesses of their own minds) in despair because the brilliant few are starved while the many are nourished, we may gain "the wisdom making passage through our slough." By despising the coward in us, and by learning Earth's lesson to "wait to see, and seeing wait," we gain the philosophy which is "Life's one match for Fate."

The poem is Meredith's definite answer to the gloomy disillusionment of such contemporaries as Hardy. It is by no means the unqualified assertion of Browning that "life means intensely, and means good." Meredith himself said, in speaking about Hardy, "I keep on the causeway between the bogs of optimism and pessimism." But from the evidence of history he held that the movement of evolution was upward; the only way in which the human race could possibly advance must be the constant exercise of the reason in conflict with the reactionary selfishness of the sensual instincts. He took issue with the disgruntled idealists by insisting that the conflict must be conducted joyfully, joy and trust being the deepest lessons of nature:

> Not what should be, but what can, as a step thereto, is the reasonable aim. You do well, even nobly, but you are one half wrong, for you go against nature, and nature says that to work soundly the creature must be in that state of contentment to which philosophy points you and poetry elevates you. You deny to man the right to be in this state while there is one miserable upon the earth.

So, despite his perception of man's shortcomings, he was able to write in his last year, "My religion of life is always to be cheerful." But he did not hold, with Browning, that the value of the struggle, and the inspiration of the cheerfulness, lay in the development of the individual soul in after-life. The struggle and the cheerfulness bear their fruit in the heritage which each man leaves in this earthly life for posterity. "I have the confidence," he wrote at seventy, "which began with hope and strengthens with experience, that humanity is gaining in the stores of mind, and that the signification of this Gift of life, that we should leave a better world for our successors, is being understood." And again, "I think that all right use of life, and the one secret of life, is to pave ways for the firmer footing of those who succeed us."

MEREDITH'S IDEAS OF GOD AND NATURE

Along with his views on the subject of human evolution, with deductions therefrom regarding religious creeds and the immortality of the soul, Meredith's poetic outlook involved his conception of God. In it he attached supreme importance to physical nature, usually symbolized by Earth, the Mighty Mother. His chief accusation against dogmatic creeds was that they turned away in fear and revulsion from Earth, setting up, instead, a supernaturalism which shapes its deity according to the dictates of human desire, in flat contradiction to the lessons of nature. His argument was to the effect that God can be perceived only by a sympathetic understanding of Earth, and never by contempt of her. Believing that progress comes from the balanced interplay of "blood, brain, and spirit," he had no respect for asceticism:

I hold that to be rightly materialistic—to understand and to take nature as she is—is to get on the true divine highroad. That we should attain to a healthy humanity, is surely the most pleasing thing in God's sight.

Any effort to exercise the human intellect divorced from the essential contact with Earth was doomed to lose sight of God immediately:

Does not all science tell us that when we forsake earth, we reach up to a frosty, inimical Inane? For my part I love and cling to earth, as the one piece of God's handiwork which we possess. I admit that we can refashion, but of earth must be the material.

To this extent, the basis of scientific materialism in his creed is clear. But we find that he sublimates the lesson of Earth into a metaphysic:

Let nothing flout your sense of a Supreme Being, and be certain that your understanding wavers whenever you chance to doubt that he leads to good. We grow to good as surely as the plant grows to the light.

Although thus in a sense agreeing with Browning in seeing progress as God's plan for humanity, Meredith does not base his perception of it on any intuitive conviction. He looks out upon the processes of nature, and perceives in the laws of growth and recurrence the testimony of the divine intention. The sonnet *Lucifer in Starlight* uses the stars, "the brain of heaven," to typify the invariable order of the universe, "the army of unalterable law"; and the same thought appears in a letter of 1878:

> To come from a gaze at the stars is to catch a glance at the inscrutable face of him that hurries us on, as on a wheel, from dust to dust. I saw beyond good and evil, to a great stillness. It seems to me that Spirit is, how, where, and by what means involving us, none can say. But in this life there is no life save in spirit. The rest of life is an aching and a rotting.

This insistence on spirit, however, is reconciled with "right materialism," the necessary love of earth and the physical life. He explains:

> I have written always with the perception that there is no life but of the spirit; that the concrete is really the shadowy; yet that the way to spiritual life lies in the complete unfolding of the creature, not in the nipping of his passions; an outrage to nature helps to extinguish his light. To the flourishing of the spirit, then, through the healthy exercise of the senses.

Fundamental, therefore, in his creed, is the perception of the spiritual as existing through all Nature, accessible by anyone who approaches her lovingly. The one essential is that man should not regard Nature from the point of view of physical comfort and material satisfactions. Whoever does so will find in her only cruelty and destruction. He used to advise his young friends "to go to our mother Nature and learn of her, and not to look upon trees, mountains, fields and lakes as merely the background of our own little ephemeral lives. He had trained himself when he walked to observe, not to feel." Here Meredith shows his divergence from Wordsworth. So long as the old religious dogmas hedged man around with a confidence in his own superiority and security, it was possible to look on Nature "as merely the background of our own little ephemeral lives" and be complacent; but after that faith had been assailed, and science had painted the "struggle for survival" in gloomy colors, Nature was apt to appear, as she did to Hardy, a blind power in whose wanton grasp man is hopelessly pinioned. Meredith insisted vehemently that such an idea arose from a mistaken view of Earth. It is only by the standards of our finite desires and selfish instincts that she appears cruel; anyone who seeks her with a true sense of her joy and love derives comfort and fortitude from her. Meredith was able to write in his old age, deprived of all the pleasures of his earlier years: "I am fairly at peace, and satisfied with nature's ways. Would you have more wisdom?"

Although as anxious as Tennyson and Browning to prove that the principle of evolution does not nullify faith in God and the human spirit, Meredith insisted on clearing away all the remnants of the systems that preceded the formulation of the new principle. The efforts toward a *via media* made by the elder poets merely showed the uncertainty with which they grasped the implications of evolution; Meredith, by basing his creed frankly on the modern theory, was able to ignore the possibility of doubt and to proclaim a coherent system of belief. He was in accord with the prevalent mood of "militant optimism" sufficiently to proclaim on his eightieth birthday: "Life is a long and continuous struggle. It is necessarily combative. Otherwise we cease. Let the struggle go on. Let us be combative, but let us also be kind." In feeling profoundly the duty imposed on every man to carry on this struggle for the sake of the race, he was nearer to Tennyson than to Browning, since the latter held the struggle to be primarily for the progress of the individual soul. Meredith went farther than Tennyson, however, in asserting that the fulfilment of the responsibility, the handing-on of one's achievements to posterity, is the soul's only form of immortality. In 1876 he said that his favorite passage in his poetry was from the opera in *Vittoria* (1866):

> Our life is but a little holding, lent
> To do a mighty labour: we are one
> With heaven and the stars when it is spent
> To serve God's aim: else die we with the sun.

In 1909, in response to a similar request for his favorite passage, he cited the lines from *The Thrush in February* (1885):

> Full lasting is the song, though he,
> The singer, passes: lasting too,
> For souls not lent in usury,
> The rapture of the forward view.

The message of the two passages is the same: the individual soul passes, but its work survives if it has obeyed the law of nature, in harmony with the rest of the physical universe, and if it has labored confidently toward the vision of future progress.

Nature, then—or, as Meredith preferred to call her, Earth—is the basis for all activities of the human mind, even those of a wholly "spiritual" character. Only through close communion with Nature can man develop his own spiritual qualities or perceive the existence of any larger spiritual entity. The reason is that Earth is in a very literal sense the "mother" of man, since he has been evolved from her through the same natural processes as those which shaped all other phenomena. In purely physical matters, the recognition of man's kinship with the lower orders of nature is shown in the poem *Melampus* to give wisdom in healing, music, and other arts. In less tangible things, the sense of kinship is equally essential. Since she is our mother, he says in the *Spirit of Earth in Autumn*, we have no right to consider ourselves superior to her, to "pretend to be aught better than she who bore us, and is our only visible friend." But this, of course, does not mean that man is to regard himself as wholly physical, for Earth is a living entity, with spirit interpenetrating every part of her, as he gleefully chants:

> Could I be sole there not to see
> The life within the life awake;
> The spirit bursting from the tree

> And rising from the troubled lake? . . . .
> Hark to her laughter! who laughs like this,
> Can she be dead or rooted in pain?
> She has been slain by the narrow brain,
> But for us who love her she lives again.
> Can she die? O, take her kiss!

In *The Woods of Westermain* he insists that her superficial beauty, witching though it be, is secondary to the spirit within, "rich past computing, past amaze"; that those who "have sight for things afield" may see "the Nurse of seed" peeping through her cloak, "showing a kind face and sweet" to anyone who "looks with the soul." Hence the gods of the Greek Pantheon may still have their place in any true modern reading of Earth, because they were conceived from a deep and loving knowledge of Nature; and in *The South Wester* he returns to this idea that the "old bards in nature wise" were right in creating personages of "pure beauty" and immortal life to symbolize the "life in orb and brook and tree and cloud."

The only way by which the living spirit of Earth can be perceived is through joy and love. *The Appeasement of Demeter* is an allegory of the essential part which joy plays in nature, and *The Lark Ascending* celebrates the joyful love of earth which includes all natural objects in its embrace until the hearer of the lark's song feels this all-pervading unity and sees "the better heart of man." And the particular value of this communion with Earth's essential joy is that thus alone can man face death without dread:

O green bounteous Earth!
Bacchante Mother! stern to those
Who live not in thy heart of mirth;
Death shall I shrink from, loving thee?
                —Spirit of Earth in Autumn

This is the theme of the long and important poem, *The Woods of Westermain*. The woods represent Nature, terrible to anyone who enters with fear or carping. Courage and love find the spirit of Nature revealed as kind and sustaining, but any trace of doubt or hate is fatal: she changes from a benevolent mother to a wantonly cruel hag, and all her processes seem a crazy and frightful saturnalia of death:

Earthward swoops a vulture sun,
Nighted upon carrion:
Straightway venom winecups shout
Toasts to One whose eyes are out:
Flowers along the reeling floor
Drip henbane and hellebore:
Beauty, of her tresses shorn,
Shrieks as nature's maniac:
Hideousness on hoof and horn
Tumbles yapping in her track . . . . etc.

Clearly the allusion is to Meredith's contemporaries who stressed the cruel and wasteful aspects of the evolutionary process, seeing Nature as a blind power in whose control we are helpless. In *The Spirit of Shakespeare* he declares that personal spleen is responsible for their fatalism:

'twas the goad of personal pain
To view in curst eclipse our Mother's mind,
And show us of some rigid harridan
The wretched bondmen till the end of time.

The same idea, that Nature appears cruel only to the mind blinded by suffering, is shown dramatically in section xxx of *Modern Love*, when the tortured lover cynically accuses a savage law of Nature for the shattering of his dream. Again in *A Faith on Trial* Meredith describes how to his selfish senses, which had temporarily overcome his philosophy, the lovely Earth "had a visage of hags; a Mother of aches and jests; soulless, heading a hunt aimless except for the meal." The responsibility of science for this pessimism is stated in the *Meditation under Stars:* if one gazes analytically at the firmament, it ruthlessly smites the heart into believing the "heavens hoar" and even "our blood-warm Earth a shuddering prey to that frigidity of brainless ray." But this is the reaction of selfishness—"it is our ravenous that quails, flesh by its craven thirsts and fears distraught." The spirit intuitively feels a unity binding the human individual with the universe, and learns

> even that we
> The specks of dust upon a mound of mould,
> We who reflect those rays, though low our place,
> To them are lastingly allied.

Thus Meredith dismisses the deductions from evolution which Tennyson years before had seen with dismay, which Arnold accepted with resignation, and which Hardy was making into a philosophic system. The sonnets *My Theme* and *Sense and Spirit* reinforce his assurance that the mind must escape from the senses, which provoke confusion and "fear-bred tales," to recognize Earth as a spiritual entity giving man life and the power to survive disaster and face death.

It is clear that Meredith confronted squarely the fact that the struggle for survival entailed suffering. The poem *Whimper of Sympathy* dismisses the "sweet sentimentalist" who would like the God he worships to intercede when the hawk kills its prey. "All around," says Meredith, "we find cold Nature slight the feelings of the totter-knee'd"; and he satirizes the desire "to fly from this tussle of foes, the shambles, the charnel," to some romantic fairyland of dewdrops and roses and starlight. Such shirking of reality has no place in Meredith's philosophy. It is only by a calm and reasoned acceptance of all the elements in Nature's process that man can grasp its law, in which his consolation lies.

THE LAW OF NATURE

The fundamental law of Nature, to Meredith, was that of the constant alternation of life and death, the regeneration always inherent in decay. Nature is never regretful over the inevitable loss of all her lovely things, for she knows that they will recur. For the operation of this law, change is essential, and dissolution must be met gladly. The idea first appeared distinctly in *Modern Love*, section xiii:

'I play for Seasons, not Eternities!'
Says Nature, laughing on her way. 'So must
All those whose stake is nothing more than dust!'
And lo, she wins, and of her harmonies

She is full sure! Upon her dying rose
She drops a look of fondness, and goes by,
Scarce any retrospection in her eye;
For she the laws of growth most deeply knows,
Whose hands bear, here, a seed-bag—there, an urn.
Pledged she herself to aught, 'twould mark her end!
This lesson of our only visible friend
Can we not teach our foolish hearts to learn?

The same theme is repeated in the *Ode to the Spirit of
Earth in Autumn*. The poet begs the Great Mother
to teach him to follow her example, which is "to kiss
the season and shun regrets." The faith to be learned
from Nature is one "that forward sets," and the poet
wishes to feel that he is "the tree and not the withered
leaf." On this analogy, death is not to be dreaded:

Into the breast that gives the rose
Shall I with shuddering fall?
Earth, the mother of all,
Moves on her steadfast way,
Gathering, flinging, sowing.

She knows not loss:
She feels but her need,
Who the winged seed
With the leaf doth toss . . . .

Behold, in yon stripped autumn, shivering grey,
Earth knows no desolation.
She smells regeneration
In the moist breath of decay.

This emphasis on the certainty of renewal inherent in
autumnal decay reappears in *Woodland Peace*, wherein the growing things declare, "We wot of life through
death, how each feeds each we spy"; and in *A Faith*

on Trial in the image "permanence sits on the grave green-grassed. . . . . By Death, as by Life, we are fed: the two are one spring."

Just as death and life are equally important for the processes of evolution, so in life the hard experiences have their place in the general plan as well as the pleasures. In the poem *Seed Time*, Nature is made to chide the weakness which longs for summer in the bleakness of autumn, on the ground that it reveals traces of the old undeveloped animal instincts: anyone who has "sowed, reaped, harvested" has learned Earth's admonition to "master the blood, nor read by chills." Those who serve Earth perceive that "the fuel, decay," brightens the fire of renewal. The conclusion, though based on very different theories, recalls *Rabbi Ben Ezra:*

> Death is the word of a bovine day,
> Know you the breast of the springing To-be.

The idea that the husbandman's work depends on his trust in Nature and his taking advantage of her harsh as well as her gentle moods is a favorite with Meredith, as in *The Day of the Daughter of Hades*, wherein the "Song of Days" is a paean of "toil and strife," "the grace of the battle for food," and

> the husbandman's heart made strong
> Through droughts and deluging rains
> With his faith in the Great Mother's love.

All this resolves itself into "the struggle for survival" in which, as the evolutionists had shown, everyone is involved. It is stated clearly in *A Faith on Trial:*

> We, quivering upward, each hour
> Know battle in air and in ground
> For the breadth that goes as it comes,
> For the choice between sweet and sour,
> For the smallest grain of our worth:
> And he who the reckoning sums
> Finds nought in his hand save Earth.
> Of Earth are we stripped or crowned.

Meredith's chief deductions from evolution are plain in those eight lines: man's essential dependence on Earth, his environment of ceaseless conflict, and his duty to choose the nobler task which will aid development.

Suffering, then, is as necessary in life as autumn in agriculture. In *Martin's Puzzle* an artless philosopher considers the apparent injustice of fate, and sees that one must either disbelieve in the existence of "a law above all" or else conclude that life is "but a trial .... some must toil, some must perish, for others below"; and yet the latter suggests the unsatisfactory principle that "the injustice to each spreads a common content." He is tempted to Hardyan pessimism, for if he seeks an explanation why "a creature put together with craft" is "then stamped on," he gets no answer from heaven: "the sky's a blue dish!— an implacable sky." But at last he grasps a clue: just as the component parts of a harmony, if taken separately, might be discords, so he may be drawing a wrong induction from "a single false note" and the universe may be "one immense Organ that rolls from devils to angels." The same idea is expressed in *The*

Promise in Disturbance, the comment of Meredith's mature philosophy on the cynicism of parts of *Modern Love.* It follows that all man's doubts and despairs arise from his failing to realize that he is but one element in the great harmony of nature, wherein the leading principles are order and sanity. *Melampus* insists that "all sane the woods revolve, the rooted life restrains disorder"; and *A Faith on Trial* reiterates that only the perfect co-ordination of the three elements in the individual can produce the right relationship of Earth and man:

> Natures at interflow
> With all of their past and the now
> Are chords to Nature without,
> Orbs to the greater whole:
> First then, nor utterly then
> Till our lord of sensations at war,
> The rebel, the heart, yields place
> To brain, each prompting the soul.
> Thus our dear Earth we embrace
> For the milk, her strength to men.

As far back as 1861, Meredith sketched his view of the necessary unity between mankind and nature in the whimsical allegory *By the Rosanna.* Representing the spirit of nature as an elusive water nymph, he inquires whether she can prove herself of any value under "the ordeal of a scrutiny of Science." He personifies contemporary civilization as a London cab driver, and suggests that it would do him good to make the nymph's acquaintance, since Science has made them equal; she must "own her parentage humanity," for "her heart comes out of the human heart," and she can only gain "the soul she yet lacks" by "wedding the cabman." This necessity of the human element, as well as the processes of external nature for the complete understanding of evolution, is made clear in *Earth's Secret:* the most elementary page of the lesson is to be found in the fields, and another "in turbid cities"; but the complete revelation comes only to those who include both, "close interthreading nature with our kind." From history they learn "what men were and have become"; but this wisdom, needful though it is, can only be valid when joined with knowledge of Her, "for Earth, that gives the milk, the spirit gives." Elsewhere Meredith uses this as a literary criterion, attributing to knowledge of Earth Shakespeare's wide tolerance, loving wisdom, and hearty laughter, his scorn of philosophy "when from her soul divorced"; and in *Manfred* explaining Byron's misanthropy as deficient communion with her.

The philosophy which bases itself on Earth is to some extent a stoic one. Earth gives no definite answer to questions regarding man's origin or destiny. Such questions spring from selfish instincts, and the effort to find answers for them only makes Earth appear terrible and inscrutable. Her processes go on, and man must accommodate himself to them. The growths of the woodland—which to Meredith always symbolizes Nature and her functions—do not make the mistake. "What is dumb we question not," they

say in *Woodland Peace*, "nor ask the hidden to un-
mask." *Meditation under Stars* is to the same effect,
and in *The Woods of Westermain* he describes at
greater length how the dragon—the selfish sensual
instincts—vainly questions Earth, who goes on with
her creative process: the unstable senses see only a
dazzling interchange of "Flow and Drought, luridness
and lustre" in endless succession, "Life and Death
each of either reaped and sown"; but when one "looks
with spirit past the sense," the underlying entity is
seen to "shine in permanence." So man's only philosophy must be submission to the inevitable law of
Earth, accepting his place in the general process of
evolution without petulant questioning. When he
does so, he is in a position to feel the existence of a
spiritual power in Earth with which he is allied, and
which is permanent beneath the vicissitudes of form.

In every phase of this concept of man's relation to
Nature the evolutionary principle is implicit. Meredith felt that the churches, as the accredited representatives of spiritual affairs, were producing by their
opposition to scientific theories the purely materialistic reaction which interpreted evolution as a blind
and cruel struggle in which man was the accidental
result of physical forces. By painting the horrors of
this gloomy view in the extremest colors, Meredith
showed the necessity for a spiritual interpretation of
Nature. Yet he held that the setting-up of an external power which could transcend the laws of Nature was a concession to the sensual instincts in man,

the primitive dread which sought refuge from Nature's apparent cruelty. Since to Meredith this selfish outlook must necessarily vanish in the course of evolution, he held that the creeds were opposing evolution's progress. In stanzas subsequently omitted from the *Ode to the Spirit of Earth in Autumn* he vigorously satirized the idea that God's favor is to be won by reviling Nature and suspecting all natural beauty as a delusion and a snare; he imagines how she must laugh at human beings as "strange perversions" who feel "confident of wings" because they have "named her Ashes" and regarded her as "a damned witch, fair to the eye, but full of foulest things." Such puritanical cant, he points out, amounts to seeking God's favor "by telling him that his prime work is vile," an obvious absurdity. On the contrary, the sole path to God is through communion with Earth, the only means of access to his footstool; and a man must love and enjoy her gifts, and "reverence the truths she teaches," since by being "true to the mother with whom we are" we may be "worthy of Him who afar beckons us on to a brighter birth."

In *Earth and Man* Meredith gave the fullest expression to his ideas of the instincts responsible for the supernaturalistic religion. Man creates "The Invisible" which he beseeches to shield him from Earth's control. A slave to the gratification of the senses, he sees the world as "his wormy home" and himself as a "wind-whipped, anywhither wave" to be destroyed with crazy wastefulness; so he escapes into a religion which must be manifested by miracles, "some proofs of slaughtered nature." The prospect of being miraculously saved from extinction is a further comfort to his conceit in that it is "by virtue of his worth, contrasting much with brutes and knaves." Such Pharisaic pretension shared with asceticism Meredith's contempt because they both seemed to him cowardly evasions of Nature's stern lesson, unintelligent survivals from primitive man and contrary to the evolutionary law decreeing the destruction of everything that has served its purpose. A religion putting personal salvation and individual immortality above the cause of racial progress was inimical to evolution, so he dismissed the orthodox religions as summarily as he dismissed the purely materialistic revulsion from them. He substituted a creed which acknowledged man's place in the physical universe without disregarding his intuitive sense of spiritual existence. Man, having been evolved in the same manner as the rest of the universe, must regard Earth with love and trust, as the visible symbol of the creative power, or deity. By doing so he comes to perceive the "unalterable law" in which he is included. His finite mind, as yet only partially liberated from the trammels of the brute—the sway of the senses—finds only bewilderment and despair if it seeks explanations of "what he is and whence he came, whither to go"; but as soon as these vain demands are relinquished, and man submits to being only a single unit in a larger organism transcending his comprehension, he discovers a spiritual entity in nature, akin to his own.

The poem *In the Woods* is an allegory of Meredith's religious development. In his journey through the dark woods (life) he puts his trust in the light within him (spirit). He has rejected safe sleep in the chrysalis (orthodox religion) and eschews all spells and charms. In his youth he had been taught to look above "with eyes of belief" for love, but it appeared intermittent and delusive; finally he looked at the earth "whereof we grow," and it said nothing of love, but gave warnings of sin and lessons of patience, explained sin and human weakness, and expounded "the struggle upward of all, and my choice of the glory of life"; and surely this revealed love indisputably. The joy of this all-embracing creed—or moral code—drawn from "this old heart of things" is proclaimed in *The Thrush in February* as keeping his spirit youthful, in company with those

> Who feel the Coming young as aye,
> Thrice hopeful of the ground we plough;
> Alive for life, awake to die;
> One voice to cheer the seedling Now.

The creed thus rooted in Earth has courage, he says in *The Woods of Westermain*, which endures even the earthquake; and it gives the sane pleasures, "sureties as the stars are sure," that do not become sensual habits. He learns from Nature, as he explains in *Outer and Inner*, that his sufferings are not accidental, being necessary for his development, so he bows to her laconic dictum "accept," seeing that the soul unfolds through blood and tears as the rose in mold.

All of this is a logical deduction from the evolutionary principle, with the single exception of the assumption that Nature possesses a spiritual element. In making that assumption, Meredith passed beyond the range of science, and depended, even as Tennyson and Browning did, on intuition. But the fact which he asserts by that sanction is more easily reconcilable with evolution than their demonstrations of God and the immortal soul, and is actually nothing more than a sublimation of the laws governing nature in general and evolution in particular.

MAN'S DUTY TOWARD EARTH AND TOWARD THE RACE

The foregoing notions of Meredith regarding Earth and man's relation to her as her physical offspring are only one-half of his theory. Taken alone, they would suggest fatalism: man, only a small cog in the great machine, cannot hope to achieve knowledge of first-causes or ultimate results, yet he is to be confident that "all's for the best." Acting on such a philosophy, one might abandon one's self altogether to the external forces, and that is the very last thing that Meredith would countenance. For he held, as Tennyson and Browning did, that evolution can be furthered by the conscious efforts of individuals. When he viewed evolution with regard to the future, he adduced an additional doctrine. The anterior course of evolution is traced in *The Woods of Westermain* by means of the lower animals—the "old-eyed oxen" who point "back to hours when mind was mud" and earth was "a slimy spine"—and such a primitive condition should have no temptations to men. Meredith felt that human evolution had reached the pinnacle of physical development, and that the intellectual and spiritual parts of man must next advance proportionately. To this end, he declared, it is the duty of each individual to devote all his efforts, and thus alone can be attained the conditioned immortality of having contributed something to the race.

Though man owes everything he possesses to Earth, Meredith adds that, in return, man is able to do Earth a service which she cannot otherwise obtain. Man has the intellectual endowment which enables him to grasp the purposes of evolution and further them. To the spiritual sustenance which Earth gives him, he can contribute mind, the poem *Nature and Life* declares. In *Earth and Man* Meredith describes how the inarticulate yearning of Earth toward harmony and beauty is fulfilled by the human race, whose efforts produce "half her loveliness" and conquer "the shapeless and the dun, their common foes." Even though blind to her inner spirit, he has puzzled out enough of her laws to create lovely things interpreting her. He has replaced the monster-haunted wildernesses of primitive times with harvest-fields and cities, and has embodied "order, high discourse, and decency." All his achievements, of course, have been based on her endowment to him; she has kindled all the instincts which prompt him onward, even the very ones which cause him to imagine a power external and averse to her. She is responsible for his revulsions from the idea of death and his "desires for happiness, for lastingness, for light," the result being the optimism and idealism which spur him to progress. All these higher impulses, as well as the animal ones, Earth has implanted in man; and, moreover, she gives him sustenance for the fight. But beyond that she is powerless—it depends on himself alone whether he shall advance:

> More aid than that embrace,
> That nourishment, she cannot give: his heart
> Involves his fate; and she who urged the start
> Abides the race.

And Earth is still doubtful as to the outcome—whether he will eventually fulfil his highest potentialities or desist and perish; she is "twi-minded of him, as the waxing tree or dated leaf." Her prayer is that he may liberate his reason from the tyranny of the senses; and when he is thus purged of "his distempered devil of Self, the glutton for her fruits," he will become "a spirit nigh divine," understanding her lesson of immortality through posterity—"live in thy offspring as I live in mine."

This transmutation of self into spirit is the theme of several poems. *The State of Age* says that a selfish

old man is a useless thing abhorred by Nature, but
that he who submits "to burn from Self to Spirit
through the lash" shall be honored by the sons of
Earth long after his "proud letter I drops prone and
void." Such willing surrender of individuality can
only be reached by active and continued participation
in the race's struggle. At this point the Darwinian
principle of "the survival of the fittest" is incorporated into Meredith's system. In *Hard Weather* he
points out that not only in primitive times did Earth
love best the stubborn fighter; now when the fight
is no longer physical—"when muscle is in mind re-
newed"—the idler is still at a disadvantage:

> Behold the life at ease; it drifts.
> The sharpened life commands its course.
> She winnows, winnows roughly; sifts
> To dip her chosen in her source:
> Contention is the vital force
> Whence pluck they brain, her prize of gifts.

Thus Meredith, consistently loyal to the "law of
Earth," defends the principle which has already partly
changed the field of man's struggle, as *Earth and Man*
asserts, from physical to mental—"has half-trans-
ferred the battle to his brain, from bloody ground."
It is part of man's stupid hatred of nature to mistake
the selective process—"her cherishing of her best-
endowed"—for the meaningless caprice of "a wanton's choice"; whereas the mind equipped with love
and insight understands the real meaning of the principle, as he states in *The Thrush in February:*

> Why the sons of Strength have been
> Her cherished offspring ever; how
> The Spirit served by her is seen
> Through Law; perusing love will show.

Meredith held that the development of the brain would be essential for showing man his true position and Earth's purpose regarding him. The thought first appeared in section xlviii of *Modern Love*, an impassioned prayer for "more brain, O Lord, more brain!" for, unless we can disentangle the "sense" from the "senses," we are bound to "mar utterly this fair garden we might win." The enlightened ones are celebrated in *Hard Weather:*

> They see how spirit comes to light,
> Through conquest of the inner beast,
> Which Measure tames to movement sane,
> In harmony with what is fair.
> Never is Earth misread by brain:
> That is the welling of her, there
> The mirror: with one step beyond,
> For likewise is it voice.

But brain, though the next great acquisition to be striven for, is not glorified in isolation. The three elements, "blood, brain and spirit," must be united to form a triad. They mark the three great stages of evolution, each emerging out of the previous one, under the guidance of Earth. *The Woods of Westermain* describes the pure and unfailing pleasures

> that through blood run sane,
> Quickening spirit from the brain,
> Each of each in sequent birth.

When the three are parted, there is unbalance and disaster; Earth is the union of them, and the individual who mirrors that union has "true felicity." Man has already progressed from the first stage into the second:

> Change is on the wing to bud
> Rose in brain from rose in blood.
> Wisdom throbbing shall you see
> Central in complexity;
> From her pasture 'mid the beasts
> Rise to her ethereal feasts.

And Earth looks forward to the third stage of the development, as it is foreshadowed in the "fittest" of the present generation. *Hard Weather* explains that she is "vowed to thresh for stouter stock" now in favoring those who serve her law without dreading her, as formerly the physically powerful; her favorites, "in strong brain her noblest born," form the starting-point for the final achievement—"the station for the flight of soul." That this spiritualized race may be evolved, the old dragon of the selfish impulses must be sublimated by a process described in *The Woods of Westermain*, when Change, despite his hugging himself, shall "wonderously renovate" him into an admirable servant; from the wedding of Change, "the strongest son of life," with the Spirit will be engendered the "vivid breed" to "bear the lights that onward speed."

Evolution being the law of Earth, the conservatism which opposes progress is flayed in *The Wisdom of Eld, Earth's Preference*, and other sonnets. Meredith bitterly satirizes the reactionary old men who are suspicious of change and try to restrain the radicalism of youth; Earth, who loves the young, prizes her beasts more than those perverted members of the "high breed" who oppose her law. He insists in *The Discipline of Wisdom* that intellect isolated from the battle of the race for progress is vain, and in *The Garden of Epicurus* he contemns the sedate and cloistered cult devoted to "the long drawing of an easeful breath" in contrast with the self-sacrifice of Christ, who entered the struggle of humanity. *A Faith on Trial* similarly insists that wisdom is won through "the combat incessant" and, if perched on a height to chew the cud of contemplation, it is "in peril of isolate scorn, unfed of the onward flood." Meredith's own philosophy completely fulfils the specification: his creed is based on the responsibility of each man to further the cause of the race, which is—as the principle of "the survival of the fittest" shows—the purpose of Earth.

The ethical law which Meredith derived from his evolutionary "reading of Earth" turns out to be practically identical with the two chief tenets of his revered friend and patron, Carlyle. His poetry is largely an exposition of the doctrines of work and leadership in the light of the evolutionary theory, though they fit so perfectly into his general concept of Earth and man that it is impossible to decide how far they are the inevitable deduction from it and how far a heritage from the elder philosopher.

Meredith put his trust firmly in the leader, or hero. In the little poem *Men and Man* he says that men collectively may be classified as either random waves or stagnant marsh, and less valuable alive than dead, since when dead they are at least not an obstruction to progress; but man, the individual hero, is recognized by the angels as their equal, and is capable of quelling the sea and draining the fen—i.e., of improving the otherwise useless majority. This Carlylean distrust of the masses is attributed in *Hard Weather* to the fact that "the champions of the race" who are "the sole humane" are the chosen of Earth who have developed mentally in accordance with her plan— "her children of the labouring brain, with understanding for their base." In *The Lark Ascending* he compares the bird's song "seraphically free of taint of personality" with the lives of men whose altruism inspires the race, "because their love of Earth is deep and they are warriors in accord with life to serve," seeking no recompense; on account of their divine self-forgetfulness their soul sings "in me and mine." This idea of the small band of heroes whose vision gives them immortality in the soul of the entire race finds its fullest expression in *The Thrush in February*. It is from the cities, he says, where the battle of life is in its most dismal, aimless, and selfish form, that the leaders emerge:

> Life was to them a bag of grain,
> And Death the weedy harrow's tooth.
> Those warriors of the sighting brain
> Give worn Humanity new youth.

Our song and star are they to lead
The tidal multitude and blind
From bestial to the higher breed
By fighting souls of love divined.

They scorn the ventral dream of peace,
Unknown in nature. This they knew:
That life begets with fair increase
Beyond the flesh, if life be true.

Just reason based on valiant blood
The instinct bred afield would match
To pipe thereof a swelling flood,
Were men of Earth made wise in watch.

Though now the numbers count as drops
An urn might bear, they father Time.
She shapes anew her dusty crops;
Her quick in their own likeness climb.

Of their own force do they create;
They climb to light, in her their root.

It is essential that these pioneers of the future race
should be willing to sacrifice themselves gladly; not
as ascetics, scorning the life of the flesh, but living
it to the full and relinquishing it without regret. *In
the Woods* contrasts "the lust after life" which clings
to it with "the lover of life" who "flings it broadcast."
This aspect, like all the others of his evolutionary
creed, is given vivid expression in *The Thrush in February*. The stanza asserting that the song survives
though the singer passes, and that the "rapture of the
forward view" is similarly permanent, has already
been quoted as Meredith's favorite; the poem goes

on to express willingness that the senses, symbolized
as a ship, should be wrecked, so long as the thought,
their cargo, survives. Only to the uninitiated does it
seem cruel that Earth should demand the death of
her lovers, since really the death of the individual is
as essential to the race's development as his life. So
long as one holds consistently as a criterion "her
thought to speed the race," one can have no doubts
nor dreads arising from the discovery that "to sacrifice she prompts her best"; for she has brought us into
existence for no other purpose:

> This breath, her gift, has only choice
> Of service, breathe we in or out.
>
> Since Pain and Pleasure on each hand
> Led our wild steps from slimy rock
> To yonder sweeps of garden land,
> We breathe but to be sword or block.

"The sighting brain," accepting "her good decree,"
knows that she is neither a lifeless clod nor a frightful
wraith, but "a flame, a stream," and that on the
stream the human race is being borne forward,

> in mid-career
> From torrent source, delirious dream,
> To heaven-reflecting currents clear.

For this progress, each generation must complete its
service by dying when it has fulfilled its purpose.
Woodman and Echo uses the symbol of the tree which
must be hewn down to make way for the harvest.

All this leads into Meredith's idea of work. To vain

questionings as to the reward which a man's efforts
will win him, Earth disdains any reply; but if he has
worked his best, he may rest content that he is fulfilling his destiny and gaining the highest reward to
which he could aspire. By such service alone can man
transcend the sensual plane and achieve anything
which survives the death of the physical body. By
applying his forces to the service of his highest ideals,
and trusting implicitly that he is thereby advancing
the purposes of the beneficent process in which he is
involved, a man makes the proper use of the physical
powers with which he is equipped. He is thus both
enjoying his sensations to the fullest, and expending
them in the way which transmutes them into spirit.
In *The Question Whither*, after saying that the "gracious gift" of sensation would be unendurable if it
continued forever limited to individual life on earth,
the poet goes on:

> Enough if we have winked to sun,
>   Have sped the plough a season;
> There is a soul for labour done,
>   Endureth fixed as reason.

> Then let our trust be firm in Good,
>   Though we be of the fasting;
> Our questions are a mortal brood,
>   Our work is everlasting.

The same idea, that work is its own reward, is repeated in *The Woods of Westermain:*

> Earth your haven, Earth your helm,
> You command a double realm;

> Labouring here to pay your debt
> Till your little sun is set;
> Leaving her the future task,
> Loving her too well to ask.

Such workers, "knowing her the Ever-new and themselves the kin of the rose," will understand the meaning of life and will feel the dragon of self thrill for service. In the sonnet *Internal Harmony* Meredith says that the person who is assured that he is making his worthiest efforts has no envy of competitors, but welcomes all who are in the same service, and acknowledges the mastery of those better than himself. He is proud to know that he is fulfilling a place in the great scheme, and has no desire for "footways laurel-strewn." To have entered the conflict and borne one's self as worthily as possible, is the only sure way to win reward and immortality. The neatest expression of his idea occurs in *The Head of Bran the Blest* as early as 1860:

> Life is but the pebble sunk,
> Deeds, the circle growing.

The creed of immortality through service to the race is Meredith's final deduction from evolution. It applies the natural law to the mental and spiritual growth of man. By serving the race without selfishness or envy, man is consciously carrying on the evolutionary purpose which in the past has acted unconsciously, and is bringing into the spiritual realm the same laws that have shaped his physical development. Thus the future perfected race will embody the immortality of all the heroes and visionaries who have sacrificed themselves to further the idea.

Interpenetrating nearly all of Meredith's poetry, the ethical implications go far afield into the future and into the spirit of man. The definite foundation, however, was unquestionably the current scientific concept of physical evolution, of which the poet gives his version whimsically in the sonnet *The World's Advance*. The course of evolution, with its relapses, is compared with that of a drunkard, who divagates often from his path, but still follows in general a forward course. Adopting Mrs. Browning's term "spiral," he modifies it to the two-dimensional to describe "the way of worms" in which the world progresses. Although anxious to "cherish the promise of its good intents," he was cautious lest one instinct should be rashly effaced before reason had ripened to replace it. In this moderate belief that the race was slowly developing the intellectual endowments toward a point where they would be adequate to the physical capacities already evolved, he was quite in accord with the scientists. The extension into metaphysical regions came when he claimed that the intellectual development was to be preparatory to a spiritual expansion, making man the perfect triad. But the basis remained Earth and her physical law; only through communion with the spirit of Earth could man reach a concept of deity, and only through conformity with Earth's law could man live a truly moral life; and this law is simply the principle of evolution. By unquestioning service and a cheerful welcome to death, man furthers the process by which Earth has already brought him to his present stage. The selfish desire to gratify the senses and cling to life, heritage from his bestial ancestry, is responsible for man's dread and hatred of Earth's ruthless law and for the creeds based on a supernatural deity eternalizing sensory existence. The new creed, based on the law of "the survival of the fittest," and on man's essential unity with Nature and dependence on her, insists, instead, that immortality can be achieved only through sacrifice of self in the service of posterity. Like Tennyson, Meredith undertook to provide a metaphysical interpretation of the new hypothesis; but by ditching all the formulas of traditional religions, he produced a system which is an organic whole, whereas Tennyson's is a sequence of tentative discussions. Meredith had developed from the Darwinian concept of man's place in the universe a new god to worship and a new heaven to strive for. Both may have been more remote than those of the previous anthropomorphism, but he found inspiration in the law of Earth that tended toward good, and the creed of service that rewarded not the individual but the race.

Chapter V

THOMAS HARDY

THOMAS HARDY resembled Meredith in completely assimilating the evolutionary theory, abandoning any attempt to reconcile it with the views of traditional religion. The two poets started from the same postulates, but the conclusions which they reached were diametrically opposed. In several instances one is tempted to suspect that a passage was written by one of them with the definite intention of controverting the arguments of the other. At any rate, they deduced from the evolutionary theory utterly different opinions as to the past and future of the universe, man's position in it, and the causes for man and the universe existing at all.

Primarily famous as novelists, both men put their quintessentialized philosophies into poetry, although disclaiming any pretensions to a consistent philosophic system. In his prefaces Hardy called his work "unadjusted impressions," and said that he was "humbly recording diverse readings of life's phenomena as they are forced upon us by chance and change." But he did admit that such a process is "the road to a true philosophy of life," and elsewhere subscribed to "the real function of poetry, the application of ideas to life," all of which implies a distinct system. Accordingly, since both Meredith and Hardy sacrificed the purely "poetic" qualities of grace and melody in favor of the concise expression of theories, there is justification for the attempt to discuss those theories and to expect at least a general consistency of outlook, even though particular examples of inconsistency in detail may be found.

THE EVOLUTIONARY BASIS OF HARDY'S PHILOSOPHY

The twelve years by which Hardy was junior to Meredith obviate any investigation of his pre-Darwinian views. He was only nineteen when *The Origin of Species* appeared, and his first published work, both in prose and in poetry, was written six years later. Moreover, his early religious training was strictly orthodox, and so thorough that it never wholly abandoned him; the paradoxical trait of high-church Anglicanism which from the days of Burton and Herrick allowed it to cohabit with positively pagan tastes is well exemplified by Hardy's lifelong affection for cathedral ritual and prayer-book diction. The early plans for making a clergyman of him were still in his mind in 1865, when he hesitantly decided that he could not honestly accept all the church's doctrines. Prior to that date he had been loyal to Toryism in politics and the Established Church in religion, as witnessed by his arguments with a fellow-apprentice of Baptist tenets and his participation in student satires of the Reform League. On the other hand, we hear of him being much impressed by *Essays and Reviews* and deciding that Newman's *Apologia* (1865) lacked logical premises. By the time he came to formulate his opinions in poetry, however, he was positive in his revolt from orthodoxy. The chief reasons for the rejection of his first novel by the publishers were its mordant satire on modern Christianity and its overweening didacticism which seemed determined to reform he world. In his poetry the same outlook was clear, and its evolutionary basis perfectly definite; nevertheless, it has been strangely neglected by commentators. Mr. Ernest Brennecke's book, *Thomas Hardy's Universe*, is typical of the general ignoring of Darwin in the effort to trace Hardy's whole system and terminology to Schopenhauer. But even if one admits the fact that the Immanent Will and its attributes were originally concepts of the German thinker, it still remains to be determined why Hardy adopted the concepts and based on them his interpretation of the universe. Mr. Brennecke's intimation that the reflective passages in Hardy's poetry are little more than a transcription into poetic form and imagery of Schopenhauer's statements—which are neither easy nor attractive to the average intelligence—evokes wonder as to the motive for such fidelity. Natural affinity of intellect is only a partial explanation: granting that when Hardy went in search of a metaphysical theory of the universe he was attracted to Schopenhauer's because of his own similar tendency toward gloom, yet the reason for his seeking any such theory at all, and for his expounding it so elaborately, is to be found in external forces rather than in native disposition.

Mr. Brennecke admits that Hardy did not encounter the ideas of Schopenhauer until about 1874 at earliest, and that his adoption of them progressed gradually until the complete assimilation occurred in *The Dynasts*. This fact strengthens the supposition that Hardy's mind was prepared by other influences before it found in Schopenhauer a nomenclature for the ideas which he had already developed. And in Hardy's young manhood it was the Darwinian theory which incited all thinking men to a revaluation of the traditional notions regarding man and the universe, disturbing all established faiths to a degree which no previous generation had ever experienced. His opinions were profoundly influenced by his friend Leslie Stephen, and in 1875 he witnessed Stephen's formal renunciation of holy orders. "Our conversation," he noted, "turned upon theologies decayed and defunct, the origin of things, the constitution of matter, the unreality of time. He told me that the new theory of vortex rings had 'a staggering fascination' for him." As early as 1870 we find him reading Comte with diligence, and in 1876 he recorded a concise cosmic perspective:

> If it be possible to compress into a sentence all that a man learns between twenty and forty, it is that all things merge into one another—good into evil, generosity into justice, religion into

politics, the years into the ages, the world into the universe. With this in view, the evolution of species seems but a minute and obvious process in the same movement.

This unhesitating acceptance of the Darwinian principle appears similarly in the *Apology* introducing *Late Lyrics and Earlier*, in a satiric allusion to spiritualism and other new creeds: "At present, when belief in witches of Endor is displacing the Darwinian theory and 'the truth that shall make you free,' men's minds appear to be moving backward rather than on." In his poetry, references to the physical action of evolution, while not frequent, are sufficient to indicate his consistent adherence. *Before Life and After* describes the primitive bestial state in which all living creatures acted instinctively, without consciousness:

> A time there was—as one may guess
> And as, indeed, earth's testimonies tell—
> Before the birth of consciousness,
> When all went well. . . . .
>
> But the disease of feeling germed,
> And primal rightness took the tinct of wrong. . . . .

Following the same idea, he mentions in *The Dynasts* (i, I, vi) that pity is a comparatively recent development, since, in the words of the Spirit Ironic, it "only came into being in what the earthlings call their Tertiary Age." Later in the play (i, VI, iii) the chorus of Ironic Spirits describes to the Pities the early prehuman types of life and the wasteful early efforts of the creative force, when abortive species developed and were superseded by types better fitted to survive:

Ere ye, young Pities, had upgrown
From out the deeps . . . .

He of the Years beheld, and we,
Creation's prentice artistry
Express in forms that now unbe

Tentative dreams from day to day;
Mangle its types, re-knead the clay
In some more palpitating way;

Beheld the rarest wrecked amain,
Whole nigh-perfected species slain
By those that scarce could boast a brain;

Saw ravage, growth, diminish, add. . . . .

As well as such references to the facts of evolution,
there are two or three poems, notably *The Mother
Mourns* and *A Plaint to Man*, in which the evolution
of man from the lowest forms of life is described with
reference to his relation to nature and God, being to
this extent comparable with Meredith's *Earth and
Man*, though utterly different in interpretation. At
present it is sufficient to quote the opening of *A Plaint
to Man*, as displaying Hardy's acceptance of evolution. The anthropomorphic god addresses human
kind:

When you slowly emerged from the den of Time,
And gained percipience as you grew,
And fleshed you fair out of shapeless slime,

Wherefore, O Man, did there come to you
The unhappy need of creating me?

This is as explicit as Meredith's "hours when mind was mud."

In explanation of the consistently gloomy view—sometimes apparently wantonly cynical and disillusioned—which Hardy took of the evolutionary process, two facts must be remembered. One is the temperamental bias already mentioned, so strong that even in a lyric celebrating auspicious love, and written at the age of thirty (four years before his imputed discovery of Schopenhauer), he concluded the poem by remarking by what a fortuitous accident he encountered his mistress, and how much more probably he might have missed her; so that the final impression is less of the lover's ecstasy than of the futility of human affairs, "what bond-servants of Chance we are all." One of his earliest poems, *Her Dilemma*, introduces his favorite theme that Humanity is mocked by the situations framed by chance and circumstance, and that all the highest human emotions are a prey to time. *On an Invitation to Visit the United States* uses the word "tragedy" as synonymous with "history." Many poems, such as *Friends Beyond*, *After the Last Breath*, *While Drawing in a Churchyard*, declare that death is the only relief, an escape from "the Wrongers," Time and Chance. Hardy always takes care to stress the material aspect of life: in *The Dynasts* (2, V, viii), when the Spirit of the Years has occasion to mention the earth, he uses the locution "this mud-moulded ball"; and such poems as *The Dream Follower* and *In a Ewe-Lease Near Weatherbury* emphasize

the fact that the human body is constantly being de-
faced and approaching the final decay of death. The
dominant impression of disillusionment and gloom in
both Hardy's poetry and his prose justifies his description of himself in *Night in the Old Home:*

A thinker of crooked thoughts upon Life in the sere,
And on That which consigns men to night after showing the day
    to them,

in contrast with his ancestors in their placid confidence, who advise him, "O let be the Wherefore! We
fevered our years not thus: take of Life what it
grants, without question!"

Though Hardy's despondency is primarily a matter
of temperament, the *Zeitgeist* must also be considered,
not only because it always influences men's mental
equipment, but also because Hardy hints that he intentionally fostered his attitude of uncompromising
disillusionment, as a necessary antidote to the extravagant optimism of his contemporaries. The poem
To Sincerity is a sarcastic stricture upon the conventional and unreasonable custom of denying the existence of the dark side of life: though youth foreknows,
and experience reveals, that life is unutterably sad
and ephemeral, custom insists on hypocritical pro-
fessions of rejoicing and faith.

—Yet, would men look at true things,
And unilluded view things,
And count to bear undue things,

The real might mend the seeming,
Facts better their foredeeming,
And life its disesteeming.

The same argument, that an honest recognition of the suffering and disappointments of life is more conducive to genuine hopefulness than is a factitious optimism, is embodied in the second poem of the group *In Tenebris*. Hardy feels himself out of place in a generation so confident that "things are all as they best may be, save a few to be right ere long," since he lacks such a clear vision. So many important people repeat it so often that he is almost convinced it must be "somewhat true," and decides that he himself is "what is wrong," with his more moderate belief:

Let him to whose ears the low-voiced Best seems stilled by the clash of the First,
Who holds that if way to the Better there be, it exacts a full look at the Worst,

Who feels that delight is a delicate growth cramped by crookedness, custom, and fear,
Get him up and be gone as one shaped awry; he disturbs the order here.

To this poem Hardy refers in the *Apology* in *Late Lyrics and Earlier*, in defending his poety from the commonest accusation leveled against it:

What is to-day alleged to be 'pessimism' is, in truth, only 'obstinate questionings' in the exploration of reality, and is the first step towards the soul's betterment, and the body's also.

After citing *In Tenebris* regarding "way to the better," he says that it must be

by the exploration of reality, and its frank recognition stage by stage along the survey, with an eye to the best consummation possible; briefly, evolutionary meliorism. Whether the human and kindred animal races survive till the exhaustion or destruction of the globe, or whether these races perish and are succeeded by others before that conclusion comes, pain to all upon it, tongued or dumb, shall be kept down to a minimum by loving-kindness, operating through scientific knowledge, and actuated by the modicum of free will conjecturally possessed by organic life.

Such a statement makes it clear that Hardy's gloomy poems are not written wholly out of a congenital penchant for misery, but rather with the definite purpose of promoting the future progress of the race by forcing public attention to present shortcomings. In a few of his poems he admits the possibility of this "evolutionary meliorism"; but a discussion of them must be postponed, as the bulk of his work is devoted to the ruthless demolition of the illusions which he considered to be barriers to such development.

REJECTION OF THE ORTHODOX VIEWS OF GOD
AND IMMORTALITY

Hardy agreed with Meredith that the traditional religions had outlived their effectiveness and were inimical to progress; but he went farther and declared that the encouraging faith which Meredith suggested as a substitute was equally unfounded. Under the influence of scientific rationalism, he early abandoned belief in the orthodox conception of God and in the immortality of the soul. He wrote in 1890: "I have been looking for God fifty years, and I think that if he had existed I should have discovered him. As an external personality, of course—the only true meaning of the word." In the poem *To Outer Nature* he says that in his youth he believed nature to be wrought by love, planned for the purpose of giving pleasure to men; but this notion, the product of conventional religious teaching, soon passed beyond recapture. *The Impercipient*, written at a cathedral service, gives utterance to his regret that he is unable to participate in the religious emotions of his fellows; it is a mystery to him why he must suffer infelicity through being unable to find their joys and share their certainty—"he who breathes All's Well to these breathes no All's Well to me"—but instead of sympathizing with his "strange destiny," they accuse him of wilfully destructive intentions. Because he himself cannot believe, it does not necessarily follow that he wishes all belief to vanish; and he asks pathetically, "O doth a bird deprived of wings go earth-bound wilfully?" Again, in *The Problem*, he wonders whether the right course is to proclaim the rationalism that is as yet accepted by only a few; and he concludes that since the traditional faiths, fallacious though they may be, conduce to human happiness, they should be left undisturbed.

In spite of such disavowals, however, he is not chary in most of his poems of proclaiming his unbelief and its reasons. His feeling that no intelligent person could really retain unshaken faith in Christianity is indicated by a memorandum of 1880, on his favorite topic of positivism:

> If Comte had introduced Christ among the worthies in his calendar he would have made Positivism tolerable to thousands who, from position, family connection, or early education, now

decry what in their heart of hearts they hold to contain the germs of a true system. It would have enabled them to modulate gently into the new religion by deceiving themselves with the sophistry that they still continued one-quarter Christians, or one-eighth, or one-twentieth, as the case might be.

In his poems he did not confine his attack to Christianity: all religions are equally trivial when compared with the vastitude of universal processes, as the Spirit of the Years points out in *The Dynasts* (1, I, vi):

> A local thing called Christianity,
> Which the wild dramas of this wheeling sphere
> Include, with divers other such, in dim,
> Pathetical, and brief parentheses;
> Beyond whose reach, uninfluenced, unconcerned,
> The systems of the suns go sweeping on.

This equality of religions, all being alike manifestations of a single human instinct, is expressed again in *Aquae Sulis*. The Roman goddess speaks from her ruined temple to the Christian god who has superseded her, and he responds that his tenure is no more secure than hers:

> "You know not by what a frail thread we equally hang;
> It is said we are images both—twitched by people's desires;
> And that I, like you, fail as a song men yesterday sang!"

So it is the anthropocentric tendency in general that Hardy is decrying; and if his attention is usually turned chiefly toward Christianity, it is because that faith is the prevailing one of his era. In *A Drizzling Easter Morning* he asserts that Christianity has not furthered progress and that the idea of resurrection has little appeal:

And is he risen? Well, be it so . . . .
And still the pensive lands complain,
And dead men wait, as long ago,
As if, much doubting, they would know
What they are ransomed from, before
They pass again their sheltering door.

Since the ideals of Christianity have failed to benefit
the race, in Hardy's opinion, it is time for religion to
be replaced by a more rational system.

In four poems he studies the progress of science in
undermining the orthodox notion of God. The most
flippant of them is *The Respectable Burgher on "The
Higher Criticism"*:

Since Reverend Doctors now declare
That clerks and people must prepare
To doubt if Adam ever were;
To hold the flood a local scare. . . . .

After enumerating a long list of miracles and other
scriptural events which are endangered by rationalistic commentary, the poem concludes:

Since thus they hint, nor turn a hair,
All churchgoing will I forswear,
And sit on Sundays in my chair,
And read that moderate man, Voltaire.

As well as this sketch, Hardy presents three less
frivolous pictures of the dissolution of traditional
beliefs. *The Sick God* describes the gradual waning
of the God of Battle and Vengeance who received his
attributes in Old Testament times, "till but a shade
is left of him." In explanation, Hardy cites two
schools of thought: one that "modern meditation"

and "penmen's pleadings" broke his spell, the other that "crimes too dire" were committed in his name. The naïveté of the primitive concept succumbs to modern tolerance and *Weltschmerz:*

> Souls have grown seers and thought outbrings
> The mournful many-sidedness of things
> With foes as friends, enfeebling ires
> And fury-fires by gaingivings!

Another poem, *God's Funeral*, symbolizes the regretful surrender of belief in God by those who have learned from science that he is a figment of the idolatrous instinct. They mournfully review the process by which the "man-projected Figure, of late imaged as we," developed and declined: at first he was jealous and fierce, then "as the ages rolled" he was endowed with justice, long-suffering, manifold mercies, and "will to bless those by circumstance accurst," until his worshipers deceived themselves into believing him their maker instead of their making;

> "Till in Time's stayless stealthy swing,
> Uncompromising rude reality
> Mangled the Monarch of our fashioning,
> Who quavered, sank: and now has ceased to be."

The mourners go on to lament for the old days of confident faith; but another party appears to contradict them, asserting that God still lives and that the "requiem mockery" is for "a counterfeit of straw." Although unable to support this view, Hardy has admiration and sympathy for its exponents, and admits that he, too, "long had prized" the superseded divinity. He feels that everyone must face the problem "how to bear such loss"; and finally he observes "a pale yet positive gleam" on the horizon, which is proclaimed by a few who stand aloof but is unseen by the mourners. Bewildered and puzzled, he mechanically follows with them "between the gleam and the gloom."

That this gleam is the "way to the Better" resulting from the "full look at the Worst" which he described in *In Tenebris*, is stated in *A Plaint to Man*. Herein the subject of *God's Funeral* is treated from the opposite point of view—it is the anthropomorphic god's lament that men ever created him, since they now destroy him. He asks why man took the virtue, power, and utility, which must necessarily reside within man himself, and attributed them to an external being. To man's reply that the concept of some superior being, remote from this "wailful world," was essential for his endurance of life, since no "local hope" existed, God responds that now, when science is destroying him, men will have to depend on their own resources, and, had they been forced to do so long before, progress would have been more rapid, for then the uncompromising fact would have been faced:

> The fact of life with dependence placed
> On the human heart's resource alone,
> In brotherhood bonded close and graced
>
> With loving-kindness fully blown,
> And visioned help unsought, unknown.

Thus we see Hardy once again declaring that progress toward humanitarian ideals is possible as soon as insincere optimism is replaced by a rational recognition of actuality.

In the foregoing poems Hardy is wholly in accord with Meredith, who was equally emphatic in condemning the anthropomorphic god as a barrier to progress, a survival from an earlier stage of evolution where it fulfilled its usefulness, but now preventing unselfish service to the race and recognition of fraternal responsibility. Still in accord with Meredith, he discards the other leading tenet of orthodox faith— the immortality of the individual soul. In fact, taking for granted that such a belief has already been exploded, he seldom even formally denies it. One of his earliest poems, *A Young Man's Epigram on Existence*, echoes the hedonistic view which Fitzgerald's *Rubaiyat* had popularized in those years, terming life "a senseless school" in which the whole time is wasted in learning how to live, with no moment left for prizes. In later poems he was more affected by the pathos of man's desire for survival after death, as in the poem called *Unknowing*, depicting the disillusionment of a lover whose dying mistress promised to revisit him but "tarries dead and dumb." The same negation is expressed in the conclusion of *Middle-Age Enthusiasms:*

> "Our thoughts, when breath has sped,
>   Will meet and mingle here!" . . . .
> "Words!" mused we. "Passed the mortal door,
>   Our thoughts will reach this nook no more."

Apart from these indications of his belief that the spirit becomes extinct when the body dies, the only poem discussing the question is *A Sign Seeker*, wherein he describes himself as familiar with natural science and desirous of proving by analogous methods the soul's survival. Despite all his efforts, he is unable to experience any of the supernatural communications by which so many people, according to their testimony, have been convinced. Regretful that he cannot attain their comforting assurance, he is forced to accept the rational view: "Nescience mutely muses: when a man falls he lies." The methods by which he gained his knowledge of geology and astronomy being of no avail when turned to psychical research, his agnosticism really amounts to denial of survival, since the negative arguments of science and common sense cannot be countered by any proofs. He admits that nothing but belief in immortality can reconcile us to the injustice and cruelty "when Earth's Frail lie bleeding of her Strong," but even so he sees it as but a figment invented by man for his own consolation. In *A Plaint to Man*, as we have seen, Hardy attributed belief in God to the same cause; in short, he considered the two tenets of orthodox religion—a personal God and the immortality of the soul—as pseudoxia evolved by man for his comfort, and rendered untenable now by scientific rationalism.

IMMORTALITY THROUGH HEREDITY

All this will recall Meredith's similar skepticism regarding the conscious survival of the individual after death; but in his substituted faith in conditioned survival through the memory of after-generations and through the individual's contribution to the race there was to Hardy a clear fallacy. The scorn which he cast on precisely that notion in at least half a dozen of his poems tempts one to think that he is intentionally discounting the Meredithian idea. In *Her Immortality* the dead woman appears in a vision to her lover and forbids him to attempt to join her by committing suicide, for the existence of a Shade depends on "its mindful ones," and by dying he would slay her; and he sees clearly the extreme brevity of such survival:

> When I surcease
> Through whom alone lives she,
> Her spirit ends its living lease,
> Never again to be.

A companion poem, even in title, is *His Immortality* which traces the rapid fading of the reflected life enjoyed by the dead man in the memories of his friends, until there remains "unperished still" only one old man's recollection of him, "a feeble spark, dying amid the dark." The identical theme appears in *The To-be-forgotten*, wherein the voices of the dead speak from the tomb and lament their short tenure of survival:

> Our future second death is near,
> When, with the living, memory of us numbs
> And blank oblivion comes.

They point out that their ancestors have utterly dis-
appeared from memory, and "are as men who have existed not"; and they anticipate the same fate as soon
as their "loved continuance" in some surviving soul
ceases. They had lived honestly and to the best of
their ability, but they could not achieve "that world
awakening scope granted the few whose memory none
lets die," and accordingly they will not be remembered beyond their generation.

By emphasizing in these poems, and others such as
The Ghost of the Past, the rapid dimming and inevitable extinction of memory, Hardy shows how ephemeral is the immortality envisaged by Meredith. Meredith's defense would be that if a man fulfilled his duty,
however humble, to his highest capacity he made a
permanent contribution to the race and thus survived
in the future generations, even though unrecognized;
but to this Hardy would give only a qualified assent.
In many poems he expresses grave doubts as to
whether any genuine contribution to the progress of
the race can be made. Once or twice he gives unexpected credence to the idea, as in the lines written on
the death of Meredith, which imply that Meredith's
work will have lasting existence:

> Further and further still
> Through the world's vaporous vitiate air
> His words wing on—as live words will.

Again, the poem *To Meet, or Otherwise* expresses the
idea often uttered by Meredith, and still more forcibly
by Browning, that action is the one thing which

counts, and that even the most trivial act, when it represents an opportunity fully realized, has an eternal existence secure from destruction:

> By briefest meeting something sure is won;
>   It will have been:
> Nor God nor Demon can undo the done,
>   Unsight the seen,
> Make muted music be as unbegun,
>   Though things terrene
> Groan in their bondage till oblivion supervene.
>
> So, to the one long-sweeping symphony
>   From times remote
> Till now, of human tenderness, shall we
>   Supply one note,
> Small and untraced, yet that will ever be
>   Somewhere afloat
> Amid the spheres, as part of sick Life's antidote.

Apart from the characteristic references to "groaning in bondage" and "sick Life," the poem might have been written by Browning, and its concept of the permanent contribution to the amelioration of life made by every deed of human tenderness appears nowhere else so clearly in Hardy's poems. One or two cautious utterances can be associated with it, such as *By the Barrows*, which says that a woman's devoted act of self-sacrifice more consecrates its scene than the mighty battles fought there. There is a trace of a Meredithian idea in *Life Laughs Onward*, wherein the poet admits that it is desirable for the old generation to yield place to the new:

Life laughed and moved on unsubdued,
I saw that Old succumbed to Young:
'Twas well. My too regretful mood
Died on my tongue.

But as a rule, as in *The Superseded*, Hardy is chiefly impressed by the pathos evoked and the futility implied when a "staunch strenuous soul" drops away without acknowledgment from his successors.

There is only one definite respect in which, according to Hardy, a man makes a permanent and unalterable imprint upon posterity. It is a demonstrable scientific fact, thus differing from all metaphysical doctrines of immortality, from the Bible to Meredith. It is the fact of heredity. By the transference of his physical characteristics, a man survives in his progeny quite independently of their conscious recollection of him. The source of this concept in the theory of evolution and the modern sciences derived therefrom is sufficiently obvious.

Hardy's poems show that he always possessed a keen interest in the workings of heredity. *San Sebastian* relates an unaccountable case of an incident in a man's experience being reflected in his daughter's physical appearance. That Hardy considered the theme, which is really a problem in genetics, suitable for poetic treatment, is evidence of the significance that he attached to heredity and its workings. When the puzzled father muses,

Maybe we shape our offspring's guise
From fancy, or we know not what,
And that no deep impression dies,

Hardy seems to be weighing the possibility of a physical process upholding the metaphysical concept of every action's eternal survival. If he could have convinced himself that it is a fact of heredity "that no deep impression dies," he might have given more frequent expression to the idea, which Browning and Meredith had proclaimed without scruples. But lacking any indubitable fact of physical science, he was chary of subscribing to it.

In another poem, *To a Motherless Child*, he discusses the point that heredity works according to mechanical principles beyond the control of human will. The speaker wishes that the child might be a perfect reincarnation of its mother, but "niggard Nature's trick of birth" does not heed such dreams in "her mechanic artistry." From this view of heredity as an automatic process propagating certain traits from one generation to the next, Hardy derives his most definite idea of immortality, as stated in the short poem entitled *Heredity*:

> I am the family face;
> Flesh perishes, I live on,
> Projecting trait and trace
> Through time to times anon,
> And leaping from place to place
> Over oblivion.
>
> The years-heired feature that can
> In curve and voice and eye
> Despise the human span
> Of durance—that is I;
> The eternal thing in man
> That heeds no call to die.

This succinctly formulates Hardy's uncompromising-
ly scientific concept of immortality. An interesting
corollary to it is provided by *The Pedigree*, a poem
depicting him deep in his hobby of genealogy and seeing a vision of his progenitors:

> . . . . dwindling backward each past each
> All with the kindred look . . . .
> Generation and generation of my mien, and build, and brow.

He realizes that all his characteristics, and consequently all his actions, were molded by his ancestors,
so that free will is an illusion:

> Every heave and coil and move I made
> Within my brain, and in my mood and speech,
> Was in the glass portrayed
> As long forestalled by their so making it. . . . .

> Said I then, sunk in tone,
> "I am merest mimicker and counterfeit!—
> Though thinking, *I am I*
> *And what I do I do myself alone.*"

Through this poem a transition is provided between
his purely physical concept of immortality and his
purely physical concept of fate, which will be considered in detail presently. In these two chief topics
of metaphysics he instituted theories based directly
on the evolutionary hypothesis and the sciences to
which it gave rise.

THE RIDDLE OF EXISTENCE

The same severely rationalistic standards which for-
bade him to believe in immortality unless he could see
definite evidence in the form of ghosts apply also to

the other primary tenet of religion—the existence of
God. His poetry reveals him in constant revolt
against passive agnosticism; although his common
sense tells him that it is the reasonable view, his temperament is forever urging him to interrogate the
sphinx of existence. Even though the result of his
cogitations is depression and lacerated sympathies,
he cannot refrain from seeking an explanation of why
the universe exists. That the solution of the riddle is
infinitely beyond human comprehension he admits
in *The Masked Face*, wherein his questions are an-
swered in an apologue:

> "There once complained a goose-quill pen
> To the scribe of the Infinite
> Of the words it had to write
> Because they were past its ken."

But despite this recognition of man's limitations,
Hardy is bound to obey the instinct which has always
driven men to seek a system explaining their place in
the world. The very fact that his mind is rationalistic impels him to impose some sort of comprehensible
significance on phenomena. And any such system entails the concept of unifying power of some sort,
spiritual or mechanical, conscious or unconscious.

As his cogitations center upon the concept of controlling power, it is natural that he should on occasion
use the terminology which the whole tradition of culture has associated with it. Accordingly, he often
symbolizes the controlling power as God, or the Lord;
but he makes it clear that his use of the words is in-

variably symbolic. As well as declaring the anthropomorphic God as a figment of the human brain, now
expelled by scientific knowledge, he denies also the
converse idea of a personal conscious power of evil
responsible for the cruelty and wastefulness of nature. The sonnet entitled *Hap* declares that if some
vengeful god were finding ecstasy in his suffering,
man could steel himself by the thought that he was
the unoffending victim of a superior power's will and
control. But all human sorrows and disappointments
are due to "crass Casualty" and "dicing Time," and
"these purblind Doomsters had as readily strewn
blisses about my pilgrimage as pain." Similarly, in
The Dynasts (2, VI, v) the Spirit of the Pities is impelled by the sight of human suffering

> To hold that some mean, monstrous ironist
> Had built this mistimed fabric of the Spheres
> To watch the throbbings of its captive lives;

but, as usual, this Spirit is deluded by sentiment.
Such a concept is as foreign to Hardy's system as is
the notion of a benignant deity. There is no conscious power, evil or good.

It is here that Hardy's concept of the controlling
power differs sharply from Meredith's. The latter in-
variably insisted that a general tendency toward good
prevailed, and that any man who submitted himself
to the tuition of nature found himself participating in
a beneficent process. Such a faith Hardy flatly contradicts: in *The Farm Woman's Winter*, for instance,
he disputes the reconciliation of optimism with pain

and grief which Meredith saw in the husbandman's welcome to the cheerless hardships of winter as essential for the processes of growth. Hardy points out that winter is more apt to kill the farmer. Another of Meredith's favorite symbols of nature's power and goodness was the woods, whereas Hardy writes *In a Wood* to show the ruthless struggle for survival at its highest intensity, the trees blighting each other with poison,

> Great growths and small
> Show them to man akin—
> Combatants all!

He escapes thankfully from the trees to the world of men, where the struggle is at least occasionally softened by cheerfulness and kind deeds.

In addition to these indirect refutations of Meredith's optimistic arguments, Hardy devotes several poems to affirming that belief in good is a ridiculous illusion. Its transitory and superficial character is shown in *A Meeting with Despair:* the poet is momentarily roused from his melancholy by the glory of a sunset sky, and decides that there is solace everywhere; but as he is reproaching himself "as one perverse, misrepresenting Good in graceless mutiny," the darkness falls and despair triumphs—"Heaven's radiant show had gone that heartened me." With the same rather pathetic tone of disillusionment, *To Life*, after describing Life's familiar sad countenance and draggled cloak and message "of Death, Time, Destiny," breaks off with the appeal:

But canst thou not array
Thyself in rare disguise,
And feign like truth, for one mad day,
That Earth is Paradise?

I'll tune me to the mood,
And mumm with thee till eve;
And maybe what as interlude
I feign, I shall believe!

Similarly, *On a Fine Morning* says that solace comes, not from recognizing the actualities of life and the monitions of Time, "but in cleaving to the Dream" and in casting a golden light on gray things; and that the poet lets the fair weather beguile him into believing "shadows but as lights unfolding"—i.e., existing imperfections as tokens of future development— and the moment of beauty "no specious show" but "part of a benignant plan, proof that earth was made for man." Thus, as antithesis to Meredith's trenchant pictures of the loveless pessimist's misery, Hardy mildly sketches the deluded optimist's fatuity. The two mutually exclusive points of view are dictated by the temperaments of the poets, and there is no standard for determining their respective validity save the reader's predilections.

Having dismissed categorically the idea of any conscious power, evil or good, determining the affairs of the universe, Hardy had to look for some other explanation of existence. The only tangible material for investigation being the phenomena of nature, he sets forth in *Nature's Questioning* the various possibilities.

To him, pool and field and tree, with a dull and constrained look, as if their early zest had been over-
borne by some severe discipline, say, "We wonder,
ever wonder, why we find us here!

> "Has some vast Imbecility
>   Mighty to build and blend,
>   But impotent to tend,
> Framed us in jest, and left us now to hazardry?

> "Or come we of an Automaton
>   Unconscious of our pains?
>   Or are we live remains
> Of Godhead dying downwards, brain and eye now gone?

> "Or is it that some high Plan betides
>   As yet not understood,
>   Of evil stormed by Good,
> We the Forlorn Hope over which Achievement strides?"

These three stanzas summarize the ideas which Hardy discussed individually in various poems dealing
with the creative force: is it a mindless power working freakishly, or an automatic process, or an originally conscious power that has lost its control? Finally, there is the optimistic possibility, entailing a transcendental plan, and Hardy includes it on condition
that it recognizes the sufferings of the present dispen-
sation. The poem does not undertake to discriminate
among the possibilities: in the closing lines Hardy declares himself "no answerer" to the queries, and declares that the only indubitable facts are "Earth's old
glooms and pains" and the perpetual proximity of
Death to "glad Life."

Unable to believe in the existence of an immortal soul, Hardy could accept neither the religious dogma that man's possession of a soul distinguished him from all the creatures expressly made to serve him nor the recent poets' suggestions that the soul might experience an evolution equivalent to that of the body; so he declared unequivocally that man has no advantages over the rest of natural phenomena. On the contrary, man is capable of degraded actions beyond the scope of animals. This thought is whimsically expressed in *Wagtail and Baby*, wherein the bird is undisturbed by powerful beasts, but flies in terror on the approach of "a perfect gentleman." In other respects, too, the lower orders of nature are in advance of the human: *An August Midnight* points out that the insects, "God's humblest," are not to be contemned, since "they know Earth-secrets that know not I"; and similarly in *The Caged Thrush Freed and Home Again*, the tiny creatures which men "count least of things terrene" realize that "men know but little more" than they "how happy days are made to be." In *The Blinded Bird* the poet goes farther, and ascribes to the bird the highest virtues, which he would never ascribe to man:

> Who hopeth, enduring all things?
> Who thinketh no evil, but sings?
> Who is divine? This bird.

Through all the poems that express his keen sympathy for animal life, Hardy insinuates that animals are nearer to the ideal than humanity is.

Two passages in his notebooks make clear how directly he blamed the evolutionary process for mankind's unsatisfactory condition. In 1881 he noted:

After infinite trying to reconcile a scientific view of life with the emotional and spiritual, so that they may not be interdestructive, I come to the following general principles: Law has produced in man a child who cannot but constantly reproach its parent for doing much and yet not all, and constantly say to such parent that it would have been better never to have begun doing than to have *over*done so indecisively; that is, than to have created so far beyond all apparent first intention (on the emotional side) without mending matters by a second intention and execution, to eliminate the evils of the blunder of overdoing. The emotions have no place in a world of defect, and it is a cruel injustice that they should have developed in it. If Law itself had consciousness, how the aspect of its creatures would terrify it, fill it with remorse!

He returned to the theme in 1889:

A woeful fact, that the human race is too extremely developed for its corporeal conditions, the nerves being evolved to an activity abnormal in such an environment. Even the higher animals are in excess in this respect. It may be questioned if Nature, or what we call Nature, so far back as when she crossed the line from invertebrates to vertebrates, did not exceed her mission. This planet does not supply the material for happiness to higher existences—other planets may, though one can hardly see how.

As usual, Hardy shows himself oppressed by the pain and frustration which his oversensitized sympathy felt to exist everywhere. In *The Dynasts* he repeated this thought, that the sense of pity was the most recent major development of evolution, and inconsistent with its blind functioning.

He does not mean, however, that this quality in

men makes them a race apart. The essential identity of mankind with the rest of nature is to him a truism. *A Thought in Two Moods* depicts a girl standing in a meadow:

> And as I looked it seemed in kind
> That difference they had none;
> The two fair bodiments combined
> As varied miens of one.

The metaphysical implication appears in *"The Wind Blew Words"*:

> ".... Behold this troubled tree,
> Complaining as it sways and plies;
> It is a limb of thee.
>
> "Yea, too, the creatures sheltering round—
> Dumb figures, wild and tame,
> Yea, too, thy fellows who abound ....
> They are stuff of thy own frame."
>
> I moved on in a surging awe
> Of inarticulateness
> At the pathetic Me I saw
> In all his huge distress,
> Making self-slaughter of the law
> To kill, break, or suppress.

The last stanza hints at a code of ethics based on man's identity with all nature; but it would promptly transcend the material plane, and so Hardy does not develop it any further.

Holding these views on the basic unity of all creation, Hardy in his earlier poems frequently personified the creative energy, as Meredith habitually did, as a feminine being, signifying maternity. In *Doom*

and She Hardy terms this figure "The Matron"—
"mother of all things made, matchless in artistry."
Again, the sonnet *At a Bridal* (1866) speaks of "the
Great Dame whence incarnation flows." In the more
articulate system, however, which finds fullest expression in *The Dynasts*, "she" is replaced by the
impersonal "it." That the feminine figure is but a
figment, produced by the human tendency of image-
making, is made clear by the Shade of the Earth, who
speaks of

> her . . . .
> Men love to dub Dame Nature—that lay shape
> They use to hang phenomena upon.

Thus the figure of personified Nature is relegated to
the same category as that of a personal God. Among
allegories of the creative power, Meredith's is no more
adequate than the Bible's.

Nevertheless, Hardy uses the figure of the mother, just as he uses the figure of God, as a convenient
representation of the creative force, since both figures
have a familiar connotation to all readers and obviate
unwieldy circumlocutions. He uses the two symbols
interchangeably, both having the same characteristics.

The most important among his descriptions of Nature's evolutionary methods, and the one most closely parallel with Meredith's *Earth and Man*, is *The
Mother Mourns*. The poet hears Nature complain
that man has ceased to have implicit trust in the perfection of her artistry, the scientific impulse having

led him to analyze her processes and discover her blunders. She admits that she initiated the development of the human mind, but without foreseeing the outcome, which occurred unobserved by her:

> "I had not proposed me a Creature
> (She soughed) so excelling
> All else of my kingdom in compass
> And brightness of brain
>
> "As to read my defects with a god-glance,
> Uncover each vestige
> Of old inadvertence, annunciate
> Each flaw and each stain!
>
> "My purpose went not to develop
> Such insight in Earthland;
> Such potent appraisements affront me
> And sadden my reign!

She blames herself for having loosened her "olden control" while she "mechanized skyward," on the assumption that no "great scope" could develop in "a globe of such grain," till she suddenly discovered that man's unchecked "mountings of mindsight" had given him a range of vision that "finds blemish throughout her domain," and even is dissatisfied with her "deftest achievement"—his own body. He contemns her inventions as "fitful, ill-timed, and inane," and reduces her teachings to gross and ignoble instincts, explaining even love as merely the reproductive urge—"a lure that my species may gather and gain." Man asserts that with the same material and means he could have invented a "more seemly, more sane" creation. In other words, the poem presents a double embodiment of the evolutionary theory: it describes the evolution of the human mind, and it points out that the most recent step in that evolution is the forming of the evolutionary hypothesis. The realization of the abortions and wastefulness of natural processes marks an irrevocable advance in man's knowledge. The poem goes on to give Nature's reason for having inaugurated the development of intelligent beings at all:

> "If ever a naughtiness seized me
> To woo adulation
> From creatures more keen than those crude ones
> That first formed my train,

> "I rue it!'"

"His guileless forerunners" failed in the attempt to fathom Nature's secrets because she "subtly could cover" her "waste aimings and futile," causing them to assume that "every best thing to best purpose her powers preordain." But now Reason and Vision have proved unruly, and man is hastening her wane by imitating her own ruthless methods in his destruction of the other species, vegetable and animal; so she resolves to produce in future only "mildews and mandrakes and slimy distortions."

The same idea of human consciousness having been evolved by mistake appears in several poems wherein God replaces Nature as the symbol of the creative force. The poet phrases it concisely in two lines of the poem *I Travel as a Phantom Now:*

> I . . . . wonder if Man's consciousness
> Was a mistake of God's.

By the Earth's Corpse describes the Lord as grieving at the sight of the earth grown chill and destitute of life. To Time's question why he should grieve, since all is the same as it was before life began, the Lord replies that he is indeed glad that the earthly scene is past—although he had planned it with keen interest —but that things can *not* be as they were:

> Written indelibly
> On my eternal mind
> Are all the wrongs endured
> By Earth's poor patient kind,
> Which my too oft unconscious hand
> Let enter undesigned.
> No god can cancel deeds foredone,
> Or thy old coils unwind!

Therefore, now that the "piteous dust" of all life "revolves obliviously," the Lord says, "that I made Earth, and life, and man, it still repenteth me!"

A slight variation of the idea is that God has forgotten earth—that he set the creative process in motion and then withdrew. *The Bedridden Peasant to an Unknown God* shows a naturally devout mind endeavoring to reconcile the orthodox God "mild of heart" with the cruelty and futility of life by the idea "that some disaster cleft Thy scheme and tore us wide apart." In *God-Forgotten* the poet dreams himself an emissary to the Lord Most High, sent by the sons of

earth to win some answer to their prayers; at first
God blankly denies all knowledge of any such place,
then dimly recalls "some tiny sphere I built long back
(mid millions of such shapes of mine)" but takes for
granted that it must have utterly perished from having "lost my interest from the first, my aims therefor
succeeding ill." He declares that he never hears any
complaints from it, and comments on human conceit
which ever thought

> that one whose call
> Frames, daily, shining spheres of flawless stuff
> Might heed their tainted ball!

On hearing of Earth's pangs, however, God expresses
compassion.

Thus Hardy points out that God cannot be endowed with both benevolence and omniscience. If he
is benevolent, he must be limited in perception and
unable to foresee the ultimate effect of his creative
activities. On the other hand, if he is acquainted with
conditions on earth, he must be indifferent to suffering. The latter possibility is canvassed in *A Dream
Question*, another interrogation of the Lord, the poet
this time demanding whether the theologians, his professed representatives, are right in asserting that he
is infuriated by the blasphemy of a man who states
the obvious dilemma of benevolence versus omniscience. The Lord replies that he is utterly indifferent
to man's opinion and that his motives can never be
comprehensible to the human mind. All the sneers
and railings of the "manikin" will not increase or take

away "one grief-groan or pleasure-gleam." If man chooses, he may assume the fourth dimension to explain the mysterious "ethic of my will."

Maintaining his parallelism of God and Nature, Hardy expressed the same idea in *At a Bridal*, which bears *Nature's Indifference* as a subtitle and which is another apparently direct contradiction of Meredith. The latter had put the improvement of the race as the highest purpose of nature, and Hardy denies that she has any such eugenic intent. The lover, seeing his mistress marrying another, laments that the exceptional offspring of which he had dreamed can never exist, but Nature answers "that she does not care if the race all such sovereign types unknows." Thus Hardy has suggested a creative power which is conscious but indifferent, whether the symbol be a God unmoved by human prayer and censure or Mother Nature unmoved by human desires.

The foregoing poems may be grouped under the category in *Nature's Questioning* which terms the world "live remains of Godhead dying downward," since they all assume that a conscious power originated the process of creation but subsequently lost control or interest. In another group he sets forth the theory that nature was framed by "some vast Imbecility mighty to build and blend but impotent to tend." Still he uses interchangeably God and Mother Nature to signify the creative force, but explains the cruelty of life as unintentional, an evil which has intruded on account of the maker's inefficiency. In *The*

Lacking Sense the poet asks of Time why the Mother works with a remorseful look instead of weaving her world-web to happy music. Time replies that she is depressed because she "has wounded where she loves," is aware of "ills misdealt for blisses," and everywhere has killed her "self-joys" with "self-smitings." The reason for "her crimes upon her creatures, these fallings from her fair beginnings," is blindness, "her vainly-veiled deficience," which brings "those fearful unfulfilments, that red ravage." Her dexterity is sufficient to amaze the scientists (as usual, Hardy calls them "seers"), but it is no more than "facile finger-touch"; and despite "each pathetic strenuous slow endeavor" she is ever pursued by her "primal doom" of being "faultful, fatal." So man, being "of her clay," should not scorn or curse "her groping skill" but should "assist her where [his] creaturely dependence can or may." The poem, with its recurrent burden of "wounding where she loves," represents Hardy's usual reading of evolution, with emphasis on the cruelty of the struggle for survival and on the waste which cancels each effort of Nature toward perfection.

The same image of Nature as blind is employed in *Doom and She;* the creating force is "matchless in artistry" but sightless, and the controlling force—Fate—is "vacant of feeling," unable to recognize joy or pain, right or wrong, and therefore incapable of answering the anxious questions anent her "clay-made creatures" which are suggested by the thought that she might find her shapings unsatisfactory and wish to undo them. As another version of Nature's unconsciousness, Hardy sometimes writes of her as laboring in sleep or in a trance: *The Bullfinches* depicts how she "works on dreaming" despite the "warrings wild" that afflict her so-called "children"; and the sonnet *The Sleep-worker* wonders, should she wake from her trance to realize "all that Life's palpitating tissues feel" in the coils that she "has wrought unwittingly, by vacant rote and prepossession strong," whether she would obliterate the whole universe in shame, "or patiently adjust, amend, and heal." Once again, there is a parallel poem using God to represent the creating power; in *New Year's Eve* the poet asks God why he ever called the earth from formless void and shaped men to suffer upon it, since so many reasons exist "why nought should be at all"; and God answers that he cannot explain his logicless labors, having wrought "sense-sealed" and without guessing that he had "evolved a consciousness" to question him, "see the shortness of his view," and "use ethic tests" which he never intended. Then, after this lucid interval,

> He sank to raptness as of yore,
>   And opening New Year's Day
> Wove it by rote as heretofore,
> And went on working evermore
>   In his unweeting way.

Hardy's alternation, in these poems, between God and Mother Nature as symbols for the creative force suggests that neither is wholly satisfactory to him. In the poem ᾽ΑΓΝΩΣΤΩι ΘΕΩι he admits being aware that such efforts at definition are vain, since the problem he tries to solve is immeasurably beyond human comprehension:

> Long have I framed weak phantasies of Thee,
> O Willer masked and dumb!
> Who makest Life become,—
> As though by laboring all-unknowingly,
> Like one whom reveries numb.
>
> How much of consciousness informs Thy will,
> Thy biddings, as if blind,
> Of death-inducing kind,
> Nought shows to us ephemeral ones who fill
> But moments in Thy mind.

Nevertheless, he undertook to expound a more detailed scheme of things, intended to illuminate the meaning of existence in accord with the evolutionary view, and for it the symbols of both maternal Nature and personal God were discarded as inadequate.

EVOLUTIONARY SIGNIFICANCE OF THE IMMANENT WILL

We have seen that to Hardy the thing of gravest import in life was the prevalence of sorrow and suffering, inflicted undeservedly on all beings; and his architectural mind impelled him to seek a reasonable explanation of such apparent caprice. The Darwinian theory of "natural selection" was generally held to be synonymous with accident, in that it proclaimed the

mere freak of chance as determining who should survive and who perish; and it was natural for Hardy to
see blind chance operating in every event of life. In
his novels he was content to accept the fact—his frequent employment of it is a commonplace of criticism
—but in his poetry he was anxious to offer explanations. So his principle of pervasive chance grew into a
fatalistic view which eventually produced a matured
scheme of the universe. His fatalism is well illustrated in *The Subalterns,* wherein the chief evils of
life—sickness, death, and bad weather—declare that
they are not willingly malicious but are compelled by
"laws in force on high." Even Death confesses himself a slave, and the poet finds consolation in "their
passiveness."

To represent this power which controls all fate,
Hardy seeks a word free of all connotation of personality. The variety of titles available is shown in the
poem named *Fragment,* wherein a reference to "one
called God" is followed by a parenthesis:

> (Though by some the Will, or Force, or Laws;
> And vaguely, by some, the Ultimate Cause.)

For the more elaborate formulation of his scheme,
Hardy did not want to retain the name of God, for
reasons stated in the Preface to *The Dynasts:*

> The wide prevalence of the Monistic theory of the Universe
> forbade, in this twentieth century, the importation of Divine
> personages from any antique Mythology as ready-made sources
> or channels of Causation, even in verse, and excluded the celestial
> machinery of, say, *Paradise Lost,* as peremptorily as that of the
> *Iliad* or the *Eddas.* And the abandonment of the masculine pro-

noun in allusions to the First or Fundamental Energy seemed a
necessary and logical consequence of the long abandonment by
thinkers of the anthropomorphic conception of the same.

To this First Energy he sometimes gives the name of
"The Absolute," as in *V.R. 1819–1901,* wherein its
function is described as "pronouncing the deedful
word whereby all life is stirred"; in the next stanza he
speaks of the same force as "the All-One." Equally
careful avoidance of personification is shown in *The
Blow,* an interesting exposition of his view of fate:

> That no man schemed it is my hope—
> Yea, that it fell by will and scope
>   Of That Which some enthrone,
> And for Whose meaning myriads grope . . . .
>
> And if it prove that no man did,
> And that the Inscrutable, the Hid,
>   Was cause alone
> Of this foul crash our lives amid,
>
> I'll go in due time, and forget. . . . .

The poem concludes with a vision of the possible ultimate consciousness and regret of this impersonal power, as in other poems a similar awakening of God, or
of the Mother, was anticipated:

> The Immanent Doer That doth not know
>
> . . . . in some age unguessed of us
> May lift Its blinding incubus,
>   And see, and own:
> It grieves me I did thus and thus!"

This phrase "the Immanent Doer" comes close to the
title which Hardy finally adopted for the Fundamen-

tal Energy; it conveys in the word "immanent" the fact that no external power is involved, but with that concept the word "doer" is not quite consistent. Accordingly, he selected at last a phrase which included the idea of causation, "the Immanent Will."

The phrase was introduced in two or three shorter poems, wherein particular aspects of its activity were mentioned. *The Unborn* describes it as the impelling cause for the phenomenon of birth; *The Convergence of the Twain* shows it as the process of fate by taking what seemed to be an utterly accidental occurrence—the loss of the "Titanic"—and declaring that "the Immanent Will that stirs and urges everything" prepared the iceberg long in advance, predestined "for the time far and dissociate," the consummation occurring when "the Spinner of the Years" commands it. As this poem seems to imply that the Will is an external power, it should be correlated with one which implies that it resides within all the phenomena through which it acts. The poem called *He Wonders about Himself* points out that the individual represents a fragment of the Will, although too insignificant to alter the course of destiny:

> Part is mine of the general Will,
> Cannot my share in the sum of sources
> Bend a digit the poise of forces,
> And a fair desire fulfill?

Thus the identification is indicated between Fate, with its apparently capricious chances, and the Immanent Will, which is the primal energy within all manifestation, producing the creative process.

In *The Dynasts* the Immanent Will is really the hero. The huge drama is an exposition of the way in which all human actions are subordinate to its control. In the *After Scene* the poet says that even the Napoleonic wars, so momentous to humanity, are a tiny incident to the Will, which includes the whole universe and evolves the suns from nebular masses:

> Yet but one flimsy riband of Its web
> Have we here watched in weaving—web Enorm,
> Whose furthest hem and selvage may extend
> To where the roars and plashings of the flames
> Of earth-invisible suns swell noisily,
> And onward into ghastly gulfs of sky,
> Where hideous presences burn through the dark—
> Monsters of magnitude without a shape,
> Hanging amid deep wells of nothingness.

Withdrawing attention from this universal manifestation of the Will to the portion of it represented by this planet, one finds in the *Fore Scene* that the Spirit of the Earth confesses Earth's productive labors to be dictated by the Will:

> I am but the ineffectual Shade
> Of her the Travailler, herself a thrall
> To It; in all her laborings curbed and kinged!

Thus the idea of Earth as the mother of all life, which seemed to Meredith a sufficient explanation of evolution, is subordinated by Hardy to the more metaphysical concept of what he calls (i, VI, iii) "the Eternal Urger." He takes particular care to insist that this primal Energy actually consists of the total of all vital activity and is not something separable from it. Recurrent interludes in *The Dynasts* present a panorama of the Will's control of human affairs, "exhibiting as one organism," in the words of the *Fore Scene*, "the anatomy of life and movement in all humanity and vitalized matter included in the display." Since every man is a unit in this organism, his sense of free will and individuality is an illusion; the Spirit of the Years explains:

> Their sum is like the lobules of a Brain
> Evolving always that it wots not of;
> A Brain whose whole connotes the Everywhere . . . .
>   . . . . the while unguessed
> Of those it stirs, who (even as ye do) dream
> Their motions free, their orderings supreme;
> Each life apart from each, with power to mete
> Its own day's measures; balanced, self-complete;
> Though they subsist but atoms of the One
> Laboring through all, divisible from none.

This subjugation of all individuals to the total is summed up in Part 3 (I, v):

> Thus do the mindless minions of the spell
> In mechanized enchantment sway and show
> A Will that wills above the will of each,
> Yet but the will of all conjunctively.

Thus Hardy establishes the first characteristic of his Fundamental Energy—that it is the sum total of all the vital activity in the universe and that, accordingly, every individual is inevitably the slave of its dispensations.

The next important characteristic is that which he

previously attributed to Nature and God—unconsciousness. The *Fore Scene* opens:

> It works unconsciously, as heretofore,
> Eternal artistries in Circumstance,
> Whose patterns, wrought by rapt aesthetic rote,
> Seem in themselves Its single listless aim,
> And not their consequence.

Several of the theories already advanced by Hardy in
shorter poems as possible explanations for the automatic, yet deft, process, such as that it tired of this
world and confines its attention to others, or that it
took offense at man's repudiation of reverence, are
mentioned only to be dismissed. It never possessed
consciousness, and never can acquire it:

> In the Foretime, even to the germ of Being,
> Nothing appears of shape to indicate
> That cognizance has marshalled things terrene
> Or will. . . . .
> Rather they show that, like a knitter drowsed,
> Whose fingers play in skilled unheedfulness,
> The Will has woven with an absent heed
> Since life first was; and ever will so weave.

Having denied consciousness to the Will, Hardy
must account for the dexterity of its workmanship
and even more for its ability to prepare predestined
events and bring them about; so he grants it a general
purpose, although the precise details which it evolves
are entirely accidental:

> In that immense unweeting Mind is shown
> One far above forethinking; purposive
> Yet superconscious; a Clairvoyancy

> That knows not what It knows yet works therewith.
> The cognizance ye mourn, Life's doom to feel,
> If I report it meetly, came unmeant,
> Emerging with blind gropes from impercipience
> By random sequence—luckless, tragic Chance,
> If ye will call it so. 'Twas needed not
> In the economy of Vitality,
> Which might have ever kept a sealed cognition
> As doth the Will Itself.

This is an apt summary of Hardy's view of evolution. The fundamental factor is the Immanent Will, constantly urging matter to assume vitality but not dictating the forms which life assumes. Human consciousness—and attendant suffering—was developed through merest accident, by natural selection. The sole metaphysical element is the Will's primary purpose to produce living matter; the course of its fulfilment is nothing but the evolutionary process. In remarking on the paradox of predestination and accident, the Ironic Spirits (i, VI, iii), after declaring that "things to be were shaped and set ere mortals and this planet met," compare that which works all to "some sublime fermenting-vat"

> Heaving throughout its vast content
> With strenuously transmutive bent
> Though of its aim unsentient.

In short, the Will causes evolution but does not determine its direction.

Although in the Preface to *The Dynasts* Hardy disclaimed any desire "to advance a systematized philosophy warranted to lift 'the burden of the mystery' of this unintelligible world," the doctrines which he labels "tentative" assume the form of a definite effort to replace the Genesis account of creation by a scheme more consistent with the evolutionary hypothesis. This required the concept of a creative power representing the "life force," divorced from any external authority. In various forms, some such pantheism appears in the work of all the poets who were promulgating a new creation-myth, but Hardy gives it a particularly conditioned character; the other poets assumed that the power instituted the evolutionary process according to a definite intention, but Hardy attributes the whole process to unmitigated chance. In spite of the metaphysical terms, such as "Immanent Will," and paradoxes, such as "purposive yet superconscious," Hardy's interpretation abides more closely to the Darwinian theory than does that of any of his poetic contemporaries.

By denying purpose to the creative force, he nullified the great nineteenth-century confidence in progress. To him, the function of the Life Force or Immanent Will was merely a constant urgency toward change; and this, after all, is the most obvious implication of evolution—that no form is static, each constantly being transformed into something else. Tennyson was impressed by the same thought all his life. This one demonstrable reality—change, irrespective of what the change produces—is the moral enforced at the end of *The Dynasts*, where Europe is shown as reverting to conditions no better than those preceding the war. The Ironic Spirits declare that the Will's aim is not "Love and Light," the rewarding of Good and the punishment of Evil, but simply "to alter evermore things from what they were before." Similarly in the *Fore Scene* the Spirit of the Years concludes from his experience that "change hath played strange pranks" but that "old Laws operate yet" and the events of the newest "dynastic and imperial" conflict "shape on accustomed lines."

The thought that all matter is in a state of flux inspires the poem called "*According to the Mighty Working*," which points out the fallacy of considering a calm night peaceful:

> Peace, this hid riot, Change,
> This revel of quick-cued mumming,
> This never truly being,
> This evermore becoming,
> This spinner's wheel onfleeing
> Outside perception's range.

The stability of all phenomena is to Hardy mere illusion, since the creative activity is constantly at work, sustaining matter through atomic motion and remodeling its forms through evolution. Change is fundamental to life.

Hardy's aptitude for seeing all the gloom and cruelty of life convinced him that this change does not entail improvement. Human nature seemed to him as barbarous as ever, and fate as perverse. He rather abruptly introduces the idea at the conclusion of *The Moth Signal*, one of his many narratives of infidelity:

> Then grinned the Ancient Briton
> From the tumulus treed with pine:
> "So, hearts are thwartly smitten
> In these days as in mine!"

The optimistic belief in progress, entertained by most
of Hardy's contemporaries, was rooted in the material
prosperity, the increasing power and knowledge,
which prevailed during the Victorian period, and the
evolutionary theory promptly dropped into place as
another article in the creed of advancement. Hardy,
however, held that the advance in mechanical efficiency was of no real significance, since it did not promote fulfilment of ideals affecting the happiness of
the race. In *The Jubilee of a Magazine*, after describing the change in agricultural implements during half
a century, he asks "what has been done to unify the
mortal lot" during the period, and finds that Truth
can indicate no advance in rightness and candor;
"events jar onward much the same." Whereas, he
says, if the old cruder mechanical devices had survived,

> And best invention been retained
> For high crusades to lessen tears
> Throughout the race the world had gained!

Being essentially humanitarian in sentiment, he re-
fused to grant the title of genuine progress to anything that does not relieve humanity of the suffering
which, in his eyes, prevails everywhere.

He was particularly depressed by the unmodified
continuance of war. *Channel Firing* says that "the
world is as it used to be" and that men, "mad as hat-

ters," devote their efforts to making "red war yet redder." The Boer war sonnets *Departure* and *Embarkation* point out that "this late age of thought, and pact, and code" has failed to mend "the self-same bloody mode" of argument. Again, the continued rarity of enlightenment and intellectual honesty is lamented in *Lausanne, in Gibbon's Old Garden*, wherein the historian's shade learns that writers are still chary of furthering Truth's advance, and still "aver the Comic to be Reverend"; he quotes the "wormwood words" of Milton, "Truth like a bastard comes into the world never without ill-fame to him who gives her birth."

Hardy's disbelief in progress extends from such particular instances to the whole realm of ideals and aspirations. In *The Church-Builder* he shows how idealism is crushed by the injustices of life, and similar pervasive disillusionment appears in *Memory and I, The Temporary the All*, and *To an Unborn Pauper Child*. He is especially miserable in the thought that if ideals could be retained and enthusiastically practiced, they might promote real progress, but that before they can reach maturity they are inevitably suppressed and extinguished, whether by mere accident or by malice. *A Commonplace Day* concludes with the idea of somebody, somewhere, feeling some impulse "of that enkindling ardency from whose maturer glows the world's amendment flows," only to have its "hopes to be embodied on the earth . . . . benumbed at birth by momentary chance or wile"; and the poet attributes his melancholy to an intuition "of this loss to man's futurity." Of the "wiles" which assail incipient ideals, he has given a fuller account in *Murmurs in the Gloom;* he denounces as opponents to progress the teachers and writers who cling to old dogmas, and wishes for "heedful ones of searching sight" to hinder the reactionary leaders and "to lead the nations vawardly from gloom to light." It is probably this recognition of possible progress being baffled that suggested *Yell'ham Wood's Story,* which modifies the declaration "that Life is for ends unknown" by asserting

> that Life would signify
> A thwarted purposing:
> That we come to live, and are called to die,
> Life offers,—to deny!

Convinced that progress is a delusion, Hardy attaches no significance to the doctrine of heroes, which was Meredith's credo. The greatest men, slaves to the Immanent Will and its aimless lust for change, exert no real influence on the world's history. At the end of *The Dynasts* the Spirit of the Years, from his observations of all the centuries, chides Napoleon:

> Such men as thou, who wade across the world
> To make an epoch, bless, confuse, appall,
> Are in the elemental ages' chart
> Like meanest insects on obscurest leaves
> But incidents and tools of Earth's unfolding;
> Or as the brazen rod that stirs the fire
> Because it must.

If this is the case, the great and memorable events of history are trivial, of no significance when compared with the most ephemeral interests of the present moment. Such an idea is whimsically presented in *The Roman Grave Mounds*, wherein the delver in the ruins proves to be no archaeologist, but a humble man burying the cat that was his only friend. *The Roman Road* pictures a spot which is important to the poet, not for its historic associations, but as the scene of his childish walks with his mother; and *By the Barrows* has a similar theme. In *Rome: Building a New Street in the Ancient Quarter* he moralizes on the vanity of human activity, which erects "frail new mansions" among the ruins of vaster structures without perceiving the futility implied.

In contrast with the transience of all man's most ambitious ventures, the only permanent thing is the endless repetition of the primitive events of birth, love, and death. This contrast of momentous events which fade and commonplace incidents which survive by recurrence is the theme of *In Time of "The Breaking of Nations"*: the annual burning of grass "will go onward the same though Dynasties pass," and the lovemaking of man and maid will continue when "war's annals will cloud into night." The whole geological development of the planet is a background for the undistinguished event of the moment, in the poem *At Castle Boterel:* the "primeval rocks" watch the petty activities of "the transitory in Earth's long order" recurring in endless cycle. Accordingly, the extinction of the individual is of no importance, according to *Autumn in King's Hintock Park:*

> New leaves will dance on high—
> Earth never grieves!
> Will not, when missed am I
> Raking up leaves.

The Tenant for Life is the comment of the sun to the poet busy at gardening, the injunction being that "it matters not," for the sun has "shined on nobler ones" than he, who are dead and forgotten.

So powerfully is Hardy affected by this sense of the recurrence of all vital activity that he occasionally exalts it into the metaphysical concept that time is an illusion. The sonnet *Rome: On the Palatine* describes the effect of a waltz tune amid the ruins as "blending pulsing life with lives long gone, till Time seemed fiction, Past and Present one." In the same way the reconstructed model of a prehistoric bird suggests the poem *In a Museum,* in which he compares the "mould of a musical bird which over the earth before man came was winging" with the voice of a living singer:

> Such a dream is Time that the coo of this ancient bird
> Has perished not, but is blent, or will be blending
> 'Mid visionless wilds of space with the voice that I heard,
> In the full-fugued song of the universe unending.

To find a parallel for the concluding line, one must go outside of Hardy's poetry and into that of the disciples of Tennyson, such as William Watson. The rest of the poem, however, utters Hardy's more frequent thought that change is really constant recurrence: the forms may differ, but the essence is the same. *In a Museum* differs only in that it deals with the desirable gift of music, whereas the other poems dwell on the suffering and injustices which are perpetual despite the superficial changes miscalled "progress."

THE ULTIMATE HOPE

The foregoing analysis of Hardy's philosophy seems anything but illustrative of the creed which he claimed for himself in the *Apology* of *Late Lyrics and Earlier*, namely, "evolutionary meliorism." If his intention was to "exact a full look at the Worst," he undeniably succeeded. His unrelieved depiction of the tragic and ironic events of life, his insistence on blind chance as the controlling force of the universe, his negation of genuine progress—all these were antithetical to the optimism of the era. In opposition to the creed of progress which his contemporaries deduced from the evolutionary theory, he insisted that it implied wanton cruelty and undirected accident as the prevailing forces of existence. Nevertheless, he felt an instinctive desire to believe in ultimate progress, in defiance of the dictates of his reason, as another part of the *Apology* indicates:

If it be true, as Comte argued, that advance is never in a straight line, but in a looped orbit, we may in the aforesaid ominous moving backward, be doing it *pour mieux sauter*, drawing back for a spring. I repeat that I forlornly hope so, notwithstanding the supercilious regard of hope by Schopenhauer, von Hartmann, and other philosophers down to Einstein who have my respect.

That this hope is not an outgrowth of his old age is aptly shown by the poem called *1967*, written when Hardy was twenty-seven, and surveying the prospect of the next hundred years,

> A century which, if not sublime,
> Will show, I doubt not, at its prime,
> A scope above this blinkered time.

Although half of the period went by without revealing to him any improvement, he still cherished the hope. The Armistice Day poem "*And There Was a Great Calm*" says that though "old hopes that earth was bettering slowly were dead and damned" by the war, the armistice reawakened the dream that men will some day be wholly given to grace. In the conclusion of 'ΑΓΝΩΣΤΩι ΘΕΩι the possibility "that listless tends to grow percipient with advance of days" is based on the unexpected spectacle from time to time of "a wrong dying as of self-slaughter." In other words, the hope of improvement depends on whether the Will can ever become conscious. In *The Sleep-Worker* he said that in such an event the Mother must either destroy all life straightway or else attempt to reconstruct it; and the latter implies hope. If human consciousness is an accidental development independent of the Immanent Will, progress depends on God's overtaking man in intelligence, as the poem *Fragment* says:

> Since he made us humble pioneers
> Of himself in consciousness of Life's tears,
> It needs no mighty prophecy

To tell that what he could mindlessly show
His creatures, he himself will know.

By some still close-cowled mystery
We have reached feeling faster than he,
But he will overtake us anon
If the world goes on.

The hope finds clear expression in *The Dynasts*. It is true that the action of the drama exemplifies the futility of human ambition and the subordination of individuals to the mindless mechanism of the Will. It is true also that the Pities, who alone cling to the optimistic view, are laughed to scorn by the more experienced Phantom Intelligences. Nevertheless, the *After Scene* concludes with the Pities victorious in the argument, and this coda leaves the final effect of the drama almost hopeful. The persistent optimism of the Pities appears at the end of the second part:

Yet it may wake and understand
Ere Earth unshape, know all things, and
With knowledge use a painless hand.

Again, in 3, IV, iv, the Pities maintain that humanity is making progress in spite of the interference of despots—"the pale pathetic peoples still plod on through hoodwinkings to light!" To justify this outlook, the Spirit of the Pities in the *After Scene* rallies all the arguments in favor of "the Inadvertent Mind" eventually gaining percipience. The evolution of the human mind is adduced as analogy:

Men gained cognition with the flux of time,
And wherefore not the Force informing them,

> When far-ranged aions past all fathoming
> Shall have swung by, and stand as backward years?

The chorus of Pities chants a hymn to their ideal Power, declaring that, in spite of our present ignorance as to the cause of unassuaged suffering, there is "food for final hope" and

> That mild-eyed Consciousness stands by
> Life's loom, to lull it by and by.

The chorus goes on to affirm that the harmony of the astronomical systems reveals a controlling force, and concludes by praising "the Alone, Whose means the End shall justify." The Spirit of the Years is moved:

> You almost charm my long philosophy
> Out of my strong-built thought, and bear me back
> To when I thanksgave thus. . . . . Ay, start not, Shades;
> In the Foregone I knew what dreaming was,
> And could let raptures rule! But not so now.

The chorus of the Years, pointing out that the fundamental question remains unanswered—"Why the All-mover urges on and measures out the droning tune of things"—clings to the old explanation that it molds as in a dream, without apprehension of how its sentient subjects fare. But the chorus of the Pities is unconvinced:

> Nay;—shall not Its blindness break?
> Yea, must not Its heart awake
> Promptly tending
> To its mending
> In a genial germing purpose, and for lovingkindness' sake?

> But—a stirring thrills the air
> Like to sounds of joyance there

> That the rages
> Of the ages
> Shall be cancelled, and deliverance offered from the darts that
> were,
> Consciousness the Will informing, till It fashion all things fair!

Thus the conclusion is raised to a plane of exultation that neutralizes some of the otherwise intolerable gloom of the drama's action and implications.

It will be noted that the keynote of the chorus is struck in the word "lovingkindness." In *A Plaint to Man* the same word is used to describe conditions when faith in a supernatural God shall have vanished:

> With loving-kindness fully blown,
> And visioned help unsought, unknown.

The word occurs again in the *Apology* to *Late Lyrics and Earlier* in the poet's prediction of earth's future: "pain to all upon it, tongued or dumb, shall be kept down to a minimum by lovingkindness, acting through scientific knowledge." One observes that in the chorus the attribute is ascribed to the Immanent Will, and in the other passages to humanity. After all, the Will is only the aggregate of all individual wills, and if the human contingent in this force were to act in unison, appreciable effects might be wrought upon the whole. A memorandum of 1890 makes the idea clear, and develops the ethical principle which we saw hinted in a stanza of *"The Wind Blew Words"*:

> Altruism, or the Golden Rule, or whatever "Love your neighbor as yourself" may be called, will ultimately be brought about I think by the pain we see in others reacting on ourselves, as if

we and they were a part of one body. Mankind, in fact, may be and possibly will be viewed as members of one corporeal frame—"the Prime Cause or Invariable Antecedent."

Thus interpreted, his concept of the Will's awakening becomes less abstruse; it joins hands with Meredith's creed of the "sighting brain" which must be extended into an attribute of all human beings. If the race unites to seek humanitarian ends, clearly recognizing the non-existence of supernatural aids and post-mortem rewards, and frankly confronting the prevalence of pain and sorrow, the course of evolution will become synonymous with genuine progress. This summarizes the poetic creeds of both Meredith and Hardy. And Hardy selected "loving-kindness" as the basis of his ethics because he felt the essential unity among all beings, and the common cause in which they all strive, implicit in the evolutionary concept.

Nurtured on Comte and Darwin, and trained in the discipline of architecture, he adopted the rationalistic principle. Deeply sympathetic by nature, he brooded on the suffering and disappointments of life. In his rationalism, evolution explained the psychological origins of faith; in his humanitarianism, evolution explained cruelty and capricious accident by the struggle for survival. But the philosophic and poetical elements in his disposition impelled him to seek for first-causes. Even while admitting that such a quest was beyond human scope, he was working out the scheme which he finally propounded in *The Dynasts*. No sooner had he constructed an image of the Fundamental Energy that seemed to him sufficiently impersonal and aimless, than he began to hint at the possibility of its becoming conscious. He could not prevent the Immanent Will from resembling the mystic unity and harmony which other poets perceived. In the invaluable *Apology* he admitted that poetry might form a *liaison* between religion and science:

> Poetry, pure literature in general, religion—I include religion because poetry and religion touch each other, or rather modulate into each other; are, indeed, often but different names for the same thing— these, I say, the visible signs of mental and emotional life, must like all other things keep moving, becoming. . . . . It may be a forlorn hope, a mere dream, that of an alliance between religion, which must be retained unless the world is to perish, and complete rationality, which must come, unless also the world is to perish, by means of the interfusing effect of poetry.

So Hardy aligned himself with the other poets of his century, from Tennyson onward. After resolutely setting his face against their mystical exaltation of progress, he was betrayed into an eventual parley with it.

Chapter VI
CONTEMPORARY POETS

W HEN the present generation was being edu-
cated, the theory of evolution had ceased to
be an intellectual cataclysm and had assumed its place in the general perspective of knowledge, taken for granted as the prevalent hypothesis,
and not of sufficient importance to worry the non-
scientific mind. Most people ignore the difficulty of
reconciling belief in evolution with orthodox faith;
they restrict their evolutionary tenets to definite scientific topics, and elsewhere are content to use the
terminology of the Bible regarding God and the soul
and the origin of life. In this compromise the majority
of the poets have been willing to join. Moral earnestness and philosophic pretensions, having monopolized
the leading poets for half a century, have gone out of
fashion; and a poet who ventures on any discussion of
ideas runs the risk of being stigmatized as Victorian.
So some of the other eternal themes of poetry have
come into their own again, and an almost childlike
simplicity of manner has replaced metaphysical sub-
tleties.

This final acceptance of the evolutionary view has
taken various forms in poetry, but falls into two main
categories: one is the frankly mystical, which con-

temns the conditions of physical life as unimportant; the other is the frankly material, which seeks to extract the full sensuous value out of phenomena, without debating problems of the spirit. The first type is represented by the Celtic poets, Yeats and A.E., exponents of the wholly spiritual theory of evolution known as reincarnation; the second type is represented by Rupert Brooke and A. E. Housman and Walter de la Mare and all the others who are keenly aware of the transience of life and the intensification of physical beauty which that transience entails.

To both groups alike the evolutionary theory has given a fresh vision of man's place in the history of the universe. Realizing the ephemeral brevity of the individual life, they realize also the significance of the larger unit—the life of the race with its constant struggle and its persistent clinging to ideals. The notion may be traced to Meredith, to whom the life of the race was of such supreme import; but with the modern poets it has lost something of its direct evolutionary connections, becoming rather an objective reality. Thus A.E., in his preoccupation with the spiritual aspect, finds in the life of the race a vision of immortality. His poem *Babylon* concludes: "For we are in the calm and proud procession of eternal things." On the other hand, Walter de la Mare sees simply the impressive contrast between the brevity of the individual life and the race's long heritage of tradition and imaginings. He writes in *All That's Past:*

Very old are we men;
Our dreams are tales
Told in dim Eden
By Eve's nightingales;
We wake and whisper awhile,
But, the day gone by,
Silence and sleep like fields
Of amaranth lie.

The same contrast is phrased by John Masefield in *Laugh and Be Merry:*

Laugh, for the time is brief, a thread the length of a span.
Laugh, and be proud to belong to the old proud pageant of man.

This perspective in which the individual appears so transient, and the procession or pageant so proud, springs from the evolutionary concept even though the connection is not expounded by the poets; they are no longer basing a metaphysical system on the concept, but merely taking advantage of its emotional connotation.

The contemporary poets, apart from the thorough mystics, are circumspect in proclaiming any adherence to supernatural faith. They prefer to avoid debatable topics by remaining within the realm of phenomena. Existence after death having been called into question, they are determined to exact the full sum of pleasure from the tangible realities of the present life. The image of old age and death, hovering in the background, makes more poignant their sense of the immediate loveliness of things. Thence comes that passionate devotion to sensuous impressions which is typical of so many recent poets, and is

well exemplified in Rupert Brooke's *The Great Lover*
and *Grantchester*. In the latter he digresses to satirize
the Meredithian search for general principles beneath
phenomena:

> Some, it may be, can get in touch
> With Nature there, or Earth, or such . . . .
> But these are things I do not know.

Most of the Georgian poets, acting on this view, have
discarded all theories. The debates and controversies
of their elders have left them only the impression that
there are no certainties beyond immediate physical
existence, and with those certainties they are content.

This last stage of the poetic absorption of evolution
being so largely negative, it can only be postulated,
without inquiry into evidence. Several of the most
prominent, however, among the contemporary poets
of England have maintained a more active interest in
the evolutionary theory.

WILLIAM WATSON

Among the successors of Tennyson, Sir William
Watson most resembles him in cogitating in lucid reflective verse upon the evolution of the universe in
the past and its possible developments in the future.
But unlike Tennyson, he is not profoundly impressed
by the responsibility of contesting doubt and defending the compatibility of science and faith. Rather, he
accepts the fact that man's religious beliefs and his
scientific theories are alike in being trivial exercises
never really penetrating the essential mystery of ex-

istence. In *The Great Misgiving* he confesses his
doubt as to whether or not there is survival after
death; in *The Captive's Dream* he points out how the
limitations imposed by our five senses prevent any
absolute knowledge; in *The Blind Summit* he reiterates that it is the doom of mortals to be "vexed with
phantoms old" and constantly baffled in trying to
perceive "the eternal landscape of the real and true."
Despite this agnostic attitude, he takes for granted
the validity of the evolutionary hypothesis, but hesi-
tates to extend it into a general theory of the universe
even on the physical plane, much less into a spiritual
principle. His chief poem on the subject is *The Hope
of the World*, and its reasoning is conveniently summarized in the prefatory Argument:

> That the evolution of Man, such as we see him, from some
> inferior form of animal life, after immeasurable ages during which
> there is reason to think that the inferior form remained unpro-
> gressive and stationary, has very much the appearance of a splen-
> did accident; that the occurrence of such a splendid accident on
> this planet affords no ground from which to infer the occurrence
> of similar splendid accidents in the experience of other inhabited
> orbs; that in the absence of any ground for such an inference, the
> theory of an upward movement or meliorative tendency as
> operating throughout nature generally, lacks support; that except
> upon this theory of the universality of the upward movement, a
> theory seen to be wanting in confirmation, no intelligible concep-
> tion of a beneficent Omnipotence can be based; and incidentally,
> that the heroic course is rather to reject than to welcome the
> solace of an optimism which apparently rests upon no securer
> foundation than that of instinctive Hope alone.

As symbols of this idea he describes in the poem "Life
and her consort Law" sitting higher than heaven,

while man seeks to enthrone the third principle of
Love as their peer, but in vain; for there is no proof

> That through all Nature's frame
> Boundless ascent benign
> Is everywhere her aim,
> Such as man hopes it here
> Where he from beasts hath risen.

The poet goes on to outline the evolution of the human race:

> In cave and bosky dene
> Of old there crept and ran
> The gibbering form obscene
> That was and was not man.
> The desert beasts went by
> In fairer covering clad;
> More speculative eye
> The couchant lion had,
> And goodlier speech the birds, than we when we began.

> Was it some random throw
> Of heedless Nature's die,
> That from estate so low
> Uplifted man so high?
> Through untold aeons vast
> She let him lurk and cower;
> 'Twould seem he climbed at last
> In mere fortuitous hour,
> Child of a thousand chances, 'neath the indifferent sky.

> A soul so long deferred
> In his blind brain he bore,
> It might have slept unstirred
> Ten million noontides more.
> Yea, round him Darkness might
> Till now her folds have drawn,
> O'er that enormous night
> So casual came the dawn,
> Such hues of hap and hazard Man's Emergence wore.

As it is only the assumption of a uniform upward process throughout the universe which warrants dependence on man's instinctive sense of immortality as proof of immortality's actual existence, Watson ascribes to the mere inveteracy of hope the arguments that half of the triumph depends on the difficulties surmounted, and that the "old dragons" which still remain in "bowers of pleasance" will cast their scales and "die into kings" through the power of a "Wizard" controlling the world. Admitting regretfully that the trusters of such felicitous hopes have more happiness, Watson chooses the harder task, to forego the faith which depreciates the world as a mere anteroom, and to endure without visionary solace "Chance and Victorious Death" and ignorance of his origin and destination. The point of view differs from Hardy's only in replacing his emotional sympathy for mortal suffering by an aloof and almost boastful stoicism.

In other poems, however, Watson draws somewhat more encouraging conclusions from the evolutionary history of man. The more immediate of them is suggested by the inspiring persistence and indomitable courage of the human creature, who never rests content but always strives onward toward some dim ideal. *The Dream of Man* celebrates the ascent of "the unwearied climber . . . . up the steps of the ages . . . . to the unknown goal," mastering his enemies as he goes. A future is envisaged wherein man has "conquered the virgin planets and peopled the desert stars," until, feeling himself familiar with all the se-

crets of nature, and seeing therein no evidence of
God's existence, he has set himself up to be worshiped
as "master of all." God attempts to humiliate him by
revealing to him his ignominious source:

> . . . . his base beginnings in the depths of time, his strife
> With beasts and crawling horrors for leave to live, when life
> Meant only to slay and to procreate, to feed and to sleep, among
> Mere mouths, voracities boundless, blind lusts, desires without
> tongue,
> And ferocities vast, fulfilling their being's malignant law,
> While nature was but one hunger, and one hate, all fangs and
> maw.

But man refuses to be abashed by the fact of his evolution, declaring "this is my loftiest greatness, that I
was born so low," and considering himself thereby
superior to God "the ungrowing." In this confidence
man goes on with his achievements till he wins the
final victory over death. But then he finds life un-
supportable with no goal to strive for; so he suppli-
cates God to restore death, and learns that man's lot
is indeed more blest than God's, since the only "joys
transcendent" are "delight of seeking" and "rapture
of striving." Herein Watson not only echoes Browning's doctrine of the glory of the imperfect, but also
shows—as certain novelists, such as Conrad, have
also done—that man's capacity for endurance and his
acceptance of conflict for its own sake form the only
gleam of encouragement in the modern evolutionary
creed.

In the *Hymn to the Sea* Watson again sings the
praises of man's indomitable spirit, ever seeking to

transcend its limitations. This discontent, apparent in human poetry as contrasted with the untroubled song of birds, is attributed in *The First Skylark of Spring* to man's growing realization of "his lack of wing" and "his iron bourn." Although occasionally voicing regret for primitive simplicity, Watson submits to the innate impulse of change as inevitable, and in *The Lost Eden* surveys the modern shift in spiritual outlook. Only now, he says, has man been driven from Eden, having stayed there so long as he imagined himself "the first of creatures, fashioned for eternity." This dream was shattered when Eve, "the adventurous soul within his soul, the sleepless, the unslaked," showed him how insignificant he really is in the world. Thus expelled from Eden by "an imperative world-thirst," he can never return from "among the infinitudes" to re-enter the narrow pale, though he often looks back to it half-regretfully when he feels

> The intolerable vastness bow him down,
> The awful homeless spaces daunt his soul.

In other words, the evolutionary theory and the consequent change in human outlook are a natural stage in the evolution of the race.

Just as we must inevitably progress beyond the comfortable and limited faiths which originated in primitive minds, so the same goading dissatisfaction with inactivity will eventually produce a golden age. This goal, toward which the world is moving despite recurrent setbacks, is described in *The Father of the*

Forest, when, "wise from all the foolish past," Earth shall see the nations unite toward "one golden end— Beauty:"

> . . . . the vision whereunto,
> In joy, with pantings, from afar,
> Through sound and odor, form and hue,
> And mind and clay, and worm and star—
> Now touching goal, now backward hurled—
> Toils the indomitable world.

Thus, on the plane of physical life, Watson believes in the race's gradual approach to perfection through the unconquerable impulse to aspire.

But the stanza just quoted betrays his hankering after the mystical pantheism of his poetic forebears, particularly Tennyson. Despite his agnosticism proclaimed in *The Hope of the World*, he sometimes extends his faith beyond the material plane. In the *Hymn to the Sea* he speaks of "Man with the cosmic fortunes and starry vicissitudes tangled"; and this entanglement, one gathers from other poems, is due to the unity and divinely appointed harmony of all nature. In the poem *England My Mother* he remarks that the instinctive love of song in man is a manifestation of his affinity with the rhythm of the universe, "Nature's self" being nothing but "an endless strife toward music, euphony, rhythm," in which trees, tides and stars participate:

> God on His throne is
> Eldest of poets:
> Unto His measures
> Moveth the Whole.

Watson is apparently using Song to symbolize the combined principles of joy and rhythm, as constituting the creative process responsible for all existence, "the choric chant of creation" which incessantly "floweth from all things"; and man is faintly echoing "the descant whereto forever dances the world." The Genesis account of creation is replaced by the idea of a rhythmic force interpenetrating all matter and shaping it into a unified whole—a convenient poetic symbol for electronic theories of matter which at the same time merges readily into a more metaphysical system.

The *Ode in May*, applying the same symbolism to the springtime's particularly fecund outpouring of creative energy, identifies its "Song of Mingling" with the original "cosmic descant." All life having been procreated by the wedding of the Sun, "the temporal lord of life," and the Earth, "the mother of men," our heritage is a strange mingling of his triumph and her travail, of spiritual greatness and physical infirmity; we are midway between the mere unconscious matter from which we have developed and the purely spiritual cosmic principle:

> We are children of splendour and flame,
> Of shuddering also, and tears,
> Magnificent out of the dust we came,
> And abject from the spheres.

Agreeing with Meredith that man is the offspring of earth, Watson adds that the spiritual element in man incarnates the principle pervading the universe.

In *The Unknown God* the poet contrasts the anthro-

pomorphic deity of the past with the divinity transcending comprehension which he envisages as interpenetrating man and all other matter, a power which
to our finite senses often seems unconscious or positively unjust, and which at any rate is beyond our
prayers and "unmeet to be profaned by praise." To
this power he gives thanks in *Vita Nuova* for having
taught him his essential unity with the "great chorus"
of nature, as "a string of that lyre of life" whose
strain builds the world. It is to this universal spirit
that the soul returns after death, as described in the
Hymn to the Sea, "into the matrix of Life darkly divinely resumed." Similarly *Lachrimae Musarum*, the
elegy for Tennyson, describes the dead poet as re-
claimed by "the spirit divine of universal loveliness"
and surviving in "the rhythm and music of the
Whole."

Using the traditional terms of religion, Watson
calls this principle of harmony "God," and its temporarily incarnated fragment "the soul"; but were the
terms of science substituted, such as "vital energy,"
"electronic attraction," his apparent mysticism would
show its identity with material principles. But he
does not preach his creed with prophetic assurance;
he sees that the old dogmatic creeds are discarded irrevocably, and he hints at possible successors to them,
but with no claim to infallibility.

ALFRED NOYES

Writing just a decade later than Watson (from 1902
onward), Alfred Noyes represents the final crystalliz-

ing of the new mystical creed. Tennyson had suggested it tentatively as reconcilable with the scientists' theories; Watson employed its terms as synonymous with those of science, so that his mystical pantheism could be taken either literally as a religion or symbolically as poetic phrasing of physical processes; Noyes uses the terms and ideas precisely as earlier generations used those of orthodox Christianity, with little recognition of any symbolic intent. The new pantheism is already traditional and is severing the umbilical cord which connected it with the intellectual necessities wherein it had birth. It is still perhaps more consistent with scientific theories than literal interpretation of the Bible can be, but it is beginning to need exegetical treatment to reveal that consistency.

It insists chiefly on man's essential identity with the rest of the universe. This unity through the general physical forces which have evolved man in common with all nature is symbolized by Noyes in *The Loom of Years:* "in spirit and flesh . . . . in body and soul" we are one with "the flower of a day . . . . the withered moon . . . . the granite mountains," and "the dream that triumphs beyond the light of the spheres," because all come from the same "Loom of the Weaver." The lyric entitled *Unity* suggests that this identity of the individual and the whole entails a sort of immortality, both because the individual is not really distinct from the total manifestation of the universe and because the analogy of the principle of recurrence in nature points to a similar recurrence of the individual incarnation. It is only to our limited intelligence that our span of life on earth seems to be isolated and finite. Actually we are "one in many, one as the waves are at one with the sea." So, whether we are reabsorbed into the general spirit of the universe, or are reborn to new earth-lives, we are eternal.

The idea of reincarnation, as the spiritual counterpart of physical evolution, which was discussed several times by Tennyson and implied more than once by Browning, appeals strongly to Noyes. It forms the motif of his "lyrical symphony" *The Progress of Love*, as uttered in the refrain:

> In other worlds I loved you, long ago:
> Love that hath no beginning hath no end.

The two possibilities, reincarnation and immediate absorption into the universal spirit, are set forth in *Michael Oaktree:*

> He had lived
> In absolute communion with the Power
> That rules all action and all tides of thought
> And all the secret courses of the stars . . . .
> So he gained
> On earth a foretaste of Nirvana, not
> The void of eastern dream, but the desire
> And goal of all of us, whether through lives
> Innumerable, by slow degrees, we near
> The death divine, or from the breaking body
> Of earthly death we flash at once to God.

Although Noyes here uses the nomenclature of religions, Buddhist and Christian, he is using the words to convey evolutionary ideas, as the same poem proves by the statement that God is the all-embracing principle of which the universe is but an illusory manifestation, in which every detail is equally important—or unimportant: those who have retained "their sense of membership in this divine Body of God" by walking in quiet communion with the universal life-spirit know that

> There is one God, one Love, one everlasting
> Mystery of Incarnation, one creative
> Passion behind the many-colored veil.

To this creative passion—the vital force, whatever it may be, which causes the phenomenon of evolution—Noyes applies the name of God.

In *The Paradox* he contrasts the old orthodox idea of a beneficent God with the modern pessimism which says that if there be a God he must be a malevolent one, "the supreme Evil," molding men of clay for a moment and then destroying them. The deity who is given a voice in the poem cannot be described by either term, since he is absolute: "Meeting and mingling in Me they become neither evil nor good." All the discords of human life are resolved into the universal harmony, "chiming like chords in a world-wide symphony"; to the omniscient mind of the Maker there is none of the diversity which appears to our finite senses. After explaining that he has assumed the manifold forms of the physical universe in order to manifest himself intelligibly to humanity, the Lord describes the spiritual evolution by which the individual gradually progresses toward identity with the Absolute. The evolution of new physical powers and senses is included in this ascent; all lives approach the single End "as unending asymptotes," the divine love having contrived for man "the glory of this forever." Life only "vanishes away from day to wider wealthier day," for "each new delight of sense" and each emotional experience "widens, relumes and recreates each sphere from a new ring and nimbus of pre-eminence." The drift of this farrago of abstruse phrases is Browning's notion of spiritual development through imperfection, specifically embodied in the Buddhistic system of advance through repeated incarnations toward ultimate union with the Absolute.

Noyes, like Watson, generally speaks of the law which controls the universe as a rhythm or harmony. In *Michael Oaktree* nature is "like one heavenly choir pealing one mystic music." *The Progress of Love* describes the music

> Through which the suns and moons and stars revolved
>   According to the song's divine decree,
> Till Time was but a tide of intervolved
>   And interweaving worlds of melody.

By this "immortal harmony which holds the warring worlds in one" the most trivial objects of the material world retain their significance in the general scheme of existence, "harmonizing with the Whole the temporal refrain." In short, the Hebraic concept of a conscious power creating the universe by a brief process of manufacture has been replaced by a concept of an all-pervading spirit which manifests itself in the apparent diversity of physical forms by means of a rhythmic principle.

Even in a poem ostensibly for children, *The Forest of Wild Thyme*, Noyes devotes an episode to the "universal rhythm and rhyme" as the basic principle of existence. He expatiates upon the fact that all our knowledge is relative to our limited senses, and that consequently the most minute forms of life are really equal in importance with the mightiest. Indeed, the theme of the whole poem is Tennyson's *Flower in the Crannied Wall*, elaborated into a fantastic search for the "tiniest flower" which shall reveal the secret of existence. "To make a rose," he says,

> It takes the world's eternal wars,
> It takes the moon and all the stars,
> It takes the might of heaven and hell
> And the everlasting love as well.

The same forces which shaped man and control his destiny were devoted to the development of every other natural object; and if their relation to any single organism could be comprehended, the mystery of life would be wholly solved.

At first acquaintance, the mysticism of Noyes seems to be far removed from scientific materialism. There are practically no direct references to the evolutionary hypothesis, except a brief passage in *The Progress of Love* which mentions the old bestial instincts still haunting the subconscious mind:

Cold incarnate memories
Of earth's retributory throes . . . .
Ancestral folds in darkness furled
Since the beginning of the world . . . .
That obscure heritage of foes . . . .
The ghostly worms . . . .

His recent poem *The Torchbearers*, it is true, deals extensively with the careers and achievements of scientists; but for their objective dramatic interest rather than for any philosophical implications. In his reflective poems he avoids reference to physical evolution, which Tennyson had vehemently debated and Watson had surveyed in concise panorama. It is not necessary for him to explain why he assumes an immanent creative principle instead of the personal God of the Old Testament; he can depend on his predecessors having made plain that a mystical faith is the only one reconcilable with modern science. By combining the electronic theory of matter and the evolutionary theory of form, Noyes gains his concept of God as the immanent force causing the action of these principles, and the universe as the result of them. In this system man is on a parity with the rest of nature; and as the poet is not prepared to surrender faith in the spiritual element in man, he must attribute it to the rest of nature also. He finds a convenient terminology in oriental mysticism, which makes all nature the "vestment of God" and the human spirit a temporarily isolated fragment of the divine essence, returning through successive incarnations toward identity with the Absolute. Two generations had sufficed

to develop this mystical evolutionary creed from a
tentative series of suggestions into an established belief. The close of *The Torchbearers* (1930) sums up the
implications of all modern science in strictly mystical terms: "the Eternal Logos . . . . breathed through
the Creation with His instant voice . . . . Now, and
forever, God makes heaven and earth."

RUDYARD KIPLING

With regard to the evolutionary theory and the religious debates resulting from it, Rudyard Kipling,
as might be expected, comes closer to reflecting the
popular mind than his poetic confrères do. Little concerned with philosophic discussions, he draws his material at will from the realms of both religion and science, without considering it his business to expatiate
upon their relationship or even to make his references
consistent. Both are important activities of the human mind, and as such both afford suitable material
for his objective treatment.

Toward the notion of man's development from the
lower forms of life he tends to be flippant, as in *The
Conundrum of the Workshops*, wherein he dismisses the
hypothesis in a single line, "We have learned to bottle
our parents twain in the yelk of an addled egg," proceeding in the rest of the poem to convey his argument
on aesthetics by the story of Adam and Eve. Nevertheless, the more recent stage of evolution—the earliest period of human emergence—has a fascination for
Kipling. In the opening poem of his first volume—the

General Summary prefixed to *Departmental Ditties*—
he speaks of "the semi-apes who ranged India's prehistoric clay," and sketches the struggle for survival
in those times, when primitive man "met the Mammoth face to face," stole his neighbor's canoe, and
"scratched the reindeer bone." *The Story of Ung* and
In the Neolithic Age likewise give pictures of life "in
that dim red dawn of man"—the "savage warfare for
food and fame and woolly horses' pelt," the force of
"the piled Biscayan ice-pack," the aurochs, the saber-
toothed tiger, the "mountainous mammoth," the
"berg-battered beaches" and "boulder-hatched hill
. . . . by the caves of the lost Dordogne." Again, the
prehistoric configuration of Europe, and its fauna, as
revealed by geological study, appear in *The River's
Tale:*

> I'd have you know that these waters of mine
> Were once a branch of the River Rhine,
> When hundreds of miles to the East I went
> And England was joined to the Continent.
>
> I remember the bat-winged lizard-birds,
> The Age of Ice and the mammoth herds,
> And the giant tigers that stalked them down
> Through Regent's Park into Camden Town.

There follows a description of the "earliest Cockney"
and his primitive culture.

A similar venture into the prehistoric, but with
clearer indications of evolutionary processes, is *The
King*, which describes the development of culture
from the most elementary stage. The Cavemen la-

ment the departure of Romance "with bone well-carved," since their own arrowheads are ignobly armed with flint and their spears tipped with jasper; and the Lake-folk in turn feel that Romance remains in "the caverns of the mountain side" and "scorns our hutted piers." Another sketch of cultural progress, with emphasis on the fact that it is enforced by the stern necessity of the struggle for survival, is given in *The Benefactors:*

> When in this world's unpleasing youth
> Our god-like race began,
> The longest arm, the sharpest tooth,
> Gave man control of man;
>
> Till, bruised and bitten to the bone
> And taught by pain and fear,
> He learned to deal the far-off stone,
> And poke the long safe spear.
>
> So tooth and nail were obsolete
> As means against a foe,
> Till, bored by uniform defeat,
> Some genius built the bow.

Two other poems dealing with the earliest acquisition of culture by the human animal are *The First Chantey*, describing man's beginning of seafaring when a fleeing savage escaped on a floating log, and the *Song of The Men's Side*, showing how the introduction of the knife relieved ancient man of his subjection to the power of wild beasts. The anthropological data upon which all these poems are based are tantamount to acceptance of the evolutionary theory.

Further back than this latest stage of evolution—
the development of human culture and intellect from
the sheer animality of "semi-apes"—Kipling seldom
ventures. Even the popular impression that the theory signifies man's kinship with the monkeys appears
only in a jocose form, as in *The Legends of Evil*, wherein the apologue of the monkeys who were deprived of
their tails and doomed to labor is told in a manner
which clearly alludes to the Darwinian theory. It
would be injudicious to do more than point out that
this poem does not refer to the tailless race as de-
scendents of the monkeys, but as their "fathers"—
i.e., representatives of an anterior parent race.
Whether any subtle scientific point is being conveyed
cannot be affirmed on the basis of so allusive and
frivolous a poem.

It is only in two or three of his later and more reflective poems that Kipling touches on the philosophic
implications of the theory instead of its picturesque
aspects. *Cities and Thrones and Powers* is an exposition of the transience of all man's achievements, reminiscent of Hardy. It recalls Meredith also, however,
in its reference to the endless recurrence of all vital
activity: as the daffodil each year confidently enters
upon its brief existence, so every human achievement
springs out of the fundamental natural forces that
propagate all life:

. . . . as new buds put forth
To glad new men,
Out of the spent and unconsidered Earth
The Cities rise again.

Arguing from the analogy of this "economy of nature," he concludes *The Sack of the Gods* with an expression of belief in the recurrence of the soul through successive incarnations:

They will come back—come back again, as long as the red Earth rolls.
He never wasted a leaf or a tree. Do you think He would squander souls?

Strong interest in the idea of reincarnation appears also in his later short stories, such as *The Finest Story in the World*.

Such lines show that Kipling belongs to the same era as Tennyson and Meredith and William Watson; but discussion of their problems does not come within his natural scope. Possibly personal conviction is not wholly absent from *The Prayer of Miriam Cohen*, wherein God is besought to refrain from revealing the guiding scheme of the universe:

Thy Path, Thy Purposes conceal
From our beleaguered realm,
Lest any shattering whisper steal
Upon us and o'erwhelm.

Whether this expresses Kipling's own view or not, it certainly accords with that of a number of the twentieth-century poets.

In one respect, however, Kipling's contact with the evolutionary idea shows itself clearly, and that is in his attitude toward religion, and specifically toward Old Testament cosmology. Although his style and imagery are saturated with those of the Authorized

Version, and he uses the Genesis creation story quite as frequently as he uses scientific data on the Neolithic age, yet his use of the anthropomorphic God has a familiarity that to earlier generations would have seemed irreverent. *The Last Chantey* is positively facetious in tone, but Kipling is able to describe the dialogue of the Lord and the "jolly, jolly mariners" without offense, for under the influence of science and higher criticism the scriptural material has ceased to be isolated and sanctified; it can appear on common ground with the rest of the race's imaginative heritage, save that it retains a particular impressiveness by reason of its connotations. Whether in *The Last Chantey* or in a more dignified poem like *The Return of the Children*, the poet uses the anthropomorphic symbolism with intentional fantasy, and the reader unconsciously accepts it in the same light.

As though to enforce this revaluation of the scriptures, Kipling has in three distinct instances written pairs of complementary poems, both poems of each pair treating the same topic, but one in the terminology of science, the other in that of religion. *The First Chantey* describes primitive man's discovery of seafaring, and *The Last Chantey* describes the Lord's final judgment on the ocean which he had created. The first of *The Legends of Evil* ascribes man's unhappiness to the acceptance of cultural evolution by the original anthropoid, while the second ascribes it to the devil's unfortunate admittance into the Ark. *The Story of Ung* recounts the origin of art in the snow-images and bone-scrivings of primitive man, *The Conundrum of the Workshops* offers an alternative theory:

When the flush of a new-born sun first fell on Eden's green and
    gold,
  Our father Adam sat under a tree and scratched with a stick
    in the mould.

In these pairs of companion-poems Kipling is testing the comparative value of science and religion for picturesque effect. Unconcerned with the actual truth of either one, he treats both as imaginative concepts. His acceptance of the scientific material has inevitably modified his treatment of the religious traditions, but his adherence to the latter has caused him to regard the scientific pretensions with levity and disrespect:

We have learned to whittle the Eden Tree to the shape of a
    surplice peg,
We have learned to bottle our parents twain in the yelk of an
    addled egg.

Neither Darwin nor the book of Genesis having really explained the mystery of existence, both are important only in so far as they stir the imagination. Kipling accepts from the scientist the dictum that man is by instinct anthropomorphic, and exemplifies it in *Evarra and His Gods;* he deduces therefrom an argument in favor of tolerance, as expressed in *Buddha at Kamakura* with its significant conclusion: "Is God in human image made no nearer than Kamakura?" and in this mood of tolerance he admits not only all re-

ligions as legitimate expressions of human instinct—
as in the ideal eclecticism of *The Mother Lodge*—but
scientific theories also. He resembles the senior poets
of his era in that he accepts both religion and science
as equally valid; but he effects the compromise more
easily than they, by declining to champion the compatibility. He is able to enjoy the phenomena of nature without discussing theories of first-causes, and
when he comes to the theories he is content to include
them all, as manifestations of the human spirit.

JOHN MASEFIELD

In their various ways, Watson and Noyes and Kipling all represent tacit acceptance of the evolutionary
principle. John Masefield, on the other hand, insists
on reconsidering the whole problem for himself, and
discarding any interpretations that have been offered
to him by others. He seeks in real anguish of spirit for
a solution in which the scientific and the supernatural
can be affiliated.

His earlier poems (*ca.* 1903) are entirely objective,
pictures of the sea and seamen with no tendency toward reflection. One would not hesitate to ascribe to
the poet the outlook which he utters in *Vagabond:*

> An' why I live, an' why the old world spins,
> Are things I never knowed.

After his seafaring, however, he became associated in
London with a group of mystics devoted to the propa-
gation of eastern occultism, a group which included
Yeats and other members of the Celtic revival. In

Biography (1911) Masefield describes the life centered about discussions

> Under strange pictures of the wakened soul
> To whom this earth was but a burnt-out coal.

In those eager debates there was no doubt of the spiritual importance of man, the supremacy of intuition as opposed to reason:

> Those glittering moments that a spirit lends
> That all may be imagined from the flash,
> The cloud-hid god-game through the lightning gash.

They looked forward to great spiritual developments still in the future, "the forts of human light not yet assailed." Under such influence he believed firmly in the spiritual evolution which proceeds unrecognized under the surface of physical life. The opening of *Biography* echoes the opening of *In Memoriam* in declaring that dead selves are cast off as the soul climbs by means of its moments of intuition:

> Men do not heed the rungs by which men climb
> Those glittering steps, those milestones upon Time,
> Those tombstones of dead selves, those hours of birth,
> Those moments of the soul in years of earth.

He did not stop, however, at this general belief in spiritual progress. A leading tenet of his circle was reincarnation, wherein the soul goes through an evolution parallel with that of the body, with accumulated experience from past lives corresponding to the hereditary traits by which the body is molded. Masefield wholly accepted this doctrine in *A Creed* (1911):

> I hold that when a person dies
> His soul returns again to earth:
> Arrayed in some new flesh-disguise
> Another mother gives him birth.
> With sturdier limbs and brighter brain
> The old soul takes the road again.

The poem expounds how all one's good or evil actions are "curse or blessing justly due for sloth or effort in the past," life being shaped by "vice indulged or overcome," and the ultimate goal of "this long war beneath the stars," after its achievements and its setbacks, being the transmutation of "this clogging mould," the body, into "kingly gold." In the same vein, he says in *Twilight*, "I know that death cannot last"; and in *The Word:*

> And may we find, when ended is the page,
> Death but a tavern on our pilgrimage.

The equally mystical idea of Watson and Noyes that the creative process is a conjuncture of rhythm and joy appears in *Laugh and Be Merry:*

> remember, in olden time,
> God made Heaven and Earth for joy He took in a rhyme,
> Made them, and filled them full of the strong red wine of His mirth,
> The splendid joy of the stars, the joy of the earth.

Before long, however, Masefield began to express a more modified metaphysic, less derivative and more indicative of personal cogitation. The poem *Truth* expresses no certainty in any survival after death except that of a man's vision of truth, "in which his soul may sail" when it "goes out alone on seas unknown,"

when death has taken toll of all other human attributes. At the end of *Fragments* this immortal vision
is identified with imaginative creation:

> The dream that fires man's heart to make,
> To build, to do, to sing or say
> A beauty Death can never take,
> An Adam from the crumbled clay.

The cautious "perhaps" and "may" with which the
poem *Truth* qualified its references to immortality, as
contrasted with the confidence of *A Creed*, were the
first indication of a growing concern with the whole
question of science and faith. The *Sonnets*, published
in 1915, and others logically sequential in later volumes, form an extensive and impassioned debate of
the problem. The whole group is reminiscent of *In
Memoriam* in being a loosely connected, and often
contradictory, series of poems centering on the conflicting opinions of evolutionary science and metaphysical faith concerning the question of human
origins and destiny. His impulse toward accepting intuitive belief in a spiritual principle is tempered not
only by his rational interest in scientific facts but also
by a prevalent melancholy which tends to dwell on
the brevity of life, the cruelty of chance, and the
physical dissolution of the body, in the vein of Hardy
and Housman.

His basic idea is an identification of the world-soul
with the beauty of all phenomena and of the individual soul with the imagination which appreciates it.
The sonnets are devoted to debating whether these

have any objective existence, and, if not, what element in the human being, unexplained by the scientists, produces the illusion. The only possible clue is within one's self; "here in the self, which withers like a flower . . . . in the flesh, the never-yet explored," is "Beauty herself"; and he succinctly shows that Beauty to him is synonymous with all terms for spiritual forces, by mentioning "the god, the holy ghost, the atoning lord" of the orthodox trinitarians, "the universal mind" of the pantheists, and the "Eternal April" of the believers in Nature's creative force. By diligent introspection he has sought to discover whether the elusive intuition of beauty is an external inspiration—"the unfeeling mud stabbed by a ray cast by an unseen splendor's great advance"—or a subconscious physical process—the glory gathering "crumb by crumb unseen, within." In any case, he is certain that the occasional moments of vision are the only significant events of life.

In describing the burial and decay of the body and the rapid fading of the "sense or wraith or essence" which survives in the memories of friends, he draws an analogy with the gradual extinction of a great heavenly body; and as the latter is really a cycle of recurrent life, since the dead sun eventually, by collision with another, produces a new active star, so it is possible that the soul survives, finding "some new delight of living without limbs," or else that "the million cells of sense" proceed to "some joy of changed experience, weight in the earth or glory in the grass"; but all this is conjecture, and even if death is total extinction, "life is a miracle." He examines the scientific definition of the body, and finds mysterious not only the existence of consciousness and intuition but also the functioning of the vital processes:

> What am I, Life? A thing of watery salt
> Held in cohesion by unresting cells,
> Which work, they know not why, which never halt,
> Myself unwitting where their Master dwells.
> I do not bid them, yet they toil, they spin;
> A world which uses me as I use them,
> Nor do I know which end or which begin,
> Nor which to praise, which pamper, which condemn.

This is the entity—"this myriad I"—which responds to beauty. If one could penetrate to the identity dwelling within the cells of the body, the soul might be discovered:

> If I could get within this changing I,
> This ever altering thing which yet persists,
> Keeping the features it is reckoned by
> While each component atom breaks or twists,
> If, wandering past strange groups of shifting forms,
> Cells at their hidden marvels hard at work,
> Pale from much toil, or red from sudden storms,
> I might attain to where the Rulers lurk,
> If, pressing past the guards of those gray gates,
> The brain's most folded intertwisted shell,
> I might attain to that which alters fates,
> The King, the supreme self, the Master Cell,
> Then, on Man's earthly peak, I might behold
> The unearthly self beyond, unguessed, untold.

Why, then, should "this atom which contains the whole, this which imagined God and is the soul" re-

quire such a wasteful, clumsy, and destructible instru-
ment as the body, unless its concerns are mainly
earthly? If it is a heavenly thing, why has it "such
heavy chains of sense"; if earthly, why such unrest
and discontent with clay? It must partake of both:
"we are neither heaven nor earth, but men—something that uses and despises both," transitional creatures who cannot enjoy the beauty of the rose without
thinking that it is imbedded in the vanished beauty
of past ages and will soon give place to future
growths. All these generations of beauty, touched by
"some leap of human brains," combine to form the
spirit of beauty providing the only true and lasting
faith—"the earth, the living church of ancient joy."
Man's power of imagination that links him with the
world-spirit is responsible for his evolution:

> O little self, within whose smallness lies
> All that man was, and is, and will become.

The poet's intuitive sense of an external spirit of
beauty corresponding to his soul becomes clearly pantheistic:

> all the summer flowers
> Were only glimpses of your starry powers,
> Beautiful and inspired dust they were.

But when he attempts to analyze, the spirit fades
from his vision.

Turning from physiology to the history of evolution, Masefield in five sonnets considers separately
the animal and vegetable forms. In the former he is
primarily impressed by the essential cruelty of the

struggle for survival, the ruthless pursuit of food, always entailing death for the prey:

> Restless and hungry, still it moves and slays
> Feeding its beauty on dead beauty's bones,
> Most merciless in all its million ways,
> Its breath for singing bought by dying groans.

From this voracious type the greedy human mind was eventually evolved:

> Roving so far with such a zest to kill
> (Its strongness adding hunger) that at last
> It cells attained beyond the cruel skill
> To where life's earliest impulses are past.
> Then this creation of the linkéd lusts
> To move and eat, still under their control,
> Hunts for his prey in thought, his thinking thrusts
> Through the untrodden jungle of the soul.

The quarry of the intellectual hunt is the reality of the external spiritual force—"to prove the Thing Within a Thing Without"—and repeatedly the searcher is baffled to find "the imagined godhead but a form of thought."

Turning to the other form of life, Masefield describes the great power of Will in the seed which enables it to take root, draw sustenance from the earth, and expand into tree or flower. He cannot decide whether in the vegetable kingdom the same ruthless struggle prevails; perhaps there is a communal instinct—a "great green commonwealth of thought"—determining the precedence of growth "by secret stir which in each plant abides,"

> Or is it, as with us, unresting strife,
> With each consent a lucky gasp for life?

He proceeds to the latest stage of human development, the discarding of belief in external, personal
gods. But even when declaring that "there is no God,
as I was taught in youth," Masefield perceives that
man's instinct to see a spiritual first-cause will not be
thwarted: "each according to his stature builds some
covered shrine for what he thinks the truth"; and
he concludes "we are God ourselves and touch God
everywhere." On this pantheism he affirms more
positively his faith in immortality; the body withers,
but "his life renews in Aprils of the soul," surviving in
the general store of universal beauty:

> Wherever beauty has been quick in clay
> Some effluence of it lives, a spirit dwells,
> Beauty that death can never take away,
> Mixed with the air that shakes the flower bells.

This spirit of beauty is the determining factor of
progress:

> Having all art, all science, all control
> Over the still-unsmithied, even as Time
> Cradles the generations of man's soul,
> You are the light to guide, the way to climb.

In a more pessimistic mood, he contrasts man's
puny interests, recurrent through endless generations,
with the rare intuitive gleams that are his only lasting
contribution to the world-soul: countless bodies have
rotted back into the soil, who "hated, fought and
killed as separate men," and all their efforts are
merged in the "gleam" which is their sole survival.

He protests passionately against the fatalism, inspired by science, which sees man helpless amid physical forces that use his emotions for furthering natural processes:

> If all be governed by the moving stars . . . .
> We are but pawns, ignobler than the grass
> Cropped by the beast and crunched and tossed aside.
> Is all this beauty that does inhabit heaven
> Trail of a planet's fire? Is all this lust
> A chymic means by warring stars contriven
> To bring the violets out of Caesar's dust?
> Better be grass, or in some hedge unknown
> The spilling rose whose beauty is its own.

In contrast with these debasing implications of modern science, he sketches also the dignity of human evolution, envisaging the occasional visits of a wandering planet as a possible influence, which

> made (men) stand erect and bade them build
> Nobler than hovels plaited in the mire,
> Gave them an altar and a god to gild,
> Bridled the brooks for them and fettered fire;
> And in another coming forged the steel
> Which, on life's scarlet wax, forever set
> Longing for beauty bitten as a seal
> That blood not clogs nor centuries forget,
> That built Atlantis, and in time will raise
> That grander thing whose image haunts our days.

In the concluding sonnets of the series he reiterates his one constant belief in the spirit of beauty as the animating force of all phenomena, "all fire, all living form, marvel in man and glory in the worm." He reviews the various possibilities that may follow death —extinction, rebirth, conscious survival, or union with the universal beauty. The final sonnet utters no de-

cision; whatever may come, ephemeral life is to be
enjoyed, the generations continue, and whether the
sequel be death or change, good or evil, "we cannot
tell."

No greater certainty is expressed in the further
sonnets and other short poems in later volumes. He is
familiar with all the current suggestions regarding the
origin of the universe:

> What was the Mind? was it a mind which thought?
> Or chance? or law? or conscious law? or Power?
> Or a vast balance by vast clashes wrought?
> Or Time at trial with Matter for an hour?
> Or is it all a body where the cells
> Are living things supporting something strange
> Whose mighty heart the singing planet swells
> As it shoulders nothing in unending change?
> Is this green earth of many-peopled pain
> Part of a life, a cell within a brain?

He can only conclude, "It may be so, but let the unknown be"; and later he reaches a similar conclusion
on the question, "What is this life which uses living
cells it knows not how nor why?" The soul is not an
external endowment but a congenital attribute; is it
therefore only a physical activity?

> It comes not from without, but from the sperm
> Fed in the womb, it is a man-made thing,
> That takes from man its power to live a term
> Served by live cells of which it is the King.
> Can it be blood and brain? It is most great,
> Through blood and brain alone it wrestles Fate.

Rather, "blood and brain are its imperfect tools"
which merely hamper it; the imagination, which is

apparently independent of the physical medium, is the "finer power" which can catch glimpses of the world-soul through the beauty of phenomena. His typical point of view is summarized in the poem called *The Passing Strange* (1920); of seventy-two lines, fifty-one are devoted to a mournful survey of human life,

> Perpetual in perpetual change
> The unknown passing through the strange.

The impermanence of the body, the transience of beauty and joy and effort, the aimless cruelty of human beings, all are included, pointing to the logical conclusion that there is neither progress nor survival. At the close, however, he points out that the spirit, like the cock at midnight, "crows from trust that death will change because it must"; the analogy of all nature suggests that there is endless change but no extinction; and anyone who keenly enjoys the physical life leaves his joy to hearten those who come after him.

The obstinate questionings of Masefield reveal the plight of one who tries to correlate the modern points of view. In the physical world he wholly accepts the evolutionary process and the biological and physiological facts attendant thereon. Like Hardy, Housman, Brooke, and their clan, he sees the pathetic brevity of life, and intensely feels the beauty of material phenomena. Not satisfied, however, with melancholy resignation, he seeks, as Tennyson did, the first-cause underlying the universe and the spiritual quality in man. From the evidence, he cannot proceed beyond agnosticism, but his mystical tendency will not be curbed. On his instinctive sense of beauty he bases a pantheistic creed, but it is proposed tentatively, with many qualms as his reason interposes queries. He cannot rise above a temperate and admittedly unverified hope for some kind of spiritual survival and racial progress dependent on the intuition of beauty. His methods are like Tennyson's; but his mood is that of the twentieth century, aesthetic where his predecessors were moral, wistful and harassed where they were confident. Reason and faith are at stalemate.

ROBERT BRIDGES

Although chronologically of the generation of Thomas Hardy, Robert Bridges requires consideration among the living poets, and as the last of them, because his poetic discussion of science and faith did not come until after the younger men had their say and because its widespread acceptance suggests that it accords with the current interest. Having been a physician by profession, Bridges must have been fully acquainted with modern scientific tenets, but most of his poetry was of classic or lyric or pastoral types in which philosophizing did not enter. In *Prometheus the Firegiver* (1883) there are clear evolutionary implications throughout the representation of the man who defied the tyranny of a traditional god and

apotheosized the cause of human progress; and
Prometheus narrates the development of the earth in
terms more scientific than mythological:

> The heaven and earth thou seest, for long were held
> By Fire, a raging power, to whom the Fates
> Decreed a slow diminishing old age. . . . .
> . . . . Forests of fire
> Whose waving trunks, sucking their fuel, reared
> In branched flame roaring, and their torrid shades
> Aye underlit with fire. The mountains lifted
> And fell and followed like a running sea,
> And from their swelling flanks spumed froth of fire;
> Or, like awakening monsters, mighty mounds
> Rose on the plain awhile . . . .
> The waters first Air brought, that in their streams
> And pools and seas innumerable things
> Brought forth, from whence she drew the fertile seeds
> Of trees and plants, and last of footed life.

In all this process, the shaping spirit of Air was counseled by Reason, and he completed the creation for
her by making man, "the best of all."

The bulk of Bridges' poetry shows no tendency to
analyze the relationship of religion and science. The
references to God sound orthodox enough, and the
general outlook is optimistic, as in *January:*

> And God the Maker doth my heart grow bold
> To praise for wintry works not understood,
> Who all the worlds and ages doth behold,
> Evil and good as one, and all as good.

This does not mean, however, that modern scientific
concepts are ignored. The first epistle in classical
prosody, entitled *Winter Delights* and published in
1903, gives a detailed and enthusiastic survey of the
whole scope of science. Although declaring himself to

"lack the wizard Darwin's scientific insight," he shows intimate familiarity with his theme. First comes geology:

Time's rich hieroglyph, with vast elemental pencil
Scor'd upon Earth's rocky crust,—minute shells slowly collecting
Press'd to a stone, uprais'd to a mountain, again to a fine sand
Worn, burying the remains of an alien organic epoch,
In the flat accretions of new sedimentary strata;
All to be crush'd, crumpled, confused, contorted, abandon'd,
Broke, as a child's puzzle is, to be recompos'd with attention.

These "very vestiges of creation," he says, are "the only commandments by God's finger of old inscribed on table of earth-stone."

Next comes astronomy, with the contrast of all human ambition for conquest with the "utter wilderness of unlimited space," and yet the power of the human mind to measure and map the universe, the triumph of Bessel in discovering Procyon and of Adams and Leverrier in discovering Neptune. Equally vivid pictures are given of the achievements of physics in computing the speed of light, using the spectroscope, and reducing to mathematical formulas "all force and all motion of all matter." Anyone who neglects these sciences, says Bridges, "is but a boor as truly ridiculous as the village clown" who thinks that the sun moves around the earth. The poet does not expect to comprehend first-causes through scientific research, but he insists that the fullest possible study of physical phenomena is the duty as well as the pleasure of self-respecting minds.

For a moment he confesses a sense of futility in face of Nature's vastitude, wastefulness, and unconcern toward the human race; but soon he decides that, since man is the highest work of Nature, "he wrongs himself to imagine his soul foe to her aim, or from her sanction an outlaw." The greatest achievement of the modern era, to Bridges, is the "new science of Man, from dreamy scholastic imprisoning set free," and based solely on physical law. He sketches the field of anthropology, remarking the paradox that we should turn to our most primitive ancestors in order to comprehend modern civilized beings. Then he goes on to surgery with its discovery of antiseptics and to medicine with its epochal strides in bacteriology.

Admitting that his generation has overstressed Nature at the expense of other human interests, he refuses to believe that spiritual Grace is doomed. Science has merely "exposed the rotten foundation of old superstition," and all the theologians "are thrown to the limbo of antediluvian idols,"

Only because we learn mankind's true history, and know
That not at all from a high perfection sinfully man fell,
But from baseness arose: We have with sympathy enter'd
Those dark caves, his joyless abodes, where with ravening brutes,
Bear or filthy hyena, he once disputed a shelter:—
That was his Paradise, his garden of Eden,—abandon'd
Ages since to the drift and drip, the cementing accretions
Whence we now separate his bones buried in the stalagma.

Bridges declares that he finds the highest inspiration in the evolutionary record,

this tale primæval of unsung,
Unwritten, ancestral fate and adversity, this siege
Of courage and happiness protracted so many thousand

Thousand years in a slow persistent victory of brain
And right hand o'er all the venom'd stings, sharpnesses of fang
And dread fury whate'er Nature, tirelessly devising,
Could develop with tooth, claw, tusk, or horn to oppose them.

Touching upon the development of religion, he begins
to suggest that it is a manifestation of man's aesthetic
sense, but breaks off with " 'tis an unsolved mystery."
We cannot judge Nature by our standards of good
and bad, beauty and ugliness; human achievements
in the arts seem so superior to the confusions and
abominations of Nature that she might feel ashamed,
were she not able to retort, "Fool, and who made
thee?" Thus ends what may be called the first real
poem of modern science, since it is the first by a man
equally trained as a scientist and a poet.

The companion epistle, *To a Socialist in London*,
applies the same evolutionary principles to the social
sciences. Bridges has no faith in the utopian vision of
social equality because it violates the law of the survival of the fittest. He assumes that our mental limitations prevent us from being able to formulate absolute ethical laws, and furthermore sees logical fallacies
in communism. He cites first the Malthusian doctrine that the world would become overpopulated,
and then goes on to portray vividly the "merciless
outrage" of destruction throughout the whole range
of living creatures:

Ah! what if all and each of Nature's favorite offspring,
'Mong many distinctions, have this portentous agreement,
MOUTH, STOMACH, INTESTINE? Question that brute apparatus,
So manifoldly devis'd, set alert with furious instinct:

What doth it interpret but this, that LIFE LIVETH ON LIFE?
That the select creatures, who inherit earth's domination,
Whose happy existence is Nature's intelligent smile,
Are bloody survivors of a mortal combat, a-tweenwhiles
Chanting a brief paean for victory on the battlefield?
Since that of all their kinds most owe their prosperous estate
Unto the art, whereby they more successfully destroy'd
Their weaker brethren, more insatiably devour'd them;
And all fine qualities, their forms pictorial, admired,
Their symmetries, their grace, and beauty, the loveliness of them,
Were by Murder evolv'd, to 'scape from it or to effect it.

To the argument that this view would produce "mere horror and despair" unless one believes that the human being is exempt from this principle by virtue of his moral ideals, Bridges retorts that the love of sport and of warfare reveals the principle still at work. The remainder of the poem insists on the permanence and value of the human love for pleasure and luxury and rank, without which life would be miserable and hopeless.

A third poem of the same period is equally significant, the one addressed *To Robert Burns*, with the subtitle *An Epistle on Instinct*. Bridges declares that "rakel Chance and Fortune blind" would have led man to destruction through the sway of sensual passion, had not Eternal Mind led him "by strait selection of pleasurable ways, to find severe perfection." Nature ruled that pleasure "should attend on every act that doth amend our soul's condition."

> Beasts that inherited delight
> In what promoted health or might,
> Survived their cousins in the fight.

Accordingly, when human reason developed, "the gains of agelong inscience" were merely sublimated into "moral conscience." Man retains the three primeval instincts—racial, self-preservative, and social—the first being the strongest, since it is essential for the survival of the species—avoided by art, unmentionable in common speech, yet tamed by reason "into a sacramental flame of consecration." We owe much to "our humble cave-folk ancestry" who, through "those hundred thousand years of budding soul," founded "the ideal bases of art and morals." Since they did not analyze philosophically, they were "saved from doubts that wreck the Will with pale paralysis." It is a waste of time for us to debate "Is Good or Pleasure our pursuit?" for instinct has determined that we shall find pleasure in doing what is good for us.

More than a quarter of a century later, Bridges expanded the ideas of these three epistles into *The Testament of Beauty*, and picked up the broken thread of the first one with regard to the aesthetic basis of faith. Many of the selfsame arguments appear, such as the praise of wine, the justification of war as inherent in progress, and the parable of the bees as proof of the stultifying effects of communism. Fundamentally, however, it resembles the earlier poems in being based solidly on the whole cycle of modern science. Bridges draws his ideas and examples, not only from astronomy, chemistry, and physics, but from the latest theories of embryology, eugenics, and psychology. He refers to Coué and Freud, is glib regarding the "mutual inexhaustible interchange of transmitted genes," and devotes most of his third book to the analysis of sex.

In particular, *The Testament of Beauty* elaborates the idea of the epistle *To Robert Burns*, that all human existence depends on the primeval instincts, which are now reduced to two, selfhood and breed, otherwise self-preservation and reproduction. The whole poem is devoted to showing how these instincts instigated evolution and still control all conduct, though now somewhat sublimated into less material forms. He shows in detail how the instinct of reproduction has the same relationship to the race as that of self-preservation has to the individual, and how it grew out of the other by means of the pack-organization for offense and defense. He insists that human reason is the direct outcome of these instincts, and that now the next step is the development of spiritual perceptions under the influence of the love of beauty. There is nothing of Masefield's mysticism involved here; spiritual beauty is, to Bridges, identical with that which causes attraction between the sexes.

He does not, however, counsel surrender to the brute impulses. They all can be degraded into mere self-indulgence, but the result of it is bound to be destruction, while the austerer type survives. Thus a severely practical and utterly evolutionary code of ethics is created: good conduct is that which betters the species, and duty and conscience are equivalent to the law of nature, the necessity of survival. The

key-word of the poem is "reason," and reason is nowise disparate from the "animal senses," since it
grew directly from them; specifically, reason is the
sublimation of the elder instinct, selfhood, while the
sense of beauty is the sublimation of the younger,
breed. He sees all nature as consistent, through the
four stages "atomic, organic, sensuous, and self-con-
scient," and man therefore as an integral part,
shaped by heredity and environment, akin to all the
prior stages.

Permeated though the poem is with scientific
thought, it is equally permeated with religious feeling.
All natural processes are referred back to the will of
God, and all the moral doctrines are supported by the
teachings of Christ. Bridges repeatedly declares that
science does not reveal first-causes, and that lack of
faith induces a despair which is inimical to evolution.
He dismisses the evidences of cruelty in nature as
examples of the folly of applying our human standards beyond their scope. Reason and spiritual perception, he insists, ought to co-operate; and invisible
influences, something like Plato's Ideas, are the most
potent forces in existence.

Thus Bridges accomplished at last what the poets
had been striving for during almost a century. He
wrote a poem in which all the tenets of evolutionary
science, including its very latest applications, were
fully and authoritatively accepted, and yet he har-
monized them with idealistic and spiritual faith such
as poets seem determined to retain.

CONCLUSION

The study of how the Darwinian hypothesis affected the poetic mind has been complicated by its far-
reaching ramifications. In part, the evolutionary theory was responsible for the religious and philosophical
disturbances of the period; in part, they brought pres-
sure from other sources to bear on the interpretation
of it. Then, so many of the modern physical and biological sciences are immediate offshoots of evolution
that their influence on the poets could not be disso-
ciated from that of the parent theory. Conversely,
the Darwinian theory was itself a synthesis of anterior
ideas with which the poets were partly acquainted.
The Origin of Species, however, both for the special-
ists and the general public, formed the focal point of
the whole development; and around it the whole
furore swirled—rationalists championing it, ecclesiasts condemning it, poets scrambling for a compromise or a new creed.

Trying to represent the new principle as the method
of God's creative activity, Tennyson and Browning
proffered a rather vague deity of love and foresight,
which was widely accepted, but which satisfied neither the melancholy agnosticism of Arnold and
Clough nor the egregious paganism of Swinburne.
Then came Meredith and Hardy, recognizing that the
terminology of the old supernaturalism could not be
remodeled to fit new concepts. The former, instinctively positive and virile, saw in the development of
life from primordial matter a law of earth acting toward a beneficent end and using men as its instru-

ments for progress; the latter, instinctively negative
and sensitive, saw in the same phenomenon an Immanent Will blindly and aimlessly obeying its urgent
need to appear in changing forms. Both poets based
their schemes on the evolutionary law of natural selection and the survival of the fittest, but Meredith
saw the struggle as glorious and progressive, Hardy
saw it as wanton and ineffectual.

Tired of the philosophic debates of all these seniors,
most of the poets of the early twentieth century regarded the topic with disfavor. They derived from it
only a general impression of the transience of physical
life, the uncertainty of any spiritual existence, and the
dignity of the race's undaunted adherence to unsub-
stantiated ideals. A few retired into a mysticism
which disdained the physical world entirely. Between
the two extremes stood two or three who maintained
the effort to establish an acceptable compromise between physical and spiritual.

In the *Sonnets* of Masefield, however, and *The
Testament of Beauty* of Bridges, the philosophizing
reappears. A new stage has been reached in the process of assimilation; it is neither the distrustful experiments of Tennyson and Browning nor the enthusiastic discipleship of Meredith and Hardy, but a tacit
acceptance on which the foundations of a new creed
of beauty and spiritual insight are apparently being
laid. Now that Darwin has been enshrined among the
saints in Dr. Fosdick's new church, it is fitting that
we should recognize his similar eventual acceptance
by the poets.

BIBLIOGRAPHY

CHAPTER I

ARBUTHNOT, JOHN. *Works,* edited by G. A. Aitkin. Oxford, 1892.

ARNOLD, MATTHEW. *Poetical Works.* London, 1890.

——. *Literature and Dogma.* London, 1873.

BEDDOES, THOMAS LOVELL. *Poems.* "Muses Library." 1907.

BYRON, GEORGE GORDON, LORD. *Poetical Works,* Oxford edition. 1916.

CARLYLE, THOMAS. *Heroes and Hero Worship.* London, 1872.

CHALMERS, ALEXANDER (ed.). *Works of the English Poets,* Vol. XVII. London, 1810.

CHAMBERS, ROBERT. *Vestiges of the Natural History of Creation.* New York, 1854.

COLERIDGE, SAMUEL TAYLOR. *Literary Remains.* New York, 1854.

——. *Poems,* Oxford edition. 1912.

DARWIN, CHARLES. *The Origin of Species.* London, 1859.

——. *The Descent of Man.* London, 1871.

DARWIN, ERASMUS. *Poetical Works.* London, 1806.

DELAGE, IVES, and GOLDSMITH, MARIE. *The Theories of Evolution,* translated by André Tridon. New York, 1912.

DE LA MARE, WALTER. *Collected Poems.* New York, 1920.

DRYDEN, JOHN. *Poems,* Oxford edition. 1910.

DUNCAN, CARSON S. *The New Science and English Poetry in the Classical Age.* Menasha, Wisconsin, 1913.

EUCKEN, RUDOLPH. *Main Currents of Modern Thought,* translated by Meyrick Booth. London, 1912.

GOETHE, J. W. *Faust,* translated and edited by A. G. Latham, "Everyman's Library." 1908.

HAZLITT, WILLIAM. *Lectures on the English Poets.* London, 1902.

HUNT, LEIGH. *Men, Women, and Books.* New York, 1847.

LUCRETIUS. *De Rerum Natura,* translated by H. A. J. Munro. Cambridge, England, 1873.

MILTON, JOHN. *Poetical Works*, Oxford edition. 1900.

ORCHARD, THOMAS N. *Milton's Astronomy*. London, 1913.

OSBORN, HENRY FAIRFIELD. *From the Greeks to Darwin*. New York, 1894.

POPE, ALEXANDER. *Poetical Works*. London, 1875.

POTTER, G. R. *Evolutionary Ideas in English Poetry Prior to 1830*, Harvard dissertation (unpublished).

RICKWOOD, EDGELL. "Thomas Lovell Beddoes," in London *Mercury*, IX (1923), 162.

SHAW, GEORGE BERNARD. Introduction to *Back to Methuselah*. New York, 1921.

SPENCER, HERBERT. *First Principles*, 6th ed. London, 1900.

SWINBURNE, ALGERNON CHARLES. *Poems*, Vol. II. London, 1905.

WELLS, H. G. *The World of William Clissold*. New York, 1926.

WORDSWORTH, WILLIAM. *Poetical Works*, Oxford edition. 1910.

CHAPTER II

The Works of Tennyson, edited by Hallam, Lord Tennyson. London, 1913.

Tennyson's Suppressed Poems, edited by J. C. Thomson. New York, 1903.

———

ALLINGHAM, H., and RADFORD, D. (eds.). *William Allingham, a diary*. London, 1907.

BROOKE, STOPFORD A. *Tennyson, His Art and Relation to Modern Life*. New York, 1894.

COLLINS, J. CHURTON (ed.). *In Memoriam, The Princess and Maud*. London, 1902.

NICOLSON, HAROLD. *Tennyson, Aspects of His Life, Character and Poetry*. Boston, 1923.

TENNYSON, HALLAM, LORD. *Tennyson, a Memoir*. London, 1897.

TENNYSON, HALLAM, LORD (ed.). *Tennyson and His Friends*. London, 1911.

WALKER, HUGH. *The Greater Victorian Poets*. London, 1895.

WARD, WILFRED. *Problems and Persons*. London, 1903.

WELD, AGNES GRACE. *Glimpses of Tennyson*. London, 1903.

CHAPTER III

Complete Poetical and Dramatic Works of Robert Browning. Boston, 1895.

Letters of Robert Browning and Elizabeth Barrett Barrett. New York, 1899.

Robert Browning and Alfred Dommett (letters), edited by F. G. Kenyon. London, 1906.

Letters of Robert Browning to Isa Blagdon, edited by A. J. Armstrong. Baylor, Texas, 1923.

BERDOE, EDWARD. *Browning's Message to His Time.* London, 1890.

CONWAY, MONCURE D. *Autobiography.* Boston, 1904.

GOSSE, EDMUND. *Robert Browning, Personalia.* London, 1890.

GRIFFIN, W. H., and MINCHIN, H. C. *The Life of Robert Browning.* London, 1910.

JAY, HARRIET. *Robert Buchanan.* London, 1903.

KINGSLAND, W. G. *Robert Browning, Chief Poet of the Age.* London, 1890.

NETTLESHIP, J. T. *Robert Browning, Essays and Thoughts.* London, 1890.

ORR, MRS. SUTHERLAND. *Robert Browning, Life and Letters.* Boston, 1891.

PALMER, GEORGE HERBERT. *The Glory of the Imperfect.* Boston, 1915.

ROBINSON, VICTOR. *Pathfinders in Medicine.* New York, 1912.

RUSSELL, FRANCES THERESA. *One Word More on Browning.* Stanford Univ., 1929.

SHARP, WILLIAM. *Life of Robert Browning.* London, 1890.

WAITE, A. E. *Paracelsus, the Hermetic and Alchemical Writings.* London, 1894.

CHAPTER IV

Poetical Works of George Meredith. New York, 1912.

Letters of George Meredith, edited by his son. New York, 1912.

Letters of George Meredith to Alice Meynell. London, 1923.

BUTCHER, LADY. *Memories of George Meredith, O. M.* London, 1919.

CLODD, EDWARD. *Memories.* London, 1916.

ELLIS, S. M. *George Meredith, His Life and Friends in Relation to His Work.* New York, 1920.

GALLAND, RENÉ. *George Meredith, les cinquante premières années.* Paris, 1923.

HAMMERTON, J. A. *George Meredith, His Life and Art in Anecdote and Criticism.* Edinburgh, 1911.

SHARP, WILLIAM. *Literary Geography.* New York, 1912.

TREVELYAN, G. M. *The Poetry and Philosophy of George Meredith.* New York, 1912.

CHAPTER V

Collected Poems of Thomas Hardy. New York, 1926.
The Dynasts. London, 1910.

ABERCROMBIE, LASCELLES. *Thomas Hardy, a Critical Study.* London, 1912.

BRENNECKE, ERNEST, JR. *Thomas Hardy's Universe.* Boston, 1924.

GARWOOD, HELEN. *Thomas Hardy, an Illustration of the Philosophy of Schopenhauer.* Philadelphia, 1911.

HARDY, FLORENCE EMILY. *The Early Life of Thomas Hardy.* New York, 1928.

———. *The Later Years of Thomas Hardy.* New York, 1930.

HEDGCOCK, F. A. *Thomas Hardy, penseur et artiste.* Paris, 1909.

SMITH, ROBERT M. "The Philosophy in Thomas Hardy's Poetry," in *North American Review*, CCXX (1924), 330.

CHAPTER VI

The Poems of Robert Bridges, Oxford edition. 1912.
The Testament of Beauty, by Robert Bridges. New York, 1929.
Rudyard Kipling's Verse, 1885–1918. Garden City, New York, 1921.
The Poems of John Masefield. New York, 1921.
Collected Poems by Alfred Noyes. London, 1910.
The Torchbearers, by Alfred Noyes. London, 1922, 1925, 1930.
The Poems of William Watson. London, 1905.

INDEX

351